For my parents, Charles and Harriett,
and Chilton Williamson.

PREFACE

The American Revolution produced at least three innovations in political thought and practice because the Founding Fathers had to justify novel institutions before a skeptical public. James Madison described how an extensive republic balanced conflicting interests and precluded the formation of a tyrannical majority faction. Madison stressed this idea to demonstrate that contrary to classical wisdom, a republican government could function, at least theoretically, in a large state. Second, to prevent further a despotic centralization of power, the Constitution provided for a "multiple representation of the people," dividing sovereignty among various organs of the State and Federal governments, all rooted in the popular will. Third, the United States instituted a written, popularly approved constitution articulating fundamental law and subjecting the government to the people, rather than vice versa. This device proved so successful that new nations for the past two centuries have used it to obtain legitimacy. These three ideas have been so widely accepted as parts of American political culture that their originality sometimes needs re-emphasis.

Yet the American Revolution produced two other intellectual innovations which have received little or no attention at all. They both occurred in the mind of Thomas Hutchinson, the last civilian royal governor of Massachusetts, and were buried with him. First, this book argues that Hutchinson, a historian of colonial Massachusetts, wrote very differently than his contemporaries of all political persuasions by providing an equitable and sympathetic judgment of diverse and contradictory positions and the individuals who espoused them. He thereby approximated the modern ideal of scholarly objectivity, unlike eighteenth century Whig and Tory historians who used history simplistically as a polemical weapon to defend their politics.

Second, Hutchinson's historical method laid the groundwork for his political theory. By trying to reconcile opposite positions on paper, he created a model for his plan to restore harmony between America and Britain. This scheme marked a second unusual feature of his thought. Rejecting natural rights,

"correct" models of government, and blueprints to
reform the British Empire, he instead insisted that any
society which had maintained peace and prosperity among
its people ought not to be tampered with even if, as
his historical studies told him, it disregarded
theoretical norms. Historical tradition became for
Hutchinson, as for Edmund Burke, a means of reconciling
the non-revolutionary elements of a society and
defending it against revolutionary challenges.

Why another book on Thomas Hutchinson? Clifford K.
Shipton, Malcolm Freiberg, and Bernard Bailyn have
already written fine, modern biographies. I must
differ, however, with some of their points. In his
great praise of Hutchinson the man and politician,
Shipton virtually identifies his principles with those
of his opponents, and attributes the revolutionaries'
dislike of him to personal malice and envy. I believe
far more fundamental differences of principle existed.
Freiberg's is a fine account of Hutchinson's career
and personal life, but does not go into his intellectual
achievements in great depth. Bailyn's biography
provides a good account of Hutchinson's public life,
but I disagree with its basic approach. First, I do
not see Hutchinson as a prudent, pragmatic politician
bewildered by revolutionary change. I view him as a
committed, consistent conservative thinker, who had
worked out all his fundamental positions on government
well in advance of the imperial crisis. Far from
being prudent and pragmatic, he frequently took
isolated and unpopular stands on matters of principle
when there was no evident need to do so. Far from
trying to adjust to events, Hutchinson cherished the
idea that he could reconcile Britain and America using
ideas that were peculiarly his own. Second,
Hutchinson was a far more original and powerful thinker
than Bailyn gives him credit for. He understood the
American Revolution far more comprehensively than just
about anyone since, and carefully raised fundamental
questions of morality and political philosophy which
anticipated the major dilemmas a world in revolution
subsequently confronted. Finally, in chapters one
through three, I present new biographical information
on Hutchinson, and in chapters four through six
analyze his historical writings in greater depth than
has been done before in order to demonstrate the
complexity and coherence of his thought.

Most of the work for this book was done at the
Massachusetts Historical Society. I thank the staff,

especially Aimee Bligh, Molly Collingwood, Winifred Collins, Gertrude Fisher, and Malcolm Freiberg, for their patient and friendly help. At the Massachusetts Archives, Leo and Helen Flaherty made research equally pleasant. The Harvard College Library and New England Historic Genealogical Society provided hospitable quarters and a few key pieces of information. I thank them all for permission to quote and cite material.

Peter Onuf, John A. Schutz, Alden T. Vaughan, and Chilton Williamson read the entire manuscript and greatly improved it by their suggestions. Members of the Boston University Colloquium in Early American History gave me the opportunity to test my ideas; Robert Gross, James Henretta, and Greg Palmer made especially valuable comments. My friend and colleague Carl Peterson was kind enough to proofread the final manuscript. I owe an intellectual debt to the late Leo Strauss and to Eric Voegelin for their approach to the history of ideas, which has guided my own.

Fellowships at the Graduate School of Columbia University and an Andrew Mellon Fellowship at Duke University helped finance completion of the work, but my principal financial and spiritual support has come from my parents. My mother uncomplainingly typed repeated drafts of this book. Nancy Riley did a superb job of preparing the final copy. My greatest debts are acknowledged in the dedication.

William Pencak

Chico, California

Abbreviations and Note on Sources

Since Hutchinson's own manuscripts and published works constitute almost all of the documentation for this study, the list of abbreviations can stand as a primary source bibliography. Other works about Hutchinson are noted below. For works which helped establish the context, see the appropriate footnotes.

"Additions-III"	Additions to volume III of the History, Proceedings of the American Antiquarian Society, XLI (1949), 11-74.
Bradford	Alden Bradford, ed., The Speeches of the Governors of Massachusetts . . . (Boston, 1818).
"Dialogue"	"Dialogue Between an American and a European Englishman," Massachusetts Archives XXVIII, 101-109, Office of the Secretary of the Commonwealth, State House, Boston. Also reprinted with an editorial apparatus by Bernard Bailyn in Perspectives in American History, VIII (1974), 368-413.
Diary	Peter Orlando Hutchinson, ed., The Diary and Letters of His Excellency Thomas Hutchinson (2 volumes: London, 1883, 1886).
Hardwicke	Letters of Thomas Hutchinson to Lord Hardwicke, Hutchinson-Hardwicke Letter Book in Frederick Lewis Gay Transcriptions (of originals at the British Museum), Massachusetts Historical Society.
History	Lawrence S. Mayo, ed., The History of the Colony and Province of Massachusetts Bay (3 volumes: Cambridge, 1936).
H	Thomas Hutchinson.

"Hutchinson in America"	In Egerton Manuscripts, #2664 at the British Museum, pagination from end. Microfilm at the Massachusetts Historical Society.
Loudoun	Letters of Thomas Hutchinson to Lord Loudoun, Loudoun Papers, Henry Huntington Library, San Marino, California, photostats at the Massachusetts Historical Society.
M	Massachusetts Archives, Office of the Secretary of the Commonwealth, State House, Boston. A typescript copy of volumes XXV-XXVII, Hutchinson letter books, prepared by Catherine Barton Mayo, is at the Massachusetts Historical Society. Pagination to the typescript.
Quincy	Josiah Quincy, ed., Reports of Cases Argued and Adjudged in the Superior Court of Judicature of the Province of Massachusetts Bay Between 1761 and 1772 (Boston, 1865).
Saltonstall Papers	Robert Moody, ed., Saltonstall Papers, 1607-1815. Collections of the Massachusetts Historical Society, LXXX (Boston, 1972).
"Stamp Act Essay"	In Massachusetts Archives, XXV, Office of the Secretary of the Commonwealth, State House, Boston. Pagination to an edition prepared by Edmund S. Morgan in "Thomas Hutchinson and the Stamp Act," New England Quarterly, XXI (1948), 461-492.
"Strictures"	"Strictures Upon the Declaration of the Congress at Philadelphia . . . . ," published in Remembrancer, IV (1776), 25-42. Reprint has been published by Boston's Old South Association as leaflet #227 (1958), edited by Malcolm Freiberg.

Burke   Abbreviates the twelve volume edition of his collected *Works*, published in Boston between 1865 and 1867.

Works about Hutchinson include:

Clifford K. Shipton, *Biographical Sketches of those Who Attended Harvard College* (Boston, 1873-   ), VIII, 149-217; Malcolm Freiberg, "Prelude to Purgatory: Thomas Hutchinson in Massachusetts Politics, 1760-1770" (unpublished Ph.D. thesis, Brown University, 1950); Bernard Bailyn, *The Ordeal of Thomas Hutchinson* (Cambridge, 1974). See also the following articles by Malcolm Freiberg: "Thomas Hutchinson: The First Fifty Years (1711-1761)," *William and Mary Quarterly*, 3d. ser., XV (1958), 35-55; "Thomas Hutchinson and the Province Currency," *New England Quarterly*, XXX (1957), 190-208; "How to Become a Colonial Governor: Thomas Hutchinson of Massachusetts," *Review of Politics*, XXI (1959), 646-656; and Lawrence Henry Gipson, "Thomas Hutchinson and the Framing of the Albany Plan of Union, 1754," *Pennsylvania Magazine of History and Biography*, LXXIV (1950), 5-35. Chapters one and two have appeared in the *New England Historical and Genealogical Register*, January 1978 and October 1982.

> Note: Throughout this work I have modernized Hutchinson's spelling and punctuation. I believe it is more important to present his ideas as comprehensibly as possible than to preserve the vagaries of eighteenth century style.

TABLE OF CONTENTS

Preface v
Abbreviations and Note on Sources ix

PART I: THE UNKNOWN HUTCHINSON

    I. A Biographical Overview 1
    II. Fighting Naval Impressment 22
    III. Chief Justice of Massachusetts 39

PART II: THE HISTORIAN

    IV. The Colonial Period 59
    V. The Constitution of Empire:
        A Theory of Sovereignty 105
    VI. The American Revolution:
        Causes and Remedies 119

PART III: THE POLITICAL THEORIST

    VII. Natural Law and Natural Right 157
    VIII. Critique of Revolutionary
        Language and Logic 197
    IX. Conclusion 217

Index 231

PART I: THE UNKNOWN HUTCHINSON

I. A BIOGRAPHICAL OVERVIEW

Shortly before death ended his unhappy six-year exile in England, Thomas Hutchinson, Massachusetts' last civilian governor under the British crown, attempted to justify his career. The most popular scapegoat on both sides of the Atlantic for the American Revolution, Hutchinson had grown tired of futile efforts to persuade any public whatever of the wisdom of his ideas or the sincerity of his principles. He therefore intended "Hutchinson in America," a history of his family since the tempestuous Anne set Massachusetts in an uproar in the 1630s, "for my own children and no part to be published to the world." Only after 1883, when Peter Orlando Hutchinson violated that confidence and published the document with some deletions, could the world, had it been curious, have learned what thoughts Hutchinson considered too intimate to share with it.(1)

Perhaps Hutchinson had some premonition of the precision with which future scholars would probe the conscious and even unconscious motives of historical figures, as he himself was probably the most acute and modern historian of pre-revolutionary America. For "Hutchinson in America" is a remarkable document, a personal testament as revealing as Benjamin Franklin's own, if less representative and ingratiating. By examining it carefully, important clues as to what Hutchinson was trying to accomplish can be ferreted out.

Hutchinson did not write an autobiography in the strict sense, although his discussion of his ancestors clearly existed only as a prologue to his self-examination. Instead, he described his forbears for the benefit of his posterity alone, carefully shutting out the rest of the world, both as readers and subjects In some cases, it would be futile to overemphasize this point, as many prominent people have interested themselves in their genealogy. But by so dwelling on his relatives, Hutchinson accurately summed up in print a process he had been practically engaged in his entire life: sequestering himself with his immediate family and a few more kin, taking such good care of them

that charges of nepotism and corruption could be
plausibly levelled against him, and ultimately
refusing to submit his behavior to be judged by any
other standards than those set by God, his ancestors,
and his descendants. And for him all these existed
as projections of his own identity.

    To what sort of a family did Hutchinson belong?
Looking back from the perspective of the American
Revolution, it appeared as the only clan in
Massachusetts which sat at the center of power from
the Glorious Revolution to the imperial crisis. The
Winthrops and Dudleys faded early in the eighteenth
century, Elisha Cooke Sr. and Jr. left no public-
spirited heirs, and Governors Jonathan Belcher and
William Phips ended their regimes in disgrace and left
no notable heirs. Hutchinson took great pride in his
heritage, perhaps too much. On April 11, 1748, <u>The
Independent Advertiser</u> poked fun at his belief that
members of his family had accomplished everything of
importance in the province's history. By the 1760s,
newspapers and pamphlets gleefully listed the multiple
offices held by Hutchinson and, through his influence,
his various unqualified relatives as proof that he
harbored imperial ambitions on the order of Alexander
the Great or Julius Caesar. When he assumed the acting
governorship in 1769, brother Foster moved from judge
of the Suffolk Court of Common Pleas to the Superior
Court and became Suffolk's judge of probate to fill
two of his old posts. Brother-in-law Andrew Oliver,
who had served as the province secretary, assumed the
lieutenant-governorship vacated by Hutchinson. Other
prominent family members included Andrew Oliver Jr.,
who sat on the Essex County Court of Common Pleas,
Peter Oliver, brother of Andrew Sr., judge of the
Superior Court, and a cousin Eliakim on the Suffolk
bench. Hutchinson also spent much of the 1760s and
70s trying to land modestly lucrative sinecures for his
own sons.

    Yet the revolutionaries' arguments that Hutchinson
sought to establish a dynasty and engross all power in
Massachusetts are simply too pat. If he were really
the devious manipulator they and later historians
agreed he was, packing the province judiciary in so
obvious a manner in the face of many better qualified
and easily offended candidates was sheer stupidity, as
was clinging to nepotism as the colonial crisis
worsened. Furthermore, if power, prestige, and pelf
were his major goals, Hutchinson sometimes behaved in

so self-denying a manner that other motivations must be found for his appointments policy.

Like most early American statesmen, Hutchinson did not consider himself a political partisan, but rather a gentleman in public life giving generously of time spent more lucratively in commerce or agriculture. In letters to his closest friends he repeatedly claimed that "I am tired of controversies"; "I have no schemes in politics"; "I am more cautious than ever of meddling in any case unless I think there will be a public mischief if I do not." He even went so far as to fear for his salvation if he did not make amends for any harm his political projects may have caused:(2)

> The temper of mind we carry out of this world we are told we shall carry into the next. You must therefore allow me to be right in my opinion of the wisdom of quitting public life before life itself, or else you must instruct me how I shall fortify myself against the dangers to which I am exposed.

Such remarks represented more than facile attempts to ease his conscience. For all his lobbying on behalf of others, Hutchinson could write in 1765 with strict truth that "I never sought or solicited any [royal] posts." Opponents' charges of megalomania are simply untrue: no evidence supports them and there is documentation to the contrary. When the Chief Justiceship fell vacant in 1760, Hutchinson's brother-in-law Andrew Oliver wrote their mutual friend Israel Williams, Hampshire County's leading statesman, that the "lieutenant-governor is so diffident of his own fitness that if he could be brought to accept of the place yet I am persuaded he will never serve in it." It took them several months to convince Hutchinson he was the best man for the job, an opinion which his service on the bench in politically uncontroversial cases suggests had considerable merit. Hutchinson only assumed the office after Governor Francis Bernard assured him that under no circumstances would the elder James Otis be appointed in the event of his refusal. The younger Otis, who had asked Hutchinson to lobby on his father's behalf, repaid his rival's courtesy by becoming Massachusetts' leading Hutchinson baiter.(3)

Hutchinson similarly had to be talked into accepting the governorship itself. He officially "desired to be excused" from the post or even to serve as acting governor when Bernard returned to England, but Colonial Secretary Lord Hillsborough's protestations of his indispensability won out over Hutchinson's reluctance. He finally accepted for reasons he revealed to his nephew Nathaniel Rogers: "The governor has wrote for leave to go to England. I should like well enough to make a trial to induce a better spirit -- I certainly have many friends more strongly attached to me than they are to him." Hutchinson's subsequent behavior confirmed that he was not dissimulating. When the Boston Massacre seemed to herald renewed violent controversy, he offered to resign even before his permanent commission arrived. But Hillsborough again instructed him to stay put, and two years of relative calm convinced him to remain. However, the disclosure of some of his private letters -- distorted by his enemies to show that he favored sweeping changes in colonial self-government -- destroyed whatever credibility Hutchinson retained and he finally did resign. Following his retirement to England in 1774 to press for abolition of the Coercive Acts, the ministry offered him other posts and a baronetcy, all of which he refused except for an honorary doctorate in civil law from Oxford, ironically awarded on July 4, 1776. Such behavior not only refutes Hutchinson's accusers but supports his own avowal that he "had no aim at honors or titles" and "would gladly give up all claim to them, and to all emolument whatsoever and to spend the remainder of my life in obscurity if upon those terms I could purchase the peace and prosperity of my country."(4) But even his voluntary surrender of power could not accomplish this end.

Furthermore, when offered his greatest opportunity to advance his family fortunes, Hutchinson turned it down. One of Earl Fitzwilliam's sons had fallen in love with his daughter Peggy, but he rejected the union. He went so far as to say that "I should certainly be highly criminal if I should countenance and encourage . . . so unequal a match." Even on patronage matters he drew the line, and argued "the precedent of a father resigning his place to his son" had the pernicious "tendency to make all offices hereditary." So great was Hutchinson's wealth -- his confiscated estate sold for ₤98,000 after he left for England -- that its income could have kept all his children comfortable for the rest of their days, enabling him to write nonchalantly that "it does not signify [much] whether I leave a few thousand pounds more or less behind me

when I die."(5) Once again, we must ask why
Hutchinson held so fanatically to his counter-productive
plural office-holding policy when he imposed strict
limits on how far his family could rise, had no need of
the income, and constantly doubted whether he should
accept or retain his own posts?

The key lies in the overwhelming psychological
importance of his family to Hutchinson. According to
"Hutchinson in America," he acquired from his father a
preference for withdrawing into a small circle of
relations and depending upon them almost exclusively for
emotional gratification. For over thirty years, Thomas
Sr. kept a Spartan table every Saturday afternoon --
codfish being the main course -- and invited the same
four close friends, two of them relatives, over and
over. Similarly, Thomas Jr. "forsook all his former
evening acquaintance" upon marrying Margaret (Peggy)
Sanford in 1734, and often thought of quitting "all
mercantile business for a happy retirement with his
wife and children." Shortly thereafter he built a
mansion in suburban Milton where he spent summers,
weekends, and as much time as possible away from his
populist opponents in the Boston town meeting and the
city's congestion, filth, noise, and disease. In this
respect, he joined a veritable exodus of upper-class
Bostonians, many of them royal officeholders, who gave
up on city life and assumed a genteel, insular
existence as aspiring English country squires in the
surrounding countryside. Unlike Hutchinson, who
retained a sense of public duty, remained in business,
and adhered to the faith of his fathers, most members
of this class simply washed their hands of responsible
office-holding and commercial activity altogether,
married and visited almost exclusively among themselves, became Anglicans, and did their best to remain
aloof from the currents of economic distress, war, and
revolution which swept Massachusetts after 1740.(6) In
one sense, faced with a governing class that had given
up the ghost, Hutchinson almost had to choose
immediate relatives to fill key posts or surrender
them to the incendiaries of the Boston town meeting by
default. Throughout the years of crisis after 1765,
he repeatedly complained of fright and apathy among his
sympathetically inclined friends.

For Hutchinson and other members of this elite, the
family functioned as a <u>Haven in a Heartless World</u>, as
Christopher Lasch has aptly described the propensity
of nineteenth and twentieth century families to turn

inward and create a stable, orderly, private environment capable of resisting the uncertainty and immorality of a world in flux. By setting their <u>Families Against the City</u>, the title of a treatise by Richard Sennett on a theme similar to Lasch's, wealthy Bostonians sought to escape America's first approximation of urban blight and chaos. In fleeing to suburbia, they also declared their preference for what Philip Greven has termed the "genteel" method of child-rearing. Children grew up under a benign but all-pervasive paternal authority, since the sheltered environment admitted no rival ideals to penetrate the family group. Yet despite, or more probably because of, this excessive protectiveness, the younger loyalists, born in the 1730s and 40s, proved a sorry lot, unable to succeed their fathers and battle on equal terms men such as Samuel Adams or James Otis, who had been trained in a harder school.(7)

Hutchinson's tragic family experiences demonstrate graphically the futility of the loyalists' efforts to insulate their loved ones from the appalling mortality and political crises of mid-eighteenth century Massachusetts. Two of his brothers and a sister died in childhood; only four of his own twelve offspring survived adolescence. His wife Peggy died in childbirth in 1754 after a long agony during which he remained almost constantly at her side. Unlike many other colonial New Englanders who lost their spouses, he never remarried. His last and favorite child, named after her mother, remained with him until she too died in 1777 at age 23. Hutchinson would not relinquish her to marry an earl's son. His own male offspring undoubtedly caused him a different although equally real grief. None of the three who survived was particularly capable: Thomas Sr. handled much of the tea business nominally managed by Thomas Jr. and Elisha, and William's intelligence was below average. The strange combination of detachment and aloofness, accompanying the meticulous care and hard work found in Hutchinson's public writings and behavior, almost suggests a man dead to the world simply filling the empty hours as best he could. After his wife's death, he thought he had lost over half his soul and took refuge in "his posts and affairs" as "the only relief from the distress of his mind."(8)

Hutchinson's nepotism can therefore be viewed not so much as a rational power ploy, but as a desperate effort to assure some future prominence to the family he loved so much. Given his self-estrangement from his contemporaries, Hutchinson needed to be needed by the family in which he had invested so much psychological capital. Hence his unwillingness to send his daughter to England or take posts outside the province: he considered his offspring the heirs to a family tradition he so pathetically sought to preserve. But even this tradition was not as glorious as Hutchinson sometimes pretended. He needed his ancestors as he needed his descendants, to be dependent on him and to exist not as individuals in their own right but as approximations to his own virtues and as vehicles for realizing his own identity and ideals. He depicted them in "Hutchinson in America" primarily as imperfect copies of the sum of all desirable qualities, which only he himself attained. Colonel Elisha, soldier, councillor, judge, merchant, and hero of the Glorious Revolution, Thomas' grandfather, appears as a paragon of piety and public spirit who was "never very successful in business." Thomas criticized him for living "upon the rents of his second wife's estate and what profit he could make from his employment in government," which was not very much. Similarly, Thomas' father "came into possession of a very handsome fortune" at age thirty-five, which had the unfortunate effect of making him "less attentive" in supporting his family than he ought to have been. A "generous, charitably disposed man," the elder Hutchinson remained in the shipbuilding business long after Boston's smart money had gone elsewhere, primarily because he did not wish to discharge his employees. Such generosity took its toll in the most crucial manner: "he lamented at his death his not being able better to provide for his widow and children," whereupon the younger Thomas, who had been a successful entrepreneur since he had made ₤500 (in the fishing business while in college, in his spare time), assured the worried man that he could rest in peace on that count.(9)

Resemblances between Hutchinson, his father, and his grandfather gave him considerable pause, as his treatment of them reveals. All three acquired large fortunes through marriage. Both Hutchinson and his father suffered from "nervous disorders," probably brought on by the chronic oversensitivity, introspection, and agonizing common to both men. With Colonel Elisha, they also tried to combine, with typical Puritan determination, success in their commercial endeavors, concern for their political obligations, and genuine religious behavior. Serving both God and Mammon was not only possible but reasonable. Hutchinson's earliest childhood memories depicted his merchant father catechizing the children morning and evening, instilling habits of frugality with his Saturday fish dinners, and only inviting merchants and clergymen, representatives of New England's finest traditions, to sit at table. Yet for all their virtues, Hutchinson's ancestors fell short. In their zeal for the public good and the next world they neglected the family, an omission the younger Thomas sacrificed every principle of political prudence to compensate for. When he assumed the patriarchy on his father's deathbed, Hutchinson assured the clan that they need never again trouble themselves on that count.

Hutchinson thus felt obliged, to anchor himself in an unstable world, to create a tradition out of two generations of worthy but flawed ancestors and a future from one generation of even less promising offspring. To satisfy his own sense of self-worth, it had to be a family dependent on his own remarkable accomplishments and synthesis of commercial, public, and religious virtues for its existence. By placing himself in solitary splendor at the apex of his heritage, Hutchinson could simultaneously bolster his propensity to cut himself off from the world while enjoying an environment totally under his control.

Familial attachment and self-estrangement from social situations reinforced each other. No sooner did Hutchinson describe his father's small, closed circle in "Hutchinson in America" than he recalled that as a boy, "even before he went to college, he chose rather to spend an evening in reading . . . than to be at play in the street with the other boys."(10) Here is no childhood full of playmates, love and affection, but only the frugal discipline of his father, adult companionship, and voluntary (so he claimed retrospectively) isolation. Hutchinson must have been rushed through his studies with little time for much else. Born on September 9, 1711, he entered Harvard at the tender age of eleven, two or three years ahead of most of his fellows, and was graduated at fifteen. Extreme youth, combined with his studiousness and great natural abilities, would have alienated him still further from any reasonably normal lot of schoolboys. His dislike of children's games indicates that he preferred transforming his loneliness into a badge of merit instead of attempting to ingratiate himself with his peers. In fact, he compensated for his immaturity in years by assuming an exaggerated maturity in behavior, a sobriety and austerity he kept all his life.

Hutchinson elevated his social isolation into a sense of moral superiority. Unlike nearly every autobiography in western history, from St. Augustine's <u>Confessions</u> to the American narratives of Franklin and Jonathan Edwards, Hutchinson's displays no "errata," to use Franklin's term, no period of trial and error, spiritual anguish, or youthful depravity preceding the mystical "conversion experience" which permanently set the reborn soul on the path of righteousness. Hutchinson rather presented himself as immaculate from the start. Even as a boy, he could not bring himself to do the slightest wrong. At Harvard, all the other students, he remembered, cheated regularly during their classroom recitations by preparing in advance translations of the Greek passages they were required to render into Latin and then hiding these in their readers. But he could not: "Young Hutchinson was tempted once to follow so bad an example, but guilt appeared so strong in his face that the president ordered him to show his book, which he did in great confusion, and received his severe reproof."(11) Of all the best sons of Massachusetts, Hutchinson alone proved incapable of dishonesty. His very being rebelled against the thought on the solitary occasion it crossed his mind. Paradoxically, therefore, only Hutchinson suffered a rebuke, not for his sins, but for those of his contemporaries. The pattern for his career thus symbolically established itself.

The two other striking incidents from his early life Hutchinson chose to emphasize in old age enhanced the self-portrait he constructed of a persecuted, isolated saint. He regretted the "gay company" he had kept as a youth, although instead of drinking, wenching, and in general making public nuisances of themselves, their most outrageous activity consisted in sailing a boat to Maine to witness the signing of an Indian treaty. Hutchinson paraded before us a sin which was not a sin at all, a solitary instance of harmless amusement. Like the boy unwilling to play or unable to cheat, this incident revealed a man determined to regard his past as unsullied. Hutchinson mentally pushed aside whatever wrong he may have done, and dwelt on pecadillos of such triviality that he emerged in his own eyes as nearly perfect. Others might reasonably interpret such posturing as the self-righteousness of one blind to his faults or consciously dissimulating. As he wrote to Nathaniel Saltonstall in 1759, he was conscious of "many many flaws which the world will never know." Perhaps he suppressed them because he knew his enemies would take care of this: he added that nevertheless "I shall appear in a worse light than I deserve."(12)

Was Hutchinson really a hypocrite, a dark, designing Machiavelli -- to collect neatly some of his opponents' favorite epithets -- who feigned friendship to America only to further his career by selling out to England? Or was he literally too good to be true, too pure to succeed in an evil world where others viciously or ignorantly projected their own flaws on him? Hutchinson clearly espoused the latter interpretation, and in old age attributed a yearning for martyrdom to the young boy. As a child, "the tragical account of King Charles' sufferings and death happened to fall into his hands; though it produced tears he went through it with much eagerness. . . . Fox's Martyrs, among his father's books, afforded him much entertainment." From the beginning, Hutchinson presented himself as a saint determined to be a sacrifice for his own unique, noble ideals. The principles themselves took a back seat, at least psychologically. On the one hand, he shed tears over high Anglican King Charles and identified "eagerly" with the monarch's execution. On the other, he admitted to being "entertained" by the tortures inflicted on the Puritans by Bloody Mary.(13)

Hutchinson similarly interpreted his own obstinance as heroism at crucial points in his life. Addressing the Superior Court the day after his house was sacked by a mob in the Stamp Act Riot of August 26, 1765, he stated: "I have nothing to fear. They can only take away my life, which is of but little value when deprived of all its comforts, all that is dear to me, and nothing surrounding me but the most pressing distress." In a letter to Lord Hardwicke in 1774, shortly after he had resigned the governorship, he depicted his standing up to the revolutionaries as proof of his unique fortitude and virtue:(14)

> I have more than once resisted the demands of a mob and would have been tarred and feathered before I would have submitted to them, but in the case of the councillors who

were resigned, as they all lived in the
country, they must have quitted their
farms and businesses and could not be
safe, which would carry with it too
great virtue to be expected in the
present age.

Hutchinson's most extreme self-praise of his sacrificial temperament occurred in an address to a grand jury in 1767. After describing the present period in provincial history as an unhappy time wherein "a man might obtain greater applause in . . . stirring up contentions, divisions, animosities, and factions" than by "promoting peace, harmony, and good order," he assumed the role of a suffering servant of Christ: "I know that it has been said by our great Lord and Savior that "Blessed are the Peacemakers, and if I might obtain His approbation, I am not anxious for any other event."(15) In the final analysis, Hutchinson viewed himself as the last bastion of good in the devil's world. He chose to endure the revolutionary crisis supported by neither party, but by his conscience and God alone.

Hutchinson's childhood identification with both Anglican and Puritan martyrs in many ways foreshadowed his career and principles. From his early days as a Bostonian representative in the General Court, trying to persuade British naval officers to release impressed American seamen, to his pathetic attempt as an exiled and repudiated governor lobbying to relax the Coercive Acts, Hutchinson devoted much of his considerable energy to achieving in practice the reconciliation of Britain and America he had accomplished symbolically through admiring martyrs for contradictory principles. Just as in his personal life he believed that he had attained the nearly impossible synthesis of commercial, civic, moral, and familial virtues, in the public realm he again courted isolation, suffering, and misunderstanding by recommending a middle course between the extremes of revolution and tyranny, combining the benefits of royal authority and colonial self-government. When speaking to Americans, he emphasized the British side, and vice versa, thereby winning the scorn of both parties and a reputation for devious, underhanded behavior. It is highly likely that such vilification reinforced his sense of self-righteousness and martyr complex.

The terms on which Hutchinson sought to keep

Britain and America together were as extraordinary as the desire itself was merely unusual. Unlike other loyalists who devised elaborate plans restructuring imperial relations and defining precisely the division of powers between colonies and mother country, Hutchinson regarded constitutional tinkering as a waste of time. (Similarly, in 1741, as he wrote in "Hutchinson in America," an old-fashioned rest in the country saved his life after the latest medical techniques had nearly killed him.)(16) The entire imperial problem could in fact be defined by the overly rigid, doctrinaire conceptions of their respective rights both Britain and America began to advance in the 1760s. For two centuries, imperial prerogatives and American liberties had coexisted, not always peacefully, to be sure, but within self-imposed limits. The healthy tension and controlled conflict between mother country and colonies formed the parameters of provincial politics. Both Charles I and the Puritans, simultaneously living in the hearts and minds of their descendants, had to survive in a tradition incorporating and transcending both if America were to remain free and prosperous.

Once again, as in his family history, Hutchinson cast himself as the unique synthesizer of virtues that had only existed in different individuals before. Recognizing the legitimate claims of both opponents and supporters of royal authority, he cast himself as the peacemaker who would preach to the unreflecting partisans of both positions that only in combination did they constitute the salt of the colonial earth. By being the great interpreter of an unknown past, a tradition he brought to consciousness for the first time, much like his family history, Hutchinson would either produce a triumphant rapprochement or, which he may even have preferred, be persecuted for peace and righteousness' sake. With the British Empire, as with his family in "Hutchinson in America," Hutchinson articulated, most untraditionally, a traditional heritage which guaranteed him the position of absolute uniqueness and moral superiority that he craved.

Hutchinson chose to identify with the totality of the Anglo-American past for two reasons. First, it defined the only plausible alternative to the courses suggested by partisans of Britain and America. It represented an approach to history shared by none of his contemporaries, who tended to view the past

simplistically as a struggle between corruption and
virtue or liberty and power. Second, it enabled him
to link his personal career with Massachusetts history
without doing violence to either. Hutchinson and his
forbears had taken almost every conceivable side on
the major issues in colonial history. He praised Anne
Hutchinson for her piety, but condemned the socially
disruptive tendencies of her doctrines. Elisha
Hutchinson, a strong supporter of the old charter in
the 1680s, and leader of the Glorious Revolution in
1689, ultimately became a mainstay of Joseph Dudley's
court party. Most of the Hutchinsons sided with the
prerogative in the early eighteenth century, although
it took Elisha's son Eliakim quite a while to come to
terms with Dudley. William, another son, deserted
most of his kin and helped Elisha Cooke, Jr. found the
Boston Caucus. Thomas himself began his career as a
friend of Governor Jonathan Belcher and at first
naturally opposed his successor William Shirley, who
had used every trick in the eighteenth century lexicon
to oust his predecessor. But Hutchinson eventually
became Shirley's "prime minister," as their enemies
sneeringly called him, because they both sought to
abolish Massachusetts' inflationary paper currency and
substitute a firm specie base. Shirley's successor
Thomas Pownall was initially friendly to Hutchinson and
secured the lieutenant-governorship for him, but they
soon became bitter rivals. Hutchinson devoted more of
his final testament to denouncing Pownall than all the
revolutionaries put together, perhaps because Pownall
probably arranged to steal the private correspondence
that ruined Hutchinson's own administration. Finally,
it took the Stamp Act crisis to unite Hutchinson's
political destinies with those of Francis Bernard, who
replaced Pownall.(17)

   Such factional inconsistency within the same
family, to say nothing of the same man, could only
escape charges of fickle self-serving if Hutchinson
assumed a standard of independent judgment above that
of any party. This he did, and reserved his greatest
praise for men like William Stoughton, Daniel Gookin,
and his own father, who "always spoke his mind without
fear either of the governor or the people."(18) Such
figures emerged only to be vilified by the opposing
sides. If Hutchinson did not, like his contemporaries
almost without exception, write the sort of history
which glorified America as a chosen nation and read
the conflicts of the American Revolution back
uncritically into the colonial past, his self-conscious

impartiality conveyed an equally clear moral message. Only by adopting his own "impartial" standpoint could the British Empire save itself. Only if everyone abandoned his own principles and adopted Hutchinson's could the strife come to an end.

In practice, Hutchinson's political career illustrated that he did not enunciate principles he failed to act upon. He was one of those rare individuals who for much of his life consistently advocated unpopular stands and adhered to a solitary course, and yet who through competence and general belief in his integrity managed to rise steadily. Only in the 1760s did his behavior arouse universal hatred and exasperation.

Almost immediately after his election as Boston representative in 1737 to fill the seat of the late Elisha Cooke, Hutchinson began to fight with his constituents. A leading supporter of efforts to put Massachusetts' currency on a silver basis -- a proposition which at the time appeared about as practical as a return to the gold standard in late twentieth century America -- the town meeting which re-elected him in 1738 instructed him to support continued emissions of paper money. Such an effort to deny his independent judgment was especially odious to the twenty-seven year old Hutchinson, who not only attacked the substance of the directive, but the very notion that a deputy's freedom of action should be cramped by the electorate: "He publicly argued against them [instructions] as iniquitous and declared that he should not observe them." The townspeople removed Hutchinson from his seat in 1739 for this outburst, but more significantly once again elected him to the house in 1742. He remained there until 1748, and presided over the body as speaker from 1746 to 1748. Renowned as one of the greatest orators of his day, he also ranked high among the handful of leading representatives in shouldering the onerous committee work most back-benchers gladly avoided, and thereby won the esteem of his colleagues despite his unpopular monetary schemes.(19)

In 1749, when Britain sent Massachusetts Ł183,000 in silver to compensate the province for its exertions in King George's War, Hutchinson found a miraculous opportunity to implement his currency program. When he proposed the adoption of a silver medium, "this caused a smile, few apprehending that he was in

earnest." But after a year's lobbying, and
parliamentary skullduggery which included persuading
the deputies to expel his leading critic, James Allen,
from the house and waiting until the opponents of the
measure had gone home for the winter, Hutchinson
obtained his bill by the narrow vote of 40-37. Again
he became unpopular: "a great part of the people was
in a fury." The town meeting ousted him as Boston's
representative by a margin of nearly three to one and
"more than once [he] was threatened with destruction
by some of the people of the town." His Boston house
burned down mysteriously during the controversy: the
fire brigade refused to appear and the spectators
cried out "let it burn." Hutchinson risked his life
by turning down the council's offer of a personal
bodyguard, giving him the distinction of being the
only private citizen in provincial history to need
official protection.(20)

Yet once again Hutchinson triumphed because of his
stubbornness. Despite some initial difficulties, the
new currency became a success, and in a short time he
"was as much praised for his <u>firm</u> as he had before been
abused for his <u>obstinate</u> perseverance." Again
Hutchinson's solitary path received positive reinforcement: elected to the council in 1749, he became
lieutenant-governor in 1758 and chief justice in 1760.
But he did not change his ways. In 1757, he became
the first person in fifty years to enter a personal
dissent on the council books when he alone opposed a
proposal to divide the town of Salem in two(21). As
chief justice, of the sixteen split decisions recorded
in young Josiah Quincy's notes on the cases,
Hutchinson stood in the minority twelve times and on
ten occasions was the sole dissenter.

During the revolutionary crisis, Hutchinson not only
advanced political principles congenial to neither side
but seemed to do so in a manner designed to maximize
his own unpopularity. How else can his private,
strenuous opposition to the Stamp Act be reconciled
with his refusal even to deny the rumors spread by his
opponents that he had authored the measure? Why
would he reopen the issue of British versus American
rights in 1772 during a period of calm over the
creation of Committees of Correspondence and undo a
policy of non-confrontation he had cultivated
successfully for two years? Hutchinson also risked
his life with surprising carelessness. On August 26,
1765, he not only refused to speak to a mob that had
come to his house inquiring about his involvement

with the Stamp Act as "an indignity to which he would not submit," but insisted on remaining in the mansion, leaving at the last moment only when his eldest daughter refused to flee without him. On the other hand, during the melee after the Boston Massacre on March 5, 1770, heedless of his own safety, he plunged into the streets in an effort to avert violence, although his presence might well have provoked the crowd instead of quieting it.(22) As these two contrasting incidents demonstrated, Hutchinson irrationally shunned or embraced popular contact when either course appeared most dangerous.

What then becomes of the portrait of Hutchinson presented both by his contemporaries and later historians of a pathologically prudent, cautious schemer who rewrote his letters over and over again, suffered a nervous breakdown in 1768 from anxiety over whether he was indeed pursuing the right course, and did not even permit his most interesting writings -- volume three of the History of the Colony and Province of Massachusetts Bay, the "Dialogue Between an American and European Englishman," a critique of the Stamp Act, and "Hutchinson in America" -- to be published during his lifetime?(23) Looked at more closely, however, it appears that Hutchinson confined his prudence to words rather than deeds; by literally worrying himself sick over what to say, when, and to whom, he could increase his sense of suffering and alienation, and ensure that he would, in fact, be poorly understood. He consciously sought out and gloried in the Ordeal of Thomas Hutchinson so described by Bernard Bailyn in his biography of that title.

If the roots of Hutchinson's thought and conduct were pathological, and even his high-minded desire to reconcile England and America arose from a self-image as the paragon of all conceivable virtues, this in no way diminishes the profundity of his thought or the fact that his program, or something like it, represented the only alternative to the American Revolution. The abnormal mind can frequently see through elements of reality taken for granted by the well-adjusted. It can plausibly be argued that in his desire to succeed or fail spectacularly on his own terms and none other, Hutchinson conceived of both history and politics in radically different ways from his contemporaries. By trying to view the history of Massachusetts in all its complexity, and appreciate on their own terms the contradictory strands that had

somehow converged to form a stable, prosperous, and
freedom-loving society, Hutchinson became one of the
first, if not the first, historian to eschew the black
and white generalizations of Whig historians or the
ponderous minutiae of antiquarians. Rendering sensible
and sensitive balanced judgments concerning the effects
of factions and individuals on political stability,
Hutchinson asked and answered the sorts of questions
only introduced regularly by academic historians in the
late nineteenth century. The proof lies in the fact
that of all contemporaneous histories of the American
Revolution, Hutchinson's is the only one used frequently
by present-day scholars almost as one of their own.
His facts and interpretations have been cited by
historians who, in almost the same breath, condemn his
political and personal behavior.

   Hutchinson also developed a political theory based
on his historical method. He insisted that the
presence of a living tradition in a society, which
constituted its very definition, was the only applicable
standard to judge it by. Unlike both British and
American Whig thinkers, Hutchinson refused to erect a
model of the good society, based on popular
representation or rights to life, liberty, property,
and the pursuit of happiness. He adopted no unitary
standard by which all the world had to be measured.
Each nation should adhere to its own past, upon pain of
self-betrayal and dissolving into chaos, tyranny, or
anarchy. Such arguments anticipated the modern
conservative view of the built-in wisdom of long-lived
social and political institutions and especially
foreshadowed the ideas of Edmund Burke.

   Hutchinson never articulated his vision of history
and politics with the precision outlined here, although
several of his works came close. Much of his thought
lies scattered in unpublished letters, recently
unearthed treatises, and his History. For all his
efforts to put his ideas into practice, Hutchinson had
little compulsion to systematize or publicize his
ideas. He claimed to have "no talent for making books"
and was amazed (or pretended to be) that his "poor
history," "designed only for the Yankees" to "save
[some facts] from oblivion," attracted overseas
notice.(24) But almost every action of his career can
be explained by his devotion to the reconciliation of
seemingly disparate positions, reverence for
Massachusetts' heritage, and a desire to assume an
absolutely unique stance wherever possible. Only such

an interpretation explains the apparent contradiction between Hutchinson's disinterested, noble idealism on some occasions and apparent duplicity and corruption on others.

Hutchinson's consistently pro-American opposition to British naval impressment and his behavior on the bench as Chief Justice of Massachusetts provide perfect examples of how he acted consistently on his principles over a thirty-year period. His conduct here cannot be squared with interpretations stressing his willingness to sacrifice his country's interests to further his ambitions, as on several occasions he stood up vigorously to abuses of imperial power. Having demonstrated Hutchinson's peculiar solitary idealism and strong defense of American rights within traditional limits, the consonance of his political and historical ideas with his actions can be readily shown.

Study of Hutchinson's principles is important for several reasons. Whether his ideas persuade or not, he has taught almost every scholar of colonial America much about Massachusetts and the causes of the American Revolution. Second, his mediating of British policy toward Massachusetts after 1765 can only be understood if the theories underlying it are fully explained. Had Hutchinson taken different stances during the Stamp Act, the Boston Massacre, and the Tea Party, the timing and immediate causes of the American Revolution, at the very least, might well have been different. Finally, Hutchinson presented his case for a traditional society forcefully enough to provoke thinking men of all political persuasions to examine seriously the foundations of order, freedom, and justice in their own time.

FOOTNOTES

1. "Hutchinson in America," 1. Material in this introductory chapter discussed more fully later in the book is cited there.

2. H to Israel Williams, June 14, 1759, July 17, 1758, Williams Papers; H to Richard Saltonstall, August 22, 1759, Saltonstall Papers, 429.

3. H to ?, December 3, 1765, M. XXVI, 373; see also H to ?, October 26, 1765, M. XXVI, 261; Andrew Oliver to Israel Williams, September 30, 1760, Williams Papers; "Hutchinson in America," 74. Hutchinson later persuaded Governor Francis Bernard to appoint the elder Otis chief justice of Barnstable County's Inferior Court of Common Pleas and its probate judge. H to Israel Williams, November 17, 1763, Williams Papers.

4. Diary, II, 79; H to Nathaniel Rogers, M. XXV, 258; Bernard Bailyn, The Ordeal of Thomas Hutchinson (Cambridge, 1974), 162, 219. Diary, I, 263.

5. H to ?, September 8, 1769, M. XXVI, 794; H to Lord Fitzwilliam, April 6, 1771, M. XXV, 589; H to ?, February 11, 1771, M. XXVII, 203; James H. Stark, Loyalists of Massachusetts (London, 1903), 174.

6. "Hutchinson in America," 41, 51; Malcolm Freiberg, Thomas Hutchinson of Milton (Milton, 1971); William Pencak and Ralph J. Crandall, "Metropolitan Boston Before the American Revolution: An Urban Interpretation of the Imperial Crisis," Bostonian Society Proceedings (1982).

7. Christopher Lasch, Haven in a Heartless World: The Family Besieged (New York, 1977); Richard Sennett, Families Against the City (Cambridge, 1970); Philip Greven, The Protestant Temperament: Patterns of Child Rearing, Religious Experience, and the Self in Colonial America (New York, 1977).

8. "Hutchinson in America," 41-45, 60; see various letters of H to William and Charlton Palmer in M. XXV-XXVII for his business activities and H to Directors of the East India Company, December 19, 1773, XXVII, 1133.

9. "Hutchinson in America," 39-41.

10. Ibid., 43-46.

11. Ibid., 48.

12. Ibid., 49; H to Richard Saltonstall, August 22, 1759, Saltonstall Papers, 429.

13. "Hutchinson in America," 48. Hutchinson ordered a new edition of Fox's Martyrs in 1767, H to ?, January 22, 1767, M. XXVI, 532.

14. Quincy, 173; Hardwicke, November 7, 1774, 2.

15. Quincy, 237.

16. "Hutchinson in America," 53-54.

17. Eighteenth century politics are described in William Pencak, War, Politics and Revolution in Provincial Massachusetts (Boston, 1981).

18. History, II, 297; I, 280; II, 7, 91.

19. "Hutchinson in America," 52-53. See John Eliot, Biographical Dictionary (Boston, 1809), 209, for Hutchinson's oratory.

20. Ibid., 58.

21. Ibid., 58; History, III, 31.

22. Quincy, 173; Bailyn, Hutchinson, 158.

23. Bailyn, Hutchinson, ch. i. has an excellent account of perceptions of Hutchinson by his contemporaries.

24. History, I, xxviii, 351; H to ?, March 26, 1765, M. XXVI, 259; History, I, xxix. Hardwicke, September 23, 1776, 120. Hutchinson originally planned volume III of his History to have "the satisfaction of being revenged on some of the

r[ascal]s" who were troubling his administration, most notably "Mr. Otis" the son, "after I am dead." (H to ?, November 30, 1763, M. XXVI, 75, and H to Ezra Stiles, July 6, 1764, M. XXVI, 172.) But his attitude changed by the time he wrote the book: Otis is in fact the only one of the patriots who comes off reasonably well: "Mr. Otis, in his calm moments, had always disavowed any design of a general revolt or of attaining to a state of independence." (History, III, 244). Otis thus became innocent by virtue of insanity. Hutchinson wrote an unknown correspondent that "I desire to forgive him and never intend to return evil for evil or to hurt his character in the least unless the vindication of my own renders it unavoidable." (H to ?, March 27, 1766, M. Arch., XXVI, 557.)

II. FIGHTING NAVAL IMPRESSMENT

With the outbreak of the War of Jenkins' Ear in 1739, the impressment of Americans into the British navy became a serious problem. In earlier colonial wars, conflict over the issue had been pre-empted, to a considerable degree, by two acts of Parliament. The first, of 1696, had stipulated that presses could be authorized only with a warrant from the colonial governor -- who in Massachusetts had to act with the "advice and consent" of a council elected by the house of representatives in conjunction with the outgoing council. The second act, passed during Queen Anne's War in 1707, had forbidden all impressment in colonial waters, but colonials and Englishmen later disagreed over whether it was perpetual or had expired with the Peace of Utrecht in 1713. The quarter-century of peace following this treaty ensured that there would be little need for impressment. But when war began again in 1739, British naval captains began to ignore parliamentary restrictions and seize Americans to man their ships.(1)

From the early 1740s until the American Revolution, naval impressment proved an intermittent obstacle to harmonious relations between Massachusetts and England. Anti-impressment riots occurred in Boston in 1741, 1745, and 1747.(2) The General Court supplied more formal objections on these occasions, and took notice of the practice in 1742 and 1756 as well.(3) The Boston town meeting presented a declaration of grievances of its own in 1768.(4) Additionally, the case of Rex v. Corbet (1769) -- in which a sailor was tried for murdering two members of a press gang -- acquired widespread notice.(5) Naval impressment surfaced as a major public issue in Massachusetts at least seven times during the thirty-year period from 1740 to 1770.

Thomas Hutchinson was actively concerned in four of these incidents (1742, 1747, 1756, 1769) and took action as the province's lieutenant-governor to redress the situation Boston faced in 1768. Furthermore, he tried to free individuals who were impressed and to work out agreements with British naval officers to regulate the practice and thereby neutralize its explosive potential. To be sure,

Hutchinson's prominence should not be attributed to any special virtue or unusual hatred of the press gang on his part. In three of the major episodes, he accidentally happened to be in a uniquely favorable position to appear as a defender of American liberty. Similarly, as lieutenant-governor and governor, he intervened because his protests would prove more effectual than those of private inhabitants. Moreover, Hutchinson was one of the few men who continuously held a position of leadership from 1740 until the Revolution. His prominence opposing impressment was a function of sheer political longevity as well as chance.

Yet while impressment only surfaced in Hutchinson's career -- as it did in the course of Massachusetts politics as a whole -- on several occasions, his activities do confirm that he did not invariably (if ever) sacrifice his country's liberties to advance his own prestige with British authorities. Rather, he sincerely tried to preserve Massachusetts' legitimate rights, acting consistently to mitigate and, in one instance, terminate the practice. Nor did he interpret provincial liberties much more narrowly than his revolutionary adversaries. But unlike them, he always sought to ensure that even if some claims of right had to be sacrificed, impressment did not become a serious stumbling block to Anglo-American relations. For despite impressment, he considered the British flag to protect more rights and material blessings than any other, and did not wish to jeopardize the situation. Hutchinson played for maximum practical relief even if it meant adopting a humble stance on occasion; he could not see the point of antagonizing the mother country with excessive zeal.

Hutchinson's first important anti-impressment activity occurred in March 1742. When Governor William Shirley failed to respond rapidly enough to the requests of Captain James Scott of H.M.S. *Astraea* to replace men lost from desertion and battle, the latter instituted a press in Boston harbor. Among those seized was a party of men returning from a short trip to inspect some lumber to be used in constructing a new house for Hutchinson. Chief among them was William Pratt, a Boston housewright worth "1500 or 2000 pounds . . . a master workman with servants under him." Pratt's brother Caleb informed Hutchinson, who had employed William, of the affair, whereupon he went to Governor Shirley and obtained a letter requesting

Pratt's release.(6)

Hutchinson then rowed out to the _Astraea_. Captain Scott, however, refused to honor the letter, stating that "his commission extended to the taking of able-bodied landmen as well as seamen," and added that "he had been very ill-used by the merchants and magistrates" of Boston, so that "if they were brought into distress or difficulty they might thank themselves for it." Scott then informed Pratt and Hutchinson that the former would not be released unless he purchased a substitute, or until Scott impressed a sufficient number of men for his crew.(7)

While on board the _Astraea_, Hutchinson met the wife of his servant, William White, a townsman who had also been impressed. Scott refused to respond to the woman's entreaties "unless she brought another man in his room," whereupon Hutchinson informed the captain "that he knew the circumstances of said White and family and that it would be impossible for the woman to procure a man" in place of her husband "though she parted with all she had and bound herself to seven years' servitude." Hutchinson thereupon returned to town to inform the governor and council of his encounter with Captain Scott. Shirley finally obtained the release of the impressed inhabitants in return for issuing warrants to replace them by non-native seamen.(8)

Hutchinson's behavior during the _Astraea_ incident established him as an opponent of arbitrary impressment. He had not only acted as the government's intermediary, but he had called attention to the incident in the first place. As Speaker of the House of Representatives, he played an even larger role in opposing a press instituted by Commodore Charles Knowles on the morning of November 17, 1947. Knowles' press provoked a riot which lasted three days; a crowd formed which seized several of his officers as hostages until the impressed men were released.

Hutchinson became the second person of importance to encounter the mob and the first to establish some sort of successful working relationship with it. Benjamin Pollard, the Sheriff of Suffolk County, had been roughed up for his peremptory demand that the mob release Lieutenant Derby of H.M.S. _Alborough_, the first officer to be taken hostage. Hutchinson, however, obtained Derby's release by assuring the crowd he did not participate in the press. This success suggests not only did Hutchinson possess influence with the general population, but also that the mob in fact consisted, in addition to foreign seamen, of native Bostonians who trusted Hutchinson and had repeatedly elected him to the house of representatives. Hutchinson then took Derby to Governor Shirley's residence to obtain protection and acquaint him with the situation.(9)

The behavior on November 17 of the house of representatives itself as directed by Speaker Hutchinson demonstrated that it fully sympathized with the demands of the mob. The house did no business that day besides appointing a committee to investigate the riot. Nevertheless, it adjourned moments before the mob entered the courthouse to press its demands. Hutchinson and other house leaders then presented an ultimatum to the governor and council. They pleaded with the reluctant Shirley -- who was incensed at the mob's attempted blackmail -- "to get the inhabitants and some of the outward bound seamen discharged." Hutchinson emerged at the height of the riot as the crowd's principal spokesman by virtue of his position as Speaker of the House as well as out of personal conviction. The following day, the General Court remained in session but took no notice of the crowd. Neither house was "willing to interpose," as Hutchinson wrote two decades later in his History, "lest they should encourage other commanders of the navy to future acts of the like nature."(10)

On November 19, having failed to negotiate the release of the captured inhabitants from Knowles, Shirley sent a letter to the General Court asking its assistance in ending mob rule. Upon its receipt, both houses adopted a series of resolutions, written by Hutchinson, condemning the outburst, instructing the militia -- which had not turned out as Shirley had ordered -- of its duty to suppress such occurrences, and pledging their support in quelling this and future uprisings. At the same time, the legislature promised to use every effort to redress the grievance of impressment. Its cooperation with the mob appears by the fact that, as Hutchinson wrote, "as soon as these votes were known, the tumultuous spirit began to subside." Knowles released many of the impressed men before he left for the West Indies on November 30.(11)

Hutchinson's account of the riot, written twenty

years later, confirmed contemporary private correspondence describing the mob as consisting of the town as a whole and approved of by leading citizens such as Hutchinson himself. Here Hutchinson revealed the complicity of the legislature, which he had hidden carefully in the resolutions he wrote in 1747. He also noted there were "several thousand" people in the crowd, which may be an exaggeration. Nevertheless, Governor Shirley and Samuel Phillips Savage confirmed that more than the handful of seamen and strangers -- blamed for the riot in all the official documents to avoid the resentment of imperial officials -- participated.(12)

Finally, Hutchinson's History explained how the riot almost escaped the control of the responsible men in town. "Some of the higher spirits" dubbed Governor Shirley's retirement to an island in Boston harbor to negotiate for the release of the men a "desertion or abdication"; they thought Shirley feared the mob and supported Knowles. Sensing insurrectionary potential, "the principal members of the house," including Hutchinson himself, began "to think more seriously of leaving the governor without support when there was not the least ground of exception to his conduct." At this point, the deputies finally summoned the militia and ordered the crowd suppressed -- requests Shirley had made three days earlier. The house's ability to dissolve the mob by fiat suggests respectable Bostonians had been involved all along.(13)

The appearance of a new newspaper in January 1748, The Independent Advertiser, confirmed Hutchinson's descriptions of the ideological cleavage produced by the riot, an observation missing in all the contemporary accounts. Founded by the twenty-five year old Samuel Adams, it justified the riot on the grounds that when government failed to protect the people, a state of nature ensued which permitted the inhabitants to defend themselves as they pleased.(14) The aftermath of the Knowles Riot therefore anticipated, in embryonic form, the Adams-Hutchinson confrontation of the revolutionary era. In both instances, Adams took advantage of British policies which hurt the colonies and proceeded to universalize grievances into planned, tyrannical usurpations of natural rights. He worked to transform specific tensions in the imperial system into an ideological confrontation. Hutchinson, on the other hand, agreed with his countrymen's analysis of their burdens, as he did in the 1760s. But he thought relief could best be obtained by a moderate course of action which prevented the development of an adversary relationship between Massachusetts and Britain, as the assembly's swift action against the Knowles mob when it began to take extreme positions indicated.

Hutchinson's activity in the Knowles crisis explains only too well why, even after the destruction of his house in the Stamp Act riots, he could insist that "mobs, a sort of them at least, are constitutional." After the Boston Massacre, he still maintained that "it may justly be said, of the people of this province, that they seldom, if ever, have assembled in a tumultuous manner unless they have been oppressed." Hutchinson recognized the people's right to oppose violently the illegal use of force by government officials, as in the Knowles Riot. He drew the line, however, at resistance to acts of Parliament, even when unjust. To threaten the legitimate, supreme legislature of the British Empire implied aiming, even if not intentionally, at an insurrection.(15)

When impressments began again during the French and Indian War, Hutchinson again took the lead. In the summer of 1756, the General Court sent a formal protest to be delivered to the King and Parliament through province agent William Bollan. On September 2, at the suggestion of the council, a committee consisting of Hutchinson, John Osborne, and Andrew Oliver of that body joined with Robert Hale, Chambers Russell, and Richard Reed of the house to draw up the document. Hutchinson almost certainly wrote the final draft, which both houses approved on September 11.(6)

Hutchinson's argument incorporated his unequivocal opposition to all forms of impressment, broad construction of colonial rights generally, and factual mastery of the issue. First, he described the situation. During the spring and summer of 1756, "all inward bound vessels [into Boston] had their men impressed." Not only "His Majesty's ships stationed in this province, but the ships at Halifax" as well took advantage of the city's proximity and abundance of seamen to "supply their deficiency of men." The navy made things even worse by seizing fishermen on the Grand Banks for the first time "to punish the province," Hutchinson alleged, for a lawsuit brought "against two seamen or petty officers of the Hornet sloop for being concerned in impressment."(17)

Hutchinson utilized arguments appealing both to British self-interest and to Massachusetts' unjust sufferings to end impressment. After recapitulating previous episodes, including one in 1745 when two veterans of the Louisbourg campaign were "barbarously murdered," he maintained that the new practice of taking sailors on the high seas must put "an end to the fishery, the most profitable branch of our business." Realizing that the state of Massachusetts' fishery might not concern the English ministry, he went on to show that "the proceeds of the greatest part of the fish that is caught center in England," since they were used to pay for colonial importations of British manufactured goods.

Hutchinson continued by condemning the fact that Britain's most loyal and cooperative province in military policy endured an excessive burden of impressment as well. He complained that "we hear of no impresses anywhere but in Massachusetts," which caused "our seamen [to] go in great number to Rhode Island and New York." As a result, these provinces could outfit many privateers, and enjoyed a flourishing trade while "the persons in trade here, are obliged to let their merchantmen lie still for want of trade." The navy had terrified the "coasting vessels, [upon] which our seaport towns depend for their provisions and fuel," out of "following their employment" as well.

To conclude, Hutchinson introduced an ingenious argument demonstrating that impressment not only was unjust, but manifested a self-contradiction in British policy which ought to be resolved. He considered it "absurd to suppose, that the inhabitants should have this privilege by charter, that even the king's governor cannot carry a man of them out of the province without the consent of the assembly" to serve in a military expedition, "and yet they must be at the mercy of every commander in the navy." If England had granted the province charter, how could it both pretend that it mattered and yet allow impressment without the assembly's consent? Hutchinson implied that impressment of any sort violated the Bay Colony's charter. By this logic, even the statute of 1696, sanctioning impressment if the governor and council alone consented, would be invalid. Hutchinson here advanced a position on impressment which he, like the colonies in general, adopted during the Stamp Act crisis of 1765. He criticized that tax for trespassing on "the most solemn engagements" which

England had made with her colonies. For Parliament to raise "monies by internal or external taxes from any part of the empire, which is not represented," could "hardly be reconciled to the constitution of the empire." Taxation, like impressment, violated the "perpetual" right of the colonies to have "assemblies of their own choosing to make laws for their government." Acts of Parliament contradicting provincial charters, which served as their fundamental law, were unconstitutional.(18)

However, the presence of illegal legislation did not warrant violent disruption of the colonial system. Nor did Hutchinson think protests stressing matters of right as strongly as possible would do the most good. He opted for a more limited remonstrance in both cases, appealing to British reason, self-interest, and generosity rather than waving a red flag before the imperial bull. In the case of impressment, he cautioned Agent Bollan not to insist upon "a prohibition of all impresses of seamen in any of the colonies," unless he thought it "convenient, at this time," to do so. He authorized Bollan to settle for measures prohibiting presses out of coasters and fishing vessels and equalizing the burden of impressment among the several colonies. Hutchinson's recommendations revealed something of the budding American nationalism which appeared among those men, such as himself and Benjamin Franklin, who had worked extensively in coordinating colonial military affairs during the French and Indian War. Although he wrote only on behalf of Massachusetts, Hutchinson hoped for an end to all American impressment.

But Hutchinson's willingness to tread softly on British toes in the interest of achieving the best practical result had its limits. His memorial concluded with a masterful, cryptic apology concealing a subtle threat. Stating the indisputable facts that "this province has ever been forward in promoting measures for His Majesty's service; they have done so to the utmost of their ability; and have been impoverishing themselves for the common benefit," both in this war and the last," Hutchinson hinted that such enthusiasm might not last forever. While using Massachusetts' ardor in the common cause as an argument that "no construction to their disadvantage . . . be made of this application," and insisting that "their disposition to promote the same service is not lessened," the province still "needed encouragement in every way that is possible." What Hutchinson really said, in his typically polite, understated fashion, was that Britain would have to meet some of Massachusetts' demands on impressment or risk some waning of its exceptional support for the war effort.

Hutchinson's letter formed the almost verbatim conclusion of the memorial agent William Bollan presented to the Lords of Admiralty, although Bollan prefaced it with equally cogent remarks of his own. He added that Massachusetts had been "planted with great toil, peril, and expense by the inhabitants," who "at all times defended it free from charge to the crown," and claimed that one-third of the eligible population had done military service in the 1740s, when the province had not only defended itself and its neighbors but captured Louisbourg and contributed troops to defend the West Indies as well. Bollan concluded that "this province producing no staple commodity, and being neither fruitful in soil, nor temperate in climate, its wealth consists in the number of inhabitants who are chiefly fishermen that are poor, and farmers who are far from rich." Bollan therefore provided the context in which Hutchinson's more specific arguments could be understood. By interrupting the trade of the most patriotic province in America, impressment hurt the colony that both deserved and could afford such treatment the least.(19)

Hutchinson's powerful but conciliatory petition met the same fate as his formal protest against the Stamp Act on grounds of inexpediency to Britain rather than American right. British officialdom did not even bother to refute the Hutchinson-Bollan case. They shunted it about from one to another and finally brushed it aside. Bollan's lobbying with the Duke of Newcastle and William Pitt, the effective heads of government in the fall of 1757, "praying their interposition to save a sinking province," met with a referral to the Admiralty Lords. There, the agent received the paltry assurance that Hutchinson's constitutional law was correct, but that national emergencies permitted the government to stretch its normal powers. Their Lordships admitted that "impresses in general are unlawful, and incompatible with the British constitution, and that nothing but extreme necessity can justify them." They even claimed that they "were made without any authority at all from the board." But to Bollan's argument that the province charter demanded that they order the practice discontinued immediately, the Lords insisted that "the charter gives the inhabitants of the province no farther right of protection with respect to impressment for service than the common law gives to all the king's subjects." Bollan protested in vain that "necessity of state" was a lame excuse. Referring to Massachusetts' heavy tax burden and declining trade, he argued that "necessity confounded would finally ruin the province." British intransigence proved as much of an obstacle to Hutchinson's conciliatory initiatives as American impatience.(20)

Impressments continued during and after the Seven Years' War, although Governor Thomas Pownall's ability to dissuade British officers from seizing inhabitants of the province alleviated matters. However, once they left their native shores, Massachusetts sailors faced the same perils as everyone else. Even Hutchinson's own nephew, Increase Mather, great-grandson and namesake of the great Puritan clergyman, was impressed in England in 1758 and remained in service until he died at the siege of Havana in 1763. In 1765, Hutchinson as lieutenant-governor interceded on behalf of Nathaniel Belknap, who had been seized and taken to Halifax. He later complained to an anonymous correspondent that "it is unfortunate that in the midst of these difficulties" that had developed with England after the war, "the Romney [the man-of-war stationed in Boston harbor] has been pressing seamen out of all inward and outward bound vessels." Even though the captain "did not take men belonging to the province who have families," yet the sailors' fear to venture forth "prevented coasters as well as other vessels coming in freely." With respect to the explosive situation in Boston politics, impressment added "more fuel to the great stock among us before." Hutchinson concluded this letter with an admonition that "it is a pity in peaceable times any pressing of seamen should be allowed in the colonies." In June 1768, however, the Romney's captain and Governor Francis Bernard worked out an agreement whereby only foreign seamen would be impressed, which Hutchinson hoped would take "much from the edge of the resentment raised against the men of war."(21)

Unable to end impressment, Hutchinson turned his efforts toward liberating individuals in cases where his official position might help. He thus became involved in the final controversial impressment incident of the colonial era. In 1769, two members of a press gang tried to seize Michael Corbet aboard the *Pitt Packet*, a vessel owned by Robert Hooper of Marblehead. Corbet resisted and killed the men. Brought to trial for murder before a special court of admiralty including Bernard, Hutchinson, Samuel Hood (commander of the North American squadron) and eleven other colonial officials, Corbet was defended by John Adams. Hutchinson, however, dominated the trial.

Before Adams began his final plea, Hutchinson moved for a recess. After four hours, the court returned to pronounce Corbet not guilty by reason of self-defense. Half a century later, Adams concocted the story that Hutchinson had arranged the acquittal to prevent him from citing the aforementioned act of 1707, which had abolished American impressment. Dora Mae Clark, echoing Adams' own judgment, agreed that "Hutchinson by his decisive action may have prevented impressment from becoming one of the main issues of the Revolution in Massachusetts. Hutchinson adjourned the court to prevent the constitutional issue of impressment from becoming a source of controversy." But the problem with the Adams/Clark interpretation is that the constitutionality of impressment had already been questioned publicly in a set of instructions from the Boston town meeting to its representatives. These resolutions had been drawn up by none other than Adams himself the year before. Hutchinson therefore must have moved the adjournment -- and, presumably, the acquittal -- for other reasons.(22)

Hutchinson clearly wished to do more than obtain Corbet's release: he himself had been responsible for digging up and presenting some obscure British statutes to Governor Bernard which insured that Corbet would be tried by an Admiralty Court. About to retire to England, Bernard, in company with Corbet's lawyers, Adams and James Otis, was perfectly willing to permit a jury trial called for by conflicting statutes. That would have acquitted Corbet with no difficulty. It thus appears that Hutchinson adopted the course he did so that he, rather than a jury, would be responsible for Corbet's release and thereby contradict the revolutionaries' propaganda that he was a tool of the ministry and an enemy of liberty. At the same time he would prevent his antagonists from capitalizing politically on the issue. In a somewhat different manner than Adams thought, Hutchinson tried to contribute to stabilizing Anglo-

American relations.

Hutchinson's plan worked perfectly. During the trial, he proved more helpful in freeing Corbet than Adams. As during the Boston Massacre trials in 1771 -- when he prevented co-counsellor Josiah Quincy from introducing evidence to show that the townspeople had planned the confrontation with the soldiers -- Adams followed a defense strategy that might well have helped the patriot cause at the expense of his client. As Adams' papers show, he considered it adequate to summon witnesses proving that an impressment had indeed been attempted; then he would simply go on to cite the act of 1707 demonstrating that it was illegal. Adams' case suffered from the serious flaw that unanimity on whether this act still applied did not exist. He knew this, for otherwise he would not have planned to bring up and refute the opinions of British Attorneys and Solicitors General that the act had expired.(23)

By merely publicizing the unconstitutionality of impressment, Adams could have martyred his client in the patriot cause. The reason Hutchinson gave for Corbet's acquittal had nothing to do with the case his attorney was prepared to present. Rather, "it appeared, that neither the lieutenant nor any of his superior officers were authorized to impress, by any warrant or special authority from the Lords of Admiralty."(24) Even though Hutchinson believed all colonial impressments unconstitutional, as his letter of 1757 proved, he realized this argument would not be accepted by the other members of the court, or the imperial administrators who might read about the case at home. But his insistence that individuals could illegally resist arbitrary acts of power carried the necessary weight. Unlike the patriots, who appeared willing to sacrifice poor Corbet to demonstrate another example of British tyranny, Hutchinson swallowed his own constitutional scruples, worked to defuse the issue and its revolutionary potential, and sought the maximum practical benefit for the man most immediately threatened. He also hoped to reap the added advantage of beginning his own governorship on a conciliatory footing.

To be sure, Hutchinson was playing with fire. The decision implied that colonials could, if necessary, resist illegal actions of British officials to the point of killing them. This implication probably explains the failure of Hutchinson or Bernard to discuss the case in their letters to the ministry. Had the revolutionaries been willing, they could have used Hutchinson's own judgment to undermine the very authority he defended. But because such a course would have required, on at least this one occasion, that Hutchinson and the other members of the Admiralty Court be presented as friends of American liberty, the impressment issue was not stressed. There were plenty of other grievances to be protested.

Hutchinson did not permit Massachusetts' ill-treatment of him to interfere with his continued efforts during his own governorship on behalf of the province's impressed inhabitants. In a letter to former Governor Bernard of August 14, 1771, he wrote that:(25)

> Our Sons of Liberty know for what purpose the men of war are stationed here and look upon them with an evil eye, but the commodore has conducted [himself] with so much prudence and kept the officers and men in such remarkable good order that we have had no sort of disturbance and no complaint <u>except what naturally flows from impresses to supply the places of runaway seamen</u>.

As governor, Hutchinson supplied the warrants required for impressments in order to prevent naval officers from taking matters into their own hands. But the letter to Bernard indicated that he hoped his ex-superior would use the fact that impressment incensed the populace to lobby for cessation of the practice.

Hutchinson's final recorded effort in opposition to impressment occurred on May 28, 1772. He wrote to Governor John Wentworth of New Hampshire to intercede for the release of a seaman of that province because he had "promised the navy he would only intercede for discharge of natives of Massachusetts."(26) The letter reveals that Hutchinson not only worried that impressment violated provincial autonomy. He also objected to its disruptive effect on the lives of ordinary men.

Hutchinson's opposition to naval impressment sheds new light on his career. First, he consistently opposed the practice over a thirty year period, which undoubtedly helps explain his intermittent popularity despite widespread opposition to his political principles. While he undoubtedly manipulated himself into the position of taking a major role in Corbet's trial, he displayed a more disinterested conduct on other occasions. Hutchinson's fight against impressment revealed the reasonings and methods he would later use to oppose the Stamp Act and other unjustifiable exertions of British authority. It also illustrated the gap that separated his conception of America's role in the empire from that of the British administration. Hutchinson agreed much more with the Americans' defense of their rights than with the British critique, but when necessary he subordinated his principles to the greater purpose of harmonizing Anglo-American relations. Unlike his opponents, he realized that unconditional assertions of right did not constitute the best method for settling differences in the imperial system.

FOOTNOTES

1. For information on impressment, see John Lax and William Pencak, "The Knowles Riot and the Crisis of the 1740s in Massachusetts," Perspectives in American History, X (1976), 163-214.

2. Events in 1741 discussed in unsigned deposition, June 9, 1741, Robert Treat Paine Papers, Massachusetts Historical Society; Journals of the House of Representatives of Massachusetts Bay (Boston, 1919 -   ), XVIII, 202 (hereafter cited as House Journals); M. LIII, 83-85. For 1745, House Journals, XXII, 204-205, 212-213; Boston Town Records (Boston, 1885), XIV, 84-85.

3. See nn. 6-9, 16 below.

4. Boston Town Records (Boston, 1886) XVI, 256-259.

5. See n. 22 below.

6. M. LIII, 195.

7. Hutchinson's deposition before the council is the source for this and the following paragraph. M. VIII, 270.

8. House Journals, XIX, 205.

9. Letter of Samuel Phillips Savage, November 21, 1747, Savage Papers I, Massachusetts Historical Society; History, II, 330; William Shirley to Lords of Trade, December 1, 1747, Correspondence of William Shirley, ed. C. H. Lincoln (New York, 1912), I, 412.

10. House Journals, XXIV, 208; William Shirley to Lords of Trade, December 1, 1747, Shirley, Correspondence, I, 415; History, II, 332. Throughout the riot Shirley tried to reconcile Knowles and Boston. He tried to free both Knowles' officers and the impressed men. In his official dispatches, he condemned the mob as he was obliged to.

11. William Shirley to Josiah Willard, November 19, 1747, Shirley, Correspondence, I, 408-409; History, II, 332; House Journals, XXIV, 212-214.

12. For a mob supported by the town, see History, II, 330-333; William Shirley to Josiah Willard, November 19, 1747, Shirley, Correspondence, I, 408-409; letter of Samuel Philips Savage, November 21, 1747, Savage Papers, I. For official dispatches condemning the mob, see Boston Records, XIV, 212-214; Shirley to Lords of Trade, December 1, 1747, Shirley, Correspondence, I, 412-418. As a member of a town committee on December 29, Hutchinson criticized the governor for publishing his letter to Willard of the nineteenth and asked him to retract his statements blaming the town and its "men of influence" for the riot. Boston Public Library, H. 92, 94.

13. History, II, 332-333.

14. William V. Welles, The Life and Public Services of Samuel Adams (Boston, 1865), I, 19.

15. H to John or Robert Grant, July 27, 1768, M. XXVI, 659; Bradford, 203.

16. House Journals, XXXIII, 164, 179-180.

17. [Thomas Hutchinson] to William Bollan, September 11, 1756, Miscellaneous Bound Manuscripts, Massachusetts Historical Society. This document is the source for the next several paragraphs. It may be attributed to Hutchinson for the following reasons: a) it is in his handwriting; b) the discussion of colonial trade resembles that found in the History, II, 340-343; c) on two other important occasions, to end the Knowles Riot (ibid., II, 332) and to protest Lord Loudoun's quartering his troops in Boston (ibid., III, 48) the General Court chose Hutchinson to draft its protest. None of these points, by itself, is conclusive; taken together, I believe they are.

18. "Stamp Act Essay," 482-483; H to Richard Jackson, October 20, 1767, M. XXV, 185.

19. Bollan's memorial is in folder 14 of the Bollan Papers, New England Historic Genealogical Society.

20. William Bollan to the Massachusetts General Court, October 1, 1757, Bollan Papers.

21. House Journals, XXXV, 267-268; 274-275. Like Shirley before and Bernard after him, Pownall worked out agreements to supply the navy with foreign seamen in return for a pledge of immunity for the province's inhabitants. H to ?, September 16, 1763, M. XXVI, 135; H to Charles Morris, July 22, 1765, M. XXVI, 235; H to ?, June 1768, M. XXVI, 647-648.

22. The information for this case is taken from Hiller Zobel, The Boston Massacre (New York, 1970), 113-131; The Legal Papers of John Adams, ed. L. Kinvin Wroth and Hiller Zobel (Cambridge, 1965), II, 280-335; History, III, 167; Dora Mae Clark, "The Impressment of Seamen in the American Colonies," Essays on Colonial History Presented to Charles McLean Andrews by His Students (New Haven, 1931), 193.

23. Zobel, The Boston Massacre, 259, 282. I do not wish to argue that Adams consciously weakened his case, which Zobel argues he did in the massacre trials. He may have presented the only case he thought possible. If Adams was doing his best, then the layman Hutchinson exhibited a more thorough knowledge of precedent in this instance.

24. History, III, 167.

25. H to Francis Bernard, August 14, 1771, M. XXVII, 353. My emphasis.

26. H to John Wentworth, May 28, 1772, M. XXVII, 907.

III. CHIEF JUSTICE OF MASSACHUSETTS

In February 1772, John Adams confided to his diary that "the liberties of this country had more to fear from one man, the present Governor Hutchinson, than from any other man, nay than from all the other men in the world." The previous June, Adams had placed the primary blame for America's sufferings on Massachusetts' governor: "his character and conduct have been the cause of laying a foundation for perpetual discontent and uneasiness between Britain and the colonies, of perpetual struggles of one party for wealth and power at the expense of the liberties of this country." Popular sentiment confirmed Adams' view: newspapers and pamphlets compared Hutchinson to Julius Caesar, Alexander the Great, Machiavelli, and the four horsemen of the Apocalypse. One print depicted him as roasting in Hell tormented by devils pursuing him with memories of his crimes. Perhaps the most extreme example of anti-Hutchinson rhetoric can be found in a letter from Nathaniel Truman to James Otis Sr., in which he appeared as the mirror opposite of Christ: "while the Son of God (in whom this abandoned wretch professes to believe) has sacrificed his own life to promote the happiness and secure the freedom of mankind, He can deliberately sacrifice the Truth and thereby his Savior to procure misery, chains, bloodshed, and death for the same species."(1)

Why was Hutchinson so detested by the revolutionaries, blamed for personally concocting the Stamp Act, instigating the garrisoning of Boston in 1768 by British soldiers, and provoking the Boston Massacre? His personal correspondence revealed that he worked behind the scenes to prevent passage of the Stamp Act, lobbied effectively for its repeal, and constantly advised his overseas superiors that their wisest course would have been to leave the colonies alone so the radicals might burn themselves out. And before the revolutionary crisis began, as Adams enviously and grudgingly admitted, "ninety-nine in an hundred . . . thought him the greatest and best man in America . . . a pious, a wise, a learned, a good man, an eminent scholar, a philosopher . . . the greatest and best man in the world."(2) Adams surely exaggerated Hutchinson's reputation to gloat more smugly over his demise, but all Massachusetts respected Hutchinson even where it disagreed with his specific policies.

Much of Hutchinson's undoing began when in 1760 he accepted Governor Bernard's offer of an appointment as chief justice of the province. By accepting the post, he awakened cries of megalomania and unprecedented engrossment of offices (he then held five). His decision in the Writs of Assistance case, refusal to open the courts after the Stamp Act, and speeches at the Superior Court urging that revolutionaries be indicted for their crimes aroused a resentment against him difficult to imagine if he had not accepted this prestigious post. But aside from these few crucial episodes, we know little about what sort of judge Hutchinson was. What precedents did he cite to reach his decisions? How did these agree with those of his fellow justices and the bar? Did he have a consistent philosophy of law? And finally, in the midst of unprecedented political crisis, was he able to keep the law above politics and, if not, what sort of goals did he hope to promote? Fortunately if ironically, the young Josiah Quincy kept a journal which coincided with Hutchinson's tenure and recorded many of his decisions and speeches.

Quincy's notes reveal that in law as in politics, Hutchinson suffered a tragic fate. Just as his political program sought to balance the irreconcilable policies of hard-line British administrators and radical American patriots, Hutchinson's notion of the function of the courts presented a third, middle road challenging the two judicial philosophies under which Massachusetts judges and lawyers operated. Like his behavior as lieutenant-governor, Hutchinson's career as chief justice succeeded in alienating almost everyone because he refused to side unequivocally with either party but held fast to his lonely course.

By 1760, Massachusetts had partially overcome its long-standing distaste for professional lawyers. Throughout most of their history, the people had regarded "pettifoggers" as self-seeking obstacles to justice, which individuals best obtained by pleading their own cases before respected figures in the community serving as amateur judges. That way, the disposition of a case could be determined on its true merits rather than through the manipulation of jurors or the flaunting of legal technicalities. By the time Hutchinson became chief justice, the situation had begun to change. An aggressive new legal profession, anxious to establish its identity, had recently emerged. To be sure, Massachusetts had enjoyed the service of a few professional lawyers since the early eighteenth century, but most of these had been connected to well-established families with commercial or landed wealth or had received legal training in England. But in the 1750s and 60s, guided by Jeremiah Gridley and Oxenbridge Thacher of the older generation, young men such as Josiah Quincy, John Adams, and James Otis Jr. began to use the law itself as both a means of social advancement and a vehicle for political protest.(3)

The tendency of Massachusetts lawyers to plead cases in the technical manner of their English counterparts, stressing precedents from Britain they considered applicable in the province, reflected a general trend of mid-century America to measure itself by British standards and values. In 1772, the lawyers formed the Suffolk Bar Association, an imitation of the English Inns of Court. About ten years earlier, they had donned the robes and powdered wigs of English lawyers and judges. In old age, John Adams blamed Hutchinson for this innovation, but this practice would have fitted poorly with Hutchinson's more traditional jurisprudence.

Another idea of law also appeared for the first time in the 1760s: the notion that Americans ought not to place their primary faith in the rights of Englishmen and the practices of British law courts, but rather in the natural rights of man. First used in a Massachusetts court by James Otis in 1761 to argue that general search warrants granted to customs officials (Writs of Assistance) were unconstitutional, the idea that man only entered society to preserve his life, liberty, and estates, also represented a British import, in this case of the social compact propounded in John Locke's Second Treatise of Government. Throughout the 1760s, lawyers and other protesters used natural rights philosophy as a last resort when no traditional precedents or English analogies existed to justify opposition to a specific policy. Writs of Assistance, for example, provided the government officers with the opportunity to confiscate property arbitrarily, and hence could not possibly have been a power granted to the state by the inhabitants when they first created civil society. Lockean theory provided Massachusetts with a means of overruling objectionable statute law.

Thomas Hutchinson thus faced a court system whose search for identity mirrored that of Massachusetts as a whole. Would the province guide itself through the troubled times after 1760 by appealing to English precedents or to universally applicable principles? Ultimately, the loyalists, like the imperial administration, chose the former course whereas the overwhelming majority of the population opted for the latter. But there was a third way. Hutchinson sought to reconcile the alternatives, in typical fashion, by rejecting them both and proposing an accommodation on his own turf: Massachusetts tradition. His response to the colonial crisis is best understood analogously with the ideas of Edmund Burke. Just as Burke tried (and managed) to impart to his countrymen a new understanding of why they should cherish traditional British liberties and reject the doctrines of English radicals and the French Revolution, Hutchinson tried (and failed) to instill a similar understanding of traditional provincial liberties and customs. Both men sought a middle road between tyranny and anarchy by erecting custom as a barrier to both despotic centralization and revolutionary natural rights.

Hutchinson embodied the very tradition he sought to define. He was one of the last of the amateur gentlemen jurists who had long decided cases on their common sense merits. These men, with whom he identified so strongly in his History, had guided the Bay Colony's destiny since the days of John Winthrop. Serving in diplomatic, judicial, legislative, and military positions, often simultaneously, they nevertheless did not earn a living from their government posts, but from trade and rural estates. And they did a tremendous job. Anyone who has even glanced at the Superior Court records in the Suffolk County Courthouse will undoubtedly be staggered at how five judges could have handled such an immense volume of business, riding circuit throughout the province for four sessions a year, all the while attending to their private affairs and other posts. As chief justice, Hutchinson sought to continue the tradition of common sense justice and to awaken his countrymen that its loss, in company with the passing of the elite which had dispensed it, would be irretrievable. Examining the specific cases for which Hutchinson's decisions survive and his pronouncements on the functions of the court system, his intellectual alienation from both the professional lawyers and natural rights theorists is apparent.

Hutchinson's career on the bench may be understood in terms of four categories. First, he stressed the absolute inviolability of statute law and insisted judges had to follow its letter, even if it offended their own principles. Second, where written law was lacking, he favored Massachusetts customary practice over natural rights, English precedents, and even his personal judgment. Third, whenever possible, Hutchinson maximized the freedom of individuals and the powers of juries, even at the expense of the legal profession and the courts themselves. But problems arose when Hutchinson had to balance parliamentary statute (which he considered unquestionable) with his devotion to local customs and rights. He tried to reconcile the two, as he did when faced with impressment or imperial taxation, by pushing provincial claims up to the point (but not beyond) where he believed they threatened to destroy the British Empire. Not only would he refuse to cross that boundary, but he made elaborate speeches from the bench at the opening of Superior Court sessions advocating juries adopt his notions of sovereignty, civil disobedience, legislative-judicial relations, and the religious foundations of the social order. These speeches disclose much of his underlying thought. But for all their logic, these orations only said one thing to the Massachusetts radicals: Hutchinson wanted the traitors punished. The addresses, combined with his support for British authority at key moments, only meant to them that Hutchinson's defense of local and personal rights was a sham to hide his true colors from the gullible populace. Distressed by the popularity of Hutchinson's easily comprehensible and fair-minded justice in politically uncontroversial cases, the revolutionaries branded his speeches as proof that he would inconsistently use whatever ideas were available to further his own pursuit of power. But upon closer study, the superficially irreconcilable elements in Hutchinson's thought appear as just the opposite: an effort to unify ideas and harmonize people who otherwise would soon be at each other's throats.

Hutchinson took as the starting point of his legal philosophy that Massachusetts' fundamental constitution -- the complex bundle of laws and customs which defined it -- ought to be unalterable, that the laws promulgated by the legislature should be "fixed, certain, and known," and finally that the courts were obliged to execute these statutes inflexibly. Hutchinson presented a three-tiered level of political authority as the cement of a stable and just society: fundamental law, statute law, and court decisions. If law failed to follow traditional principles "the

subject can never know what laws to obey." And if
execution failed to follow law, "let the body of laws
be ever so good, if they are not executed, 'tis worse
than a state of nature, and we are more secure than in
a society where we depend upon the laws for our
protection which are not put in force." The preservation of any state and the happiness of its subjects
depended on its ability to maintain its own true
principles as these had developed over time. What sort
of constitution had evolved mattered less than its
preservation. The experience of revolutionary
Massachusetts taught Hutchinson "where the fundamentals
of a constitution are unsettled and vague the people
must be miserable indeed."(4)

The "dignity and support of the executive courts"
formed a primary cornerstone of maintaining both legal
and social stability. The courts represented the level
at which most inhabitants experienced law directly,
and were judges to interpret statutes wrongly or act
unjustly, government would become odious. Undoubtedly,
the fact that the loyalists' last chance for combatting
the Massachusetts revolutionaries rested in the courts
influenced Hutchinson's stand here. But a reason also
developed logically out of his argument. As he warned
a grand jury, "let the respect due to these courts be
lost, let their dignity not be kept up by a support of
authority, and all government will soon be at an end."
Even liberty depended on knowing what laws to obey and
on the certainty of their execution. No contradiction
between "liberty" and "power" as postulated by Whig
history could be maintained in any real polity. Such
a struggle would destroy the state, which was defined
by laws that simultaneously granted and yet limited the
freedom of inhabitants.(5)

Upholding legal authority meant that the integrity
of the legislature, courts, and judges could not be
criticized. Hutchinson explained that if libels
against the government and officials went unpunished,
the public would lose respect for authority: "the
restraint of the press, in the prevention of libels,
is the only thing which <u>preserves</u> your liberty."(6)
Without popular support for the authority of
government, anarchy would result and no sort of
freedom could exist. Libels were also objectionable
because they destroyed the government's freedom --
the power to do good for its subjects without worrying
about malicious attacks in newspapers or pamphlets.
Aspersions on public officials, if allowed, would make

an objective judgment of their performance by the electorate impossible. Hutchinson did not, to be sure, rule out all differences of opinion on political questions. But he insisted that even in disagreeing with the policies of an official or content of a law, individuals refrain from urging disobedience or attacking the integrity of institutions, judges, and lawmakers.

But if Hutchinson insisted courts had to be immune from criticism, this in turn imposed on them a solemn obligation to uphold the constitution unquestioningly and behave in an honorable manner above reproach. To define and execute the fundamentals of Massachusetts law was no easy task: as Hutchinson told the legislature, "His Majesty expects from me, on the one hand, that I make no invasion upon any of your rights, but on the other hand, that I give up none of his prerogatives." For the province of Massachusetts as he had known it to continue to exist, both had to be balanced. Hutchinson's willingness to uphold royal authority in unpopular situations is well known, but he proved equally unwilling to violate popular rights. When it was rumored by the revolutionaries that he might accept a royal commission as chief justice to supplant his provincial one, he regarded the accusation with scorn. He retorted that it amounted to a charge of "bribery, corruption, and unfaithfulness." Judges who brought themselves and their offices into contempt in this way were "the most abandonedly wicked of all men."(7)

But the sword cut both ways. When faced with a law he found personally obnoxious and even unconstitutional, such as the Stamp Act, Hutchinson believed he had no choice but to enforce it. Were he to refuse, this would "lead directly to a state of slavery" and "the will of the judge would be law." Proceeding with remorseless logic, he went on to argue that if the "arbitrary will of the judge is law," then "the authority of the executive courts is brought into contempt," and under these circumstances, with every man governing his behavior in accordance with the supposed mentality of particular judges instead of by universally agreed on laws and customs, great "mischief will infest society."(8)

In explaining his doctrine of absolute obedience to law (provided it did not violate Christian morality, which will be discussed later), Hutchinson at one point remarked that "the judge should never be the

legislator." His political opponents misinterpreted
this statement to oust the members of the superior
court from the provincial council -- conveniently
ignoring the fact that most of the representatives who
voted for the measure held lesser judicial appointments
themselves. The issue for Hutchinson was not one of
personnel but of function. He would have been totally
uninterested in a provision forbidding judges to sit in
the legislature, such as the United States Constitution
contains, but he knew full well that "mischief" would
result if the judiciary proceeded to interpret a law
in a previously unheard of fashion and enforce it
against the opinion of government and society. Unlike
James Otis -- who hoped that the provincial courts,
like the British Common Law Courts, would interpose
themselves between the colonies and Parliament by
declaring acts against the fundamental principles of
English law invalid -- Hutchinson believed judicial
review an invitation to social disorder.(9)

For Hutchinson, the judge was a judge of the
"executive courts" -- the passive executant of laws
made by an unquestionably sovereign legislature.
When the Massachusetts General Court presented him with
an argument for divided sovereignty, he retorted that
"you are equally unfortunate in your notions of the
mutual check and dependence which each branch of the
legislature ought to have upon the other, as also in
the nature of a free government, and of the English
Constitution." The only division of power lay in the
fact that King, Lords, and Commons, or in Massachusetts
governor, council, and assembly, all had to assent to
legislation. But once they were agreed, no legitimate
check existed. The governor and courts were bound in
duty to execute the laws with automatic precision. To
argue otherwise, Hutchinson expostulated, would "make
a very essential change in your constitution," which
he always dreaded.(10)

But Hutchinson's understanding of the Massachusetts
constitution went beyond mere adherence to the letter
of the charter, parliamentary sovereignty, and the
dictates of the Massachusetts legislature. He
believed the "fundamentals" also embraced those customs
which had flourished under these powers and proven
themselves beneficial. Here a judge had discretion,
for common law and traditional practices had to be
determined and decided upon where the statutes were
silent. As Hutchinson told a grand jury, it not only
had to keep the laws "inviolate" but "the manners of
the people unpolluted." The courts were custodians

of *mores* (morals and customs) as well as law. The only word of approbation the "European" has for the "American" in a dialogue between two fictional characters written by Hutchinson is that "I am glad to find you will allow acts for regulating your trade by force of long usage are become part of your constitution."(11)

Hutchinson put his belief in tradition to work in the courtroom. He almost invariably disagreed with his colleagues, who cited English precedents and assumed they applied to Massachusetts. Hutchinson, however, was a historian and politician, not a lawyer. He gave clearly understandable opinions which rarely mentioned English authorities, and instead relied on Massachusetts practices. He devoted himself, usually unsuccessfully, to conserving and articulating an authentic American tradition.

Hutchinson summed up much of his judicial philosophy in a speech to a grand jury of February 1763: "Custom shall not be placed in opposition to law, but it may be a circumstance going to interpret" it in cases of ambiguity. For example, in the case of Bromfield v. Little (1764), in which the plaintiff insisted merchants had a right, on customary grounds, to interest on debts older than a year, Hutchinson, alone among his colleagues and the lawyers, exhibited no concern for English custom but only for Massachusetts practice. His minority opinion read that "'tis agreeable to natural equity that interest should be allowed, and I am glad it is growing into a custom." However, custom by its nature implied universal consent and acceptance, and "growing into a custom" was a different thing from a custom itself: "the rule is that both parties ought at the time of contraction to understand it so, and I doubt whether it is so general as that it can be supposed to be the case." Hutchinson refused to hurry matters along and thereby place his own opinion in advance of an evolving commercial practice. Other instances, fortunately, proved unambiguous. In a case involving the renegotiability of merchants' notes, Hutchinson again stood alone in arguing from custom: "if this action should be barred, it seems to me that half the trade must be extinguished, for it presently rests upon such bills."(12)

Hutchinson found himself in a genuine quandary in the case of Baker v. Mattocks (1763), when it appeared to him that custom and even court cases had contradicted the obvious meaning of a law. A descendant of Governor Joseph Dudley sought to break an entail placed by the late governor on his estate. When a majority of the court voted entail could in fact be broken, Hutchinson decided not to vote and instead made a speech reflecting his difficulty in setting his own interpretation of statutory law against the customary understanding of it:

> It seems evident to me that it is the spirit of the English law, that all inheritances should follow the method of fee simple. If it was now a thing entirely upon the law I should have not the least difficulty of thinking. Fee tail, as well as fee simple, was partable [divisible]: but it has been so long thought otherwise here, and this has been the uninterrupted contemporaneous exposition of the law, and many judgments of the court founded on it, that it creates a great difficulty. I am glad the point is determined without me, for how such a custom can prevail against plain law, I doubt.

Hutchinson also confronted a challenge from James Otis on this case, who prefaced his plea with a bit of natural rights philosophy: "the manner of succession, if traced to its original, is merely arbitrary, the law of nature is a stranger to it; by that, no man has a right to more than his life." The Dudley case epitomized Hutchinson's concern for provincial practice in the face of two reforming challenges -- from aspiring common lawyers and Anglicized judges, on the one hand, and from a natural rights theorist relying on English philosophical radicalism on the other.(13)

Hutchinson's second guiding principle was that courts existed to protect individual liberty and preserve public order, not to increase their own power and that of the legal profession by permitting technicalities in pleading and precedent to obstruct common sense justice. As he told a jury: "Where the law is in any case doubtful, and the equity of it plain, you should verge toward equity." For example, in <u>Oliver v. Sale</u> (1762), where an indentured Negro servant had been sold on the false understanding that he was a slave, Hutchinson brushed aside Otis' objection that the "rule of merchandise" (the colonial equivalent of truth-in-advertising) only obliged a seller of manufactures not to misrepresent his wares. The chief justice asked: "Is there not as palpable a fraud, when a man sells a Negro as a slave whom he knows to be free, as when he sells a bag of feathers and assures them to be hops?"(14)

In Hanlon v. Thayer (1764) Hutchinson again stood for common-sense decency when a creditor sued a widow for her husband's debts and insisted on taking her entire wardrobe except for one dress, Hutchinson alone among the Superior Court sought to ensure her a minimum standard of living. Citing precedents he himself had set as Suffolk Judge of Probate to prevent the exploitation of widows, he argued that "I always thought it to have been the custom in such cases as this, for the wife to have her clothes; in cases that have come before me as judge of probate I never knew it denied the wife where the estate was insolvent." Hutchinson then disagreed with a decision of the English Lord Chief Justice Sir Matthew Hale, which the other judges cited to show that the woman was only entitled to one suit of clothes, or all that was "necessary." He differed (in the most apologetic terms, Quincy noted, given his respect for the English common law): "this may be one of those cases where the justice says a thing obiter, or suddenly; for one gown can never be supposed sufficient -- must she go naked while that is washing?" In short, "it was safer to verge towards convenience than to strain the word necessity." Justices Peter Oliver and John Cushing, though they admitted the harshness of Hale's decision, construed it as legally binding. Hutchinson lost the case and the woman lost her clothes.(15)

Even the famous Writs of Assistance case in 1761 -- where Hutchinson drew the wrath of the Bostonian merchant community by ignoring James Otis' argument that search warrants which did not specify specific persons and locations were unconstitutional -- may be viewed as the unfortunate aftermath of Hutchinson's own libertarian efforts. I use the term "Writs of Assistance" out of conventionality. Attorney Jeremiah Gridley, who argued against Otis, knew better:

> This is properly a Writ of Assistants, not assistance; not to give the officers a greater power, but as a check upon them. For by this they cannot enter into any house without the presence of the sheriff

or a civil officer, who will be always
supposed to have eye over and be a check
upon him.

The use of the writs in Massachusetts was a recent reform, less than five years old. Hutchinson himself had been responsible for this, although his disinterestedness may be questioned. When his brother Elisha was threatened with an unassisted search by the customs house, he persuaded Governor William Shirley that the Superior Court had to consent for a writ to be issued. Hutchinson reasoned that the Superior Court could exercise the powers of a British Exchequer Court in this instance, as no other provision existed for the writs by law. He regarded the issue as whether customs officials could search with or without local supervision, not whether they had a right to search at all, which the Navigation Acts clearly allowed. He had no way of knowing Otis' reasoning would be upheld in Britain in the famous general warrants case involving John Wilkes. On the matter of naval impressment too, Hutchinson used his legal acumen to free Michael Corbet, a sailor accused of murdering two members of a press gang, on the grounds no warrant existed to justify the seizure.(16)

In addition to his efforts to construe the law favorably for Massachusetts inhabitants in specific instances, Hutchinson also tried to maximize their general legal rights. He never allowed, for instance, that the judge had power to lay down the law for a jury and merely permit it to decide the facts of the case in accordance therewith. This had been traditional practice in Massachusetts. But for up-and-coming lawyers such as John Adams, it put too much trust in the layman. Adams argued that "every intelligent man will confess that cases frequently occur in which it would be very difficult for juries to determine the question of law." In fact, one of the few times Hutchinson tried (unsuccessfully) to dismantle a custom involved extending the powers of the jury at the expense of the judges. In <u>Norwood v. Fairservice</u> (1763) the question arose whether the court or the jury had the right to decide if an altered deed was admissible as evidence. Hutchinson argued that although "the custom has been otherwise . . . I think 'tis time it was altered." In a case two years later where the validity of a deed came into question, he insisted that "the court could not determine the weight of the evidence of the witness, but the jury are the sole judges."(17)

In another instance in which the extent of colonial rights arose, the case of <u>Scolley v. Dunn</u> (1763), Hutchinson dissented from the rest of the court and tried to expand the meaning of a phrase in the province charter granting appeals from the Superior Court to the Privy Council. The clause permitted appeals "in cases that may deserve the same . . . . in any personal action, wherein the matter in difference doth exceed the value of £300 sterling." The chief justice thought the key phrase was "all cases which deserve it," which "£300 sterling" explained but did not determine. He insisted that appeals should be allowed in "all cases which deserve it." In the same case, Hutchinson also maintained that if the owner of a ship agreed to ransom the master (should he be captured by privateers or an enemy vessel in wartime) and failed to do so, the Superior Court rather than the admiralty had jurisdiction, since the contract was made on land. <u>Scolley v. Dunn</u> illustrated Hutchinson's proclivity for individual rights over government power, even when it meant undermining the unquestionable authority of his own court, and his determination to uphold local over British authority where plausible.(18)

Laymen respected, even venerated, Hutchinson the judge whatever they may have thought of Hutchinson the politician. Two women as patriotic as Jane Mecom, Benjamin Franklin's sister, and Mercy Otis Warren, who hated Hutchinson with the passion of her brother James Otis and burlesqued him mercilessly in her plays and essays, agreed that he was a humane, fair, and competent judge of probate. So did Ezekiel Price, a noted merchant, Son of Liberty, and secretary of a Boston merchants' club founded in 1764. But Hutchinson's justice easily would have dispensed with the emerging legal profession on which revolutionary leaders such as John Adams, James Otis, and Josiah Quincy depended for their incomes and prestige. Peter Oliver described his kinsman's performance on the bench in a manner that explains why laymen and professionals would have such vastly different reactions to Hutchinson:(19)

> As judge of probate, the widow and orphan repaired to him as their guardian, and the doors of his office and his house also, were ever unlatched to their petitions for relief and advice. His placid temper and his

> invincible patience seemed marked out
> by the God of Nature for the discharge
> of this most difficult office, where
> litigants appeared, who were uninstructed
> in all the forms necessary to conduct
> their cases . . . . [He once remarked]
> "it gives me so much pleasure to relieve
> the widow and fatherless, and direct them
> what steps to take in managing their
> estates; and also in reconciling contending
> parties."

Thanks to Hutchinson, executors of estates and others with inheritance problems could bypass the struggling legal profession entirely and obtain free advice. Hutchinson's eagerness, in the most trivial individual disputes as in Anglo-American relations, to "reconcile contending parties" also ensured fewer cases would be litigated.

In the Superior Court, Hutchinson behaved with an equal lack of professionalism, whatever his other virtues. Oliver wrote that he:[20]

> Seemed to be all intuition. The ablest
> councillors at the bar, and some very
> able ones there were, seemed astonished,
> and would often, when they were
> antagonists in important cases, and were
> divided in their opinions in drawing a
> special verdict, refer the draft to him.
> When in a few minutes, he would return a
> legal one, to the acceptance of both
> parties.

Oliver may have exaggerated his praise of a fellow-loyalist and close relative somewhat, but the tone of envy in John Adams' criticism of Hutchinson is unmistakable: "a man whose youth and spirits and strength have been spent in husbandry, merchandise, politics, nay in science or literature will never master so immense and involved a science as law."[21] But Hutchinson tried. He did not base his opinions on common sense morality and custom because he had failed to master the technical requirements of his post. His papers reveal that he bought every law book his agents and friends could find in England, and the willingness of the elder practitioners at the bar to refer their disputes to him for arbitration bears out this judgment. Still, here again Hutchinson appeared as a reconciler, which must undoubtedly have rankled a profession based on an adversary method of arguing.

But if Hutchinson's defense of traditional provincial and individual rights in politically non-controversial cases could not be gainsayed, neither could his support for parliamentary authority and institutions such as the Admiralty Court when the Massachusetts radicals challenged their jurisdiction. Hutchinson regarded this body as a constituent part of Massachusetts' government. He did not hold the power to undermine its just authority. In 1761, shortly after he upheld the Writs of Assistance, he persuaded the Superior Court to approve an appeal by the Admiralty Court against a judgment by the Suffolk Inferior Court of Common Pleas. The local tribunal had ruled an admiralty seizure invalid on the practical if not exactly 'legal ground that they "must put a stop to these proceedings of the customs house officers; if they did not there would be tumult and bloodshed for the people can bear them no longer." Hutchinson, however, ruled that "the Court of Admiralty was part of the constitution of the province, it being expressly provided for in the charter." Similarly, in 1766, he refused to reopen the Superior Court unless the hated stamps appeared on legal documents, as the Stamp Act required. John Adams expressed both the rage of the province in general and the special anger of the legal profession: "I was but just getting into my gear, just getting under sail, and an embargo is laid upon my ship. . . . I have groped in dark obscurity, till of late, and had just become known and gained a small degree of reputation, when this execrable project was set on foot for my ruin as well as that of America in general."(22)

Another aspect of Hutchinson's judicial behavior infuriated Adams: his use of speeches opening sessions of the court to persuade jurors to enforce the laws to suppress rioters, silence libels against public officials, and investigate conspiracies like the non-importation agreements. Had Hutchinson been successful the supporters of government -- driven from the legislature and town meetings, and challenged by the informal government of revolutionary organizations -- could have used their one remaining bastion, the courts, to halt the resistance movement without having to call in the army and thereby admit their own powerlessness. Loyalist judges in the county courts, notably Israel Williams of Hampshire, followed Hutchinson's precedent of lecturing jurors on their responsibilities.(23)

It is possible to argue, as Adams did, that by making such addresses Hutchinson used the court as "harangues . . . to scatter party principles in politics" for the purpose of annihilating his political opponents.(24) But he himself would have maintained that he really did the reverse and showed how the political issues of his day implicated the social, religious, legal, and moral order in ways the revolutionaries either ignored or rationalized away. He argued that revolution required slandering law-abiding public officials such as himself, using religion and the clergy to justify revolt, denying under oath complicity in rioting and smuggling, and consistently acting on principles which would lead to the destruction of all civilized society. Hutchinson detected the beginnings of such disintegration in contemporary Massachusetts. These speeches are a major source for his fundamental political theory that only respect for moral, statutory, and traditional law can hold a society together short of the tyrannical abuse of force.

Hutchinson probably acquired his jurisprudence from the English common lawyers, who conceived of law as a dynamic, flexible interaction between traditions which the supreme legislature ought not to violate while insisting on the unquestioned sovereignty of the legislature itself. Unlike Massachusetts' lawyers, however, Hutchinson did not read Common Law to cite specific precedents, but he approached the law as a historian who applied the common lawyers' method of understanding the English constitution to his own interpretation of the province's.

Their notion of tradition, as described by J. G. A. Pocock, involved many of the ideas found in Hutchinson's judicial opinions. They insisted that "rights are not justified by abstract reason, but as an inheritance under positive laws," and that "custom was constantly being subjected to the test of experience, so that if immemorial it was always up to date, and that it was ultimately rooted in nothing other than experience." Law existed as it had evolved historically, not as it supposedly had existed at some point in the past, or as it could be interpreted by citing particular cases and reading selected documents to prove some point arbitrarily. The greatest of these theorists, Sir Mathew Hale, was "accustomed to viewing each moral problem on its merits as it came before him, and to viewing it as entangled in the exceedingly complex web of practical social reality. This caused him to doubt whether "there exist universally valid patterns of thought with which natural reason may legislate for society."(25)

Pocock also stresses that Edmund Burke acquired his respect for custom and morality and his distrust of metaphysical speculation about rights not embodied in a particular constitution from the common law: "Burke says clearly of his doctrine of traditionalism that it was a way of thinking which existed in the consciousness of his time and had existed for so long that it itself was traditional."(26) Pocock's research into the philosophical assumptions of the common law reveals that Burke's contribution to political theory was to apply doctrines that seventeenth century English lawyers evolved to defend English law from the centralizing propensities of the Stuart monarchy to all cases whatsoever, and to transform their justification of a body of law into a generally applicable theory of politics.

But unlike Burke, when Hutchinson adopted the method of the common lawyers in articulating an authentic tradition for Massachusetts, he paradoxically made use of a theory most untraditional and revolutionary within the province itself. What Leo Strauss has written of Burke is even more applicable to Hutchinson: "it requires a much greater effort to articulate a hitherto unarticulated situation in its particular character than to interpret it in the light of precedents which have been articulated already."(27) Before Hutchinson, the people of Massachusetts had understood their constitution to consist of their charter, which they read in a simultaneously broad yet inflexible manner to score points against British officials who sought to undermine the assembly's powers. Hutchinson tried to demonstrate the error of this perception. The true constitution consisted of a configuration of customary relationships within the province's government and social structure and between Massachusetts and England. Hutchinson's adaptation of British thought therefore lay not in the content of his arguments, as it did for both other loyalists and radicals, but in his methodology. He sought to replace linguistic analysis of documents and uncritical citation of precedents with the comprehensive socio-political development of a state as the means of understanding its constitution. This book explains Hutchinson's appreciation of Massachusetts' constitution, how it developed in the seventeenth and eighteenth centuries, how he believed the American Revolution perverted it, and how he reached general conclusions about politics by observing his own society.

FOOTNOTES

1. Lyman Butterfield, ed., The Diary and Autobiography of John Adams (Cambridge, 1960), II, 34, 55; the print referred to appears on the cover of Bernard Bailyn, The Ordeal of Thomas Hutchinson (Cambridge, 1974); Nathaniel Truman to James Otis, Sr., July 10, 1773, Otis Papers, Box III, Massachusetts Historical Society.

2. Butterfield, ed., Adams Diary, I, 306.

3. See especially John M. Murrin, "The Legal Transformation: The Bench and Bar of Eighteenth Century Massachusetts," in Stanley N. Katz, ed., Colonial America: Essays in Political and Social Development (Boston, 1971), 417-449. Also source for the next paragraph.

4. H to ?, February 14, 1767, M. XXVI, 543; H to William Bollan, April 19, 1768, M. XXVI, 627; Quincy, 234, 243.

5. Quincy, 246.

6. Ibid., 266.

7. History, III, 403; Quincy, 313, 247.

8. Quincy, 234.

9. History, III, 408. For Otis see James R. Ferguson "Reason in Madness: The Political Theory of James Otis," William and Mary Quarterly, 3rd ser. XXVI, (1979), 194-214.

10. History, III, 408.

11. Quincy, 176; "Dialogue," 103.

12. Quincy, 40, 50, 108.

13. Ibid., 71-77.

14. Ibid., 32, 40.

15. Ibid., 102-104.

16. Ibid., 57; History, III, 67.

17. Quincy, 191, 240; Butterfield, ed., *Adams Diary*, II, 4.

18. Quincy, 78-81.

19. Peter Oliver, *Origin and Progress of the American Rebellion*, ed. Douglass Adair and John A. Schutz (San Marino, CA, 1961), 33; Hiller Zobel, *The Boston Massacre* (New York, 1970), 9-11.

20. Oliver, *Origin*, 33.

21. Butterfield, ed., *Adams Diary*, I, 168.

22. Francis Bernard to Board of Trade, August 6, 1761 and August 28, 1761, Bernard Papers, II, 45-52: Sparks Manuscripts, Harvard College Library; Butterfield, ed., *Adams Diary*, I, 265.

23. Undated draft of speech in Williams' handwriting, Box I, Williams Papers.

24. Butterfield, ed., *Adams Diary*, I, 281.

25. J. G. A. Pocock, "Burke and the Ancient Constitution," in *Politics, Language, and Time* (New York, 1971), 207, 210, 218.

26. *Ibid.*, 205

27. Leo Strauss, *Natural Right and History* (Chicago, 1953), 306.

PART II. THE HISTORIAN

IV. THE COLONIAL PERIOD

Western man has rarely written history purely to express a disinterested love of the past. By the eighteenth century, when Hutchinson wrote his History of the Colony and Province of Massachusetts Bay, history had flourished for centuries as the handmaiden of religion, morality, and politics. Even the best historians simplistically cited examples from the past to prove how the great drama of human destiny worked itself out in accordance with the desires of their own sect or party.

Medieval chroniclers, for instance, believed that man could not change the grand design of history through his own efforts, and subordinated history to morality. They revealed how God rewarded virtue and punished vice in this world as well as the next. The course of history rested solely in the hands of the Almighty, and religious events such as the Flood, the Exodus, the Incarnation, and the Apocalypse marked the stages in humanity's progression toward salvation.(1)

With the Renaissance and Reformation, man joined providence as an active agent in the historical process. Both Humanists and Protestants interpreted the Middle Ages as a "Dark Age" dissolving before a new era destined to restore the glories of either classical antiquity or primitive Christianity. Adherence to an unchanging moral law no longer guaranteed well-being in this world and redemption in the next. The individual also had to participate in the correct movement to create a better life on earth. A variety of ideologies pressed history into service to justify their exclusive claims to define humanity's future.

The sixteenth century thus established a three-part paradigm for the interpretation of history. An idealized past had once existed, which gave way to the present, evil order of things, that was about to be supplanted by

an emerging future which would restore the
glories of the past while at the same time
transcending them. When Hutchinson published the
first two volumes of his History in the 1760s,
most historical writing reflected either the
secular or sacred version of this model. The
finest contemporary European scholars, Voltaire,
Hume, and Gibbon, agreed with Bolingbroke's
aphorism that history embodied "philosophy
teaching by examples."(2) In varying degrees,
they praised the destruction of religious bigotry
and superstition, which had so long enslaved
Europe, once the Renaissance had ushered in a new
age of reason. Voltaire claimed that "there are
only four ages in the history of the world which
really count": ancient Greece, ancient Rome, the
Renaissance, and the Age of Louis XIV. Hume's
historical confidence belied his philosophical
skepticism. As Friedrich Meinecke has remarked,
his historical work addressed itself to the
"question as to how this rare and fortunate state
of things had come about in [eighteenth-century]
England." And Gibbon believed that with the fall
of Rome Christianity and barbarism had triumphed
in the west while the hopelessly corrupt
Byzantine Empire reigned in the east. Only the
modern age had begun to reverse a millennium of
decline.(3)

Eighteenth-century Americans held visions of
history much like their European contemporaries.
A secular and a sacred model of human development
existed side by side, each of which conceptualized
history primarily as a struggle between good and
evil. The Puritan founders of New England interpreted their effort to found a holy society by
means of "typology." They regarded contemporary
events as "types" of Biblical occurrences which
foreshadowed them. The wilderness of America
served as a "type" of the wastes of Sinai, the
people of New England as a "type" of the Jews in
the Old Testament, and men such as John Winthrop
and William Bradford were freely compared with
Moses. The Puritans consciously modelled themselves on both the ancient Hebrews and the
primitive Christians, and believed they had a
comparable role in God's plan for the world. Now
that the Reformation had begun, the emerging
Kingdom of the Saints could supplant the evils
of Popery and superstition. Both Cotton Mather

and Jonathan Edwards convinced themselves not only that the millennium was at hand, but that they would be personally and significantly instrumental in hastening its arrival.(4)

Secular historical interpretation in eighteenth-century America conformed to a pattern Herbert Butterfield has labelled the "Whig interpretation of history."(5) History became a battleground between power and liberty. The former represented the corruption, in both the political and moral sense, of kings and courts, while the latter encompassed the country, the people, Parliament, and virtue. "Liberty" was embodied in such institutions as the Anglo-Saxon Witan or Parliament, Magna Carta, and the common law; "power" or "tyranny" appeared under the several guises of Norman kings, feudalism, and the Stuart monarchy, and fairly described the political condition of most countries at most times in history. For "Old Whigs," the Glorious Revolution of 1688 marked the final triumph of "liberty" and Parliament in English history. The more radical "New Whigs," however, lamented that the potential benefits of the coup against James II had failed to materialize as the eighteenth century witnessed the revival of "power" through the subtle but insidious corruption of Parliament by the court.(6)

The Whig interpretation of history provoked a contrary Tory model, pioneered by the Earl of Clarendon in his History of the Rebellion and Civil Wars in England, written in the 1660s but not published until 1702. Tory history stood Whiggery on its head. Clarendon raised "power" to the dignity of authority and reappraised "liberty" as licentiousness. The court took on the positive attributes of order and stability, while the country stood for faction and anarchy. Americans did not avail themselves of Tory history until the war for independence, when it became the vehicle through which several of Hutchinson's fellow loyalists expressed their resentment against the new American republic.(7)

In short, Thomas Hutchinson wrote in a world where history existed as a polemical weapon to defend various philosophies and ideologies.(8) As Friedrich Meinecke has shown, even the finest eighteenth-century European historians only made tentative approaches toward "historism," which he defined as "the substitution of a process of individualizing observation for a generalizing view of human forces in history." J. H. Plumb has similarly described the true historical attitude as the attempt "to try and understand what happened, purely in its own terms and not in the service of religion or national destiny, or morality or the sanctity of institutions." Not until history emerged as a university discipline at the end of the nineteenth century did "professional historians begin to reduce their generalizations to professional areas of interest" and "the pursuit of scholarship became more important than the interpretation of history." Yet it took time: Plumb also notes that "no outstanding historian of the nineteenth century . . . did not accept a large structural interpretation of the destiny of man, and usually of his nation too." Nevertheless, many of the characteristics Plumb and Meinecke stipulate as essential for a true historical attitude appear in Hutchinson's work.(9)

"Historism" had few other forerunners. John Lukacs describes the "erudites" or "antiquarians" of late seventeenth century France, most notably Mabillon and Tillemont, as "the first modern academic historians." But even they "were not concerned to rewrite history nor to reinterpret the past; they [only] wished to purify and authenticate and make available what [sources] existed." Herbert Butterfield has also called attention to a number of German scholars at the University of Göttingen in the late eighteenth century, and also to Edmund Burke's unfinished Abridgement of English History as forerunners of modern historical writings.(10) Even though these writers became more influential in the course of historiographical development than Hutchinson -- whose insights went unappreciated even in America -- they only began to write after he had completed his work, and of course there was no mutual influence.

Given this context, the appearance of a work such as Hutchinson's History in the mid-1760s was remarkable. Modern historians of revolutionary America almost invariably praise and cite it, even if they condemn Hutchinson's political behavior in the next breath.(11) Any historian who disputes Hutchinson's analysis of a particular event usually feels obliged to offer impressive contradictory documentation, proof that his interpretations are still taken seriously. Can a similar use of Hume, Voltaire, and Gibbon by late twentieth century historians of England, France, or Rome be imagined? Hutchinson's judicious appraisals of characters and events, frequent citation of primary source material -- which unfortunately ceased halfway through volume two, the point at which the Stamp Act rioters destroyed both his house and his collection of documents -- and lucid writing suggest a work of modern history.

To be sure, Hutchinson wrote such "objective" and "analytic" history out of a profound psychological need to reconcile the diverse aspects of Massachusetts' political heritage. However, such a temperament and prejudice produced balanced judgments assessing the faults and virtues of different public figures, movements, and policies with a reasonable degree of fairness. Unlike those of his contemporaries, Hutchinson's biases functioned toward the attainment of a disinterested examination of the past, although even he -- as will be examined -- had his blind spots where for political and personal reasons he abandoned his usual method of sympathizing with contrary positions on every issue.

Hutchinson's History not only contains valuable information, interpretations, and an advanced methodology, but it also reveals the major ideas of his social and political theory as applied to practical situations. Since he completed most of the first two volumes before the revolutionary crisis began, an examination of the History establishes that one can legitimately treat Hutchinson's efforts to reconcile America and Britain as founded on a coherent system of beliefs, rather than a hodgepodge of contradictory reflections shot off to different correspondents and audiences once the colonial crisis began. Hutchinson's more theoretical pronouncements in pamphlets, letters, and volume three of the History, which deal directly with the Revolution, therefore represent the full

flowering and thinking through of principles
he had first discovered in his historical studies.

Most significantly, Hutchinson's <u>History</u>
stressed that a government such as that of
seventeenth century Massachusetts, founded on
principles which ought not to work in theory --
intolerant churches which forced conformity or
overly popular colonial societies with exaggerated
ideas of independence -- can paradoxically be the
basis of a stable and good social order.
Hutchinson deduced from this analysis that states
do not attain practical legitimacy because they
adhere to certain forms and ideals, or because
they originate in a particular way. Only the
quality of life -- manifested by stability over
time, prosperity, and morality as concomitants of
liberty -- a regime has developed for its
subjects can justify it. Whether any given state
meets this test can only be ascertained through
studying it historically, rather than examining
the supposed fundamentals upon which any just
government should rest.

Moving one step further, Hutchinson's
recognition that different ideals could motivate
equally legitimate states led him to appreciate
diversity both throughout the world and within his
own society. If contradictory political
principles held in different situations, men ought
to tolerate other customs, religions, races, and
points of view if they do not threaten the
foundations of an acceptable government or appear
criminal. By abstracting this theory of politics
from his study of colonial Massachusetts, Hutchinson turned history into a conservative weapon
defending traditional social orders against
revolutionaries.

* * * * * * *

The words paradox, irony, and diversity best
pinpoint Hutchinson's view of history. He
consciously tried to consider every side of
nearly every question from both a sympathetic and
a critical standpoint. As he wrote in his
preface, such a method remarkably suited his
purpose of "guarding against every prejudice."
Realizing that "in writing the history of my

own country" impartiality would not come easily, he tried to compensate for any bias: "I hope by shunning one extreme, I have not run upon another."(12) He made an effort not only to take a hard look at his prejudices, but he went one step further and questioned even his tendency to be critical.

Of course, Hutchinson could no more overcome his bias than any historian. His sensitivity to the faults and virtues of contrary viewpoints produced a different sort of history than most of his contemporaries, one admirably suited to his political goals. If they read him carefully, Americans would think seriously about British arguments for Parliamentary supremacy while British administrators would tolerate a greater measure of colonial liberty. In general, Hutchinson hoped his revelations of the frailties shared by all men and societies would promote appreciation of different visions of the common good. By revealing American liberty as a historical process rather than the "self-evident truth" proclaimed in the Declaration of Independence, Hutchinson made history the test of political theory and an accepted tradition the measure of a good society. On the personal level, by advancing such an unusual theory of Anglo-American relations, he fulfilled his need to alienate himself from his contemporaries and to ensure that they either pilloried him (unjustly) or accepted his premises as the only possible basis of reconciliation.

Hutchinson began his narrative with a discussion of the Puritan founders. Surprisingly for a loyalist, he set a positive tone. He admired their willingness to sacrifice material well-being in England for spiritual and political liberty. "Arbitrary measures" taken by the Stuart kings drove them from their native shores. Hutchinson dismissed the notion that economic hard times induced the first settlers to emigrate, since "persons of rank and good circumstances in life" abandoned "the conveniences and delights of England" to endure hardship and suffering. Far from seeking worldly gain, the Puritans went to "great expense, without any returns" in planning a colony from which they "had no rational prospect of any profit." Every American settlement before theirs had produced tremendous mortality rates, usually well above half the population. Despite their faith in Divine Providence the Puritans had no way of knowing they would prove the first exception. The strength of Hutchinson's conviction that his ancestors' disinterested idealism matched his own appeared in his almost poetic description of the journey undertaken by Thomas Hooker and his band from Massachusetts to Connecticut. They travelled through "hideous swamps and very high mountains" with "no pillows but Jacob's and no canopy but the heavens." (No other passage in Hutchinson's thousand-odd page History employed such flowery language.) He then clinched his argument for the pioneers' idealism by noting that when persecution ceased "after 1640, we hear of no great emigration from England to America."(13)

Yet even here, Hutchinson did not hesitate to admit exceptions to his analysis. If the first settlers were heroes, successors of a different stripe, "merchants and others, for the sake of gain," soon followed.(14) Within a few years, the ability of the spiritually-minded founders to create a stable commonwealth based on lofty ideals attracted those cramped by limited economic opportunity at home. Hutchinson's discussion of motives for colonization thus synthesized the two main interpretations which historians have since advanced: religious persecution and material self-interest. He combined them by arguing that the former theory applied to the original settlers, but that the latter soon became important.

Hutchinson thus initially set two patterns which prevailed throughout the three volumes of his magnum opus. First, he managed to reconcile what future historians have sometimes considered mutually contradictory interpretations of the major issues of colonial history. He would have found merit in Samuel Eliot Morison's, Perry Miller's, and Edmund S. Morgan's works on Puritan intellectuality and idealism while not totally rejecting Larzer Ziff's and James T. Adams' contention that, for some if not all settlers, religion cloaked a desire for wealth and power.(15) Second, far from being an uncomplicated supporter of royal power, Hutchinson's ultimate verdict on the migration, while qualified and balanced, favored the New Englanders. He shared his political opponents' pride in their common heritage, and for many of the same reasons.

Hutchinson also reached a paradoxical conclusion in his account of the society the Puritans established upon their arrival. In apparently independent discussions of their lack of toleration, relations with England, and domestic institutions, he drew similar judgments. In each instance he faulted the principles on which the colonists acted: they were religious bigots, they denied Britain its proper authority, and they overemphasized popular control over church and state. But they nevertheless created as free, stable, and prosperous a society as any in the world. Hutchinson subtly made a theoretical point about politics few in the eighteenth century found congenial. Political theory is an inductive discipline. The structure of particular states constituted the only legitimate field for gathering data to determine the correct nature of political institutions and the obedience due them. Each nation worked out these matters for itself as it developed its traditional institutions. Conversely, deductive schemes of politics based upon the nature of man, the "correct" form of government, or the original purposes of a social contract had no basis in reality.

Let us turn first to Hutchinson's discussion of the Puritan faith. In theory, he condemned religious persecution and attacked the accusers of Anne Hutchinson and her fellow Antinomians for falsely insinuating that they "held principles which admit and introduce all kinds of immorality, and which make no distinction between vice and virtue." By inquiring into men's consciences instead of simply concerning themselves with civic obedience, the Puritans were "deluded that the honor of God required them to punish his creatures for differing from themselves." Massachusetts' execution of several Quakers in the early 1660s drew from Hutchinson the exclamation: "May the time never come again, when the government shall think that by killing men for their religion they do God good service."(16)

But the story is not that simple, as it was for Hutchinson's fellow loyalist historian Peter Oliver, who condemned Puritan intolerance as "unnatural" and even questioned their religious sincerity by viewing their effort to exclude dissenters from the colony as a ploy "to avail themselves of as much independence of the parent state as they dared to." Hutchinson understood perfectly well that "liberty" may have meant something different to seventeenth century New Englanders than it did to their posterity. He could deplore the sins of his ancestors without hating them as sinners. "Bigotry and zeal prevailed among Christians of every sect or profession" in the seventeenth century, each of which "denied to the others what all had a right to enjoy, liberty of conscience." Even though Hutchinson regarded toleration of political and religious diversity as desirable, he also recognized that such an outlook had developed historically. The Puritans had to be judged by the standards of their age, not of his. In a typically balanced sentence, he wrote that "I know of nothing that can be urged in any wise tending to excuse the severity [of the anti-Quaker laws] except" -- and what an enormous exception it is -- "human infirmity, and the many instances in history of persons of every religion being fully persuaded that the indulgence of any other was toleration of impiety, and brought down the judgment of heaven." The Puritans shared their vices with all humanity; their virtues, as will soon appear, Hutchinson believed to be distinctively their own.(17)

Not only would toleration have been historically impossible for the Puritans, but they could have justified most of the so-called "persecutions" in any age as necessary for social control. Hutchinson only mentioned Roger Williams' "singular" religious tenets in passing, but laid great stress on how his political beliefs threatened the infant colony's very existence. Most especially, Williams had persuaded John Endicott, a magistrate and member of his church, to cut the cross, which he thought represented idolatry, out of the British flag. With the revocation of the charter and the dispatch of a fleet to dissolve the Bay Colony an ever-present fear in the 1630s, Williams' conduct flew in the face of the magistrates' careful efforts to present their settlement as loyal and only moderately reformist. Similarly, Anne Hutchinson's principles "involved the colony in disputes and contentions" which would have "produced ruin both to church and state" had not the "vigilance of some, of whom Mr. Winthrop was chief," prevailed, and "turned the ruin from the country upon herself." In particular, her followers' refusal to fight under "unconverted" magistrates and chaplains jeopardized the colony's safety during the Pequot War. Hutchinson justified conviction of Hingham Reverend Peter Hubbard in 1645 for sedition when he denied the magistrates' power to overrule a community decision as the government's authority "could not otherwise have been maintained." Hubbard's criticisms could well have set a precedent that would have torn the colony apart. And if Massachusetts went too far in punishing the earliest Quakers, their disruptive conduct made them "proper subjects of either a madhouse or a house of correction."(18)

Hutchinson treated the Antinomian controversy with particular astuteness. He recognized the feminist, urban, and upper-class aspects of the dissidents which Lyle Kohler and Emery Battis have recently stressed. Trouble started when Anne Hutchinson began to meet with between sixty and eighty women and criticized the clergy for their lack of faith. Most of Boston, especially the "principal inhabitants" and including some clerics and magistrates, soon joined her congregation. Many left the colony with her rather than surrender their principles. Hutchinson therefore viewed Antinomianism as a manifestation of individualism by upper-class Bostonians, especially women, who chafed under Puritan rule.(19)

But Hutchinson's effort to be fair to both the Puritans and their opponents did not even stop with his weighing of toleration and social stability. If he deemed the suppression of threats to the state as necessary and excusable, he recognized "valuable qualities" in many of its critics when regarded from either their own standpoints or his personal tolerationist propensities. Even Roger Williams never showed any "revengeful resentment" for his banishment, repeatedly warned his former persecutors of the approach of hostile Indians, and defended Massachusetts' charter along with Rhode Island's while

a special agent in England. Sir Harry Vane, the
Antinomian governor who left for England when
Massachusetts banished his followers, may have been a
"young and inexperienced . . . obstinate and self-
sufficient" magistrate, but he showed "a true
Christian spirit of forgiveness" by standing up for
the colony when English Parliamentarians in the 1640s
thought it had carried its intolerance too far. Many
of the other Antinomians also belied the excuse used
to banish them by serving faithfully in official posts
in other colonies or, as some returned, in
Massachusetts itself. The Quakers, too, after their
first excesses, "became in general an orderly people .
. . of good morals, friendly and benevolent."
Hutchinson may even have carried his desire to see the
other side a bit too far with respect to Samuel Gorton,
a troublemaker who managed to get thrown out of Rhode
Island as well as Massachusetts for stirring up the
Indians, among other things. Volume one of the History
contains Gorton's self-vindication because Hutchinson
believed he deserved equal time as earlier writers had
almost universally criticized him.(20)

Interestingly, Hutchinson praised nearly all the
Puritans' opponents for their private morality while
recognizing that the political consequences of such
principles led to chaos. Could he have been arguing
for the incompatibility of personal morality and
political success, or identifying with a tragic
necessity that condemned the finest spirits of
seventeenth century New England to be sacrificed to a
social order that could not adopt their advanced,
enlightened ideals? Given Hutchinson's zeal to martyr
himself on the altar of his own unpopular principles,
one plausible explanation of his balanced portrait of
the Puritans and their adversaries was his need to
populate the past with prototypes of himself.

Hutchinson maintained the even-handed outlook he
exhibited with respect to the Puritans and their
domestic opponents in his treatment of England's
relations with Massachusetts. He reached the same
judgment in both cases. On the one hand, the colony,
according to his own principles, operated on all the
wrong assumptions. On the other, Massachusetts
somehow managed to attain a mixture of social
stability, political liberty, and economic prosperity
which it extended to the entire British Empire.

Hutchinson differed sharply from those of his

contemporaries who looked upon the charter granted to John Winthrop as the foundation of colonial liberties. The document authorized no government even remotely resembling the one which developed. First of all, the Massachusetts Bay Company had no right to transfer the seat of governance from England to America. Since its charter omitted the usual location (London) for the company thanks to Winthrop's bribery of the appropriate official, this was a poor excuse to justify self-government. The sort of polity which evolved, where the people elected officials on a franchise restricted to church members, revealed "that they thought themselves at full liberty, without any charter from the crown, to establish any sort of government as they thought proper . . . as if they had been in a state of nature." Hutchinson considered this "a very strange apprehension of the relation they should stand in to Great Britain," in addition to blatantly violating the structure specified within the charter itself. Having removed from England, they held themselves bound only by "what they called voluntary civil subjection, arising merely from compact." This meant Massachusetts owed obedience to England only in those instances where the charter or subsequent voluntary acts of their own confirmed it, leaving them free in all other cases. For example, Massachusetts passed its own equivalent of the British Navigation Acts on the grounds Britain's could not bind the colonies. Laws such as this clearly showed "the wrong sense they had of the relation they stood in to England."(21)

But while Hutchinson could not condemn the seventeenth century Bay Colony's feeble pretense of formal autonomy enough, he still praised the practical consequences of the government effusively. Massachusetts "nourished and cherished" New Hampshire -- added illegally to the colony, which had no right to extend its boundaries by charter -- which accounted for that province's rapid achievement of a prosperous economy. However "extravagant" the people's notions of liberty, they made "no ill use" of their privileges. Furthermore, Massachusetts became the foundation of Britain's own commercial expansion. Hutchinson both opened and concluded volume one of the History, written while he knew Britain was considering colonial taxation, with eloquent pleas urging the continuance of traditional colonial rights -- not for their own sake, an argument he realized would carry little weight in Britain -- but for their

71

benefits to the mother country:(22)

> The addition of wealth and power to Great Britain in consequence of this <u>first emigration</u> of our ancestors, exceeds all expectation. They left their native country with the strongest assurances that they and their posterity should enjoy the privileges of free natural born English subjects. May the wealth and power of Britain still increase, in proportion to the increase of her colonies; may those privileges never be abused; may they be preserved inviolate to the greatest posterity. ...It is a happy thing, that a fondness for freeholds to transmit to posterity, with privileges annexed to them, excited so many of the <u>first planters</u> of America to hard labor, and supported them under hard fare. A great part of this vast continent, filled with wild beasts and savage men scarcely superior to them, now affords the necessaries and conveniences of a civilized life, equal to the like tracts of improved country in other parts of the globe. History affords us no instance of so great improvements in so short a time.

Hutchinson's American nationalism clearly appeared in these passages, but he directed much more of his praise toward Massachusetts in particular -- "first emigration," "first planters" -- than to British North America in general. He viewed the Bay Colony as an Atlas which bore the weight of the empire on its shoulders. "By hard labor and hard fare" it managed to create the famous "Triangle Trade" and ship its fish and agricultural produce to the West Indies after only a few years. New England merchants then traded the produce of the staple colonies to England for manufactured goods, which stimulated the home economy enormously. Massachusetts' efforts not only directly spurred the British West Indies' sugar production by supplying them with foodstuffs that would have taken acreage away from the valuable cash crop, but thereby created markets for the industries of the British Isles. Englishmen who justified colonial taxation and regulation on the grounds that Britain had established the conditions for colonial prosperity, at great cost to itself, had put the cart before the horse. Hutchinson disposed of this argument in one sentence: "The collections made in the colony [of

Massachusetts], after the [Great] Fire of London for the relief of the sufferers there, and upon other occasions, for the relief to diverse of the plantations" did "not fall much, if anything short, of the whole sum that was bestowed upon the colony from abroad" to establish it initially.

During the eighteenth century, in addition to its commercial importance, the province took on a major role in imperial defense. Although not threatened immediately with invasion itself after 1700, Massachusetts proved so eager to undertake several expeditions to annihilate the French in Canada, most of which the crown had not even solicited, that "it went to greater expense and had lost more of its inhabitants than all the other colonies upon the continent taken together."(23) By taxing or otherwise alienating Massachusetts' affections, Britain risked killing the goose that laid the golden egg.

Because colonial prosperity supported England and not vice versa, Hutchinson criticized British attempts to curtail Massachusetts' liberty in the seventeenth century as harshly as he opposed similar efforts in his own day. He had an effective retort to every English charge that the colony sought to throw off the imperial connection entirely. True, Massachusetts failed to return its charter to England in 1638, as required by a quo warranto, and made a series of excuses for not doing so. But if England acquiesced at the time and made no further mention of the subject for decades, why should anyone put up a fuss over a century later? How could the British have faulted Massachusetts' independent coinage, since for over twenty years neither Parliament, Cromwell, nor even King Charles II raised any objections? By allowing such a custom to develop, Britain could not destroy it without endangering beneficial commercial practices. The Bay Colony committed no crime by failing to proclaim Charles II as king in 1660, as no monarch had previously ascended the throne during its thirty year history, and the settlers had no idea what ceremonies were required. Far from sheltering Goffe and Whalley, two regicides of Charles I, the colony sought to apprehend them as soon as it learned they were among the seven whom Charles II did not pardon.(24)

Hutchinson even found favor with the colony's peaceful resistance to the Royal Commission of 1664, sent by Charles II to inquire into abuses of the

charter. In a narrative which presented both the
commissioners and the colonists in a fair light, he
concluded that Massachusetts ought not to be thought
"culpable for refusing entirely to submit to the
absolute authority of the commissioners."
Capitulation would "have suspended their charter"
which only legal procedures could revoke. Mere
decisions of appointed officials, even if sent by the
crown or Parliament, could not legitimately supersede
liberties established by long usage. However,
Massachusetts followed the best course in fighting such
an incursion. Throughout the Commissioners' stay, the
General Court revealed "not an obstinate, perverse
spirit, but a modest steady adherence to what they
imagined, at least, to be their just rights and
privileges." And the Commission proved ineffective.
Hutchinson thereby established the inquiry of 1664 as
a paradigm for a prudent, moderate course Americans
could use to counter contemporary British threats to
traditional rights.(25)

Hutchinson likewise stressed that nothing
Massachusetts did caused Britain to revoke its charter
in 1685. King Charles had been liquidating corporate
charters throughout the empire to eliminate opposition
to his absolutist ambitions. Nevertheless, tempering
his judgments as almost always, Hutchinson believed
some change in the old charter government desirable.
He considered Charles' requests for religious
toleration completely "reasonable." And the Puritans'
insistence that they had to approve any applicable
British legislation, while a pleasing principle "in
speculation," could not "bear the test when adopted by
English subjects." But such reforms would only have
brought about a constitution similar to the eighteenth
century's. Hutchinson had no good words for the
arbitrary manner in which the Stuarts effected their
changes. He found that "Nero concealed his
tyrannical disposition more years than Sir Edmund"
Andros, Massachusetts' first royal governor, "and his
creatures did months." These "harpies" not only
increased the fees of officers to exorbitant heights
and nullified all land titles to make people pay for
new ones, but they provoked the "greatest grievance"
of all by levying taxes and passing laws without an
assembly.(26) Under these circumstances,
Hutchinson found the Glorious Revolution of 1688
praiseworthy, as did all true Whigs in Britain and
America. It represented the resistance of lawful
authority to the lawless acts of officials (King James

and his minions) who had exceeded their rightful powers.

Hutchinson's account of Anglo-American relations demonstrated how the seventeenth century averted the sort of imperial crisis which brewed even as he wrote. Americans had formed unwarranted conceptions of their liberties while creating a free and prosperous society on that very basis. By threatening to abridge colonial rights, Britain jeopardized its own power, which rested on a colonial trade encouraged by those very privileges. But with the exception of Andros' brief regime, Britain failed to impose an effective and hence stifling sovereignty over its colonists. The Americans resisted firmly and moderately without putting the social order that guaranteed their liberty in jeopardy.

In describing the internal political institutions of Puritan society, Hutchinson reiterated the same point he made in discussing its intolerance and relations with Britain. The fundamental principles were all wrong, but they worked very well in practice: "however defective this constitution may appear in theory, we shall seldom meet with an instance where there has been so steady and so general an adherence to the principles upon which it was founded." The form of a government mattered much less than its faithful preservation. Among the theoretical faults Hutchinson found and dismissed included popular election of all ministers and government officials by church members. This provided the real benefit that "the constitution of church government was adopted to the constitution of civil government" and insured cooperation between clerical and lay leaders. Similarly, Hutchinson found in the election of ministers potential for animosities and "subdivisions ad infinitum." But practice did not realize potential, and "much harmony" subsisted, "not only in particular churches," but between one church and another, for fifty years together."(27)

Hutchinson's interpretation of Puritan society as stable, just, and motivated by honest religious sentiments foreshadowed the consensus of twentieth century scholarship. He had little use, however, for some modern historians' notion of "declension" -- that a period of spiritual decline and moral depravity set in after the first generation. Unlike them and the second-generation Puritans, Hutchinson "found

no evidence of any extraordinary degeneracy." He
dismissed some suggested explanations of
Massachusetts' fear that virtue had fled their land,
such as the belief that God had afflicted them with
smallpox or French and Indian attacks as punishment for
their sins, on the grounds that such evils appeared
periodically. Only "the hazardous state of their
charter" provoked such anxiety. Hutchinson slyly
noted that the first generation itself "lamented being
born too soon to see New England in its most
flourishing state." In fact, far from degenerating,
the eighteenth century maintained and added to the
piety and prosperity of the seventeenth.
Hutchinson depicted his own society as the culmination
of a spiritual and political tradition successfully
established by the Puritans, just as he presented
himself as the personal apex of its achievements in
his "Autobiography."(28)

    Hutchinson's heritage, however, was complex.
Despite his sympathy for the Puritans, he also understood the positions of English administrators and New
England sectarians who opposed them. He brought home
the unpleasant features of their rule more poignantly
than most modern scholars who have also taken their
part. Hutchinson thereby managed to think himself into
the various mentalities of an earlier age and
synthesize in advance what ultimately emerged as pro-
and anti-Puritan schools of historiography.

    Such an interpretation differed from the image of
the Puritan founders presented by nearly every other
historian looking back at them from the American
Revolution. Unlike his contemporaries, Hutchinson did
not find seventeenth century resistance to Britain
anticipatory of the final breach with England. Instead,
he bent over backwards -- undoubtedly too far -- to
show that despite a form of government almost
completely repugnant to the laws of England, the
Puritans did not behave with excessive recalcitrance.
By insisting on limited and non-revolutionary conflict
between England and New England, between dissenters
and establishment in the seventeenth century,
Hutchinson, like his contemporaries, held up the past
as a model for the future.(29)

    Hutchinson assumed the Puritans' mantle in practice
as well as theory. At age twenty-six, in 1737, he
joined Boston's New Brick Church. Only a minority of
adult males bothered to become fully communicant

church members by the mid-eighteenth century, but Hutchinson remained the congregation's leading financial contributor until he left for England in 1774, and took an active role in its affairs. In particular, he chaired the committee which brought "New Light" revivalist minister Ebenezer Pemberton to Boston in 1754. Hutchinson's preference for an emotional, fervent variety of Congregationalism most often espoused by the lowly and young may appear strange, but it undoubtedly flowed from his identification with the personal, vital religion of his ancestors as opposed to the more "genteel" form practiced by his contemporaries.(30) It also gave him yet another opportunity to alienate himself and strike off on an unusual course for a man of his station. By identifying himself so strongly with the Puritans, Hutchinson employed them as initiators of a living tradition rather than as models for political revolution.

* * * * * * * *

Eighteenth century Massachusetts presented Hutchinson with the reverse problem of the seventeenth. He regarded the charter granted by King William and Queen Mary in 1691, which combined a royal governor, elected assembly, and a council chosen by the other branches of the legislature, as a nearly ideal solution to the problem of reconciling liberty and authority, America and England. Writing on the eve of that government's dissolution, he confidently asserted that "seventy years' practice under a new charter, in many respects to be preferred to the old, has taken away not only all expectation, but all desire of ever returning to the old."(31) Yet even this constitution, nearly ideal in theory, produced practical difficulties Despite general stability, factional strife arose; the council proved insufficiently independent of the other two branches; town government, especially in Boston, reflected an overly popular bias; and paper money disputes divided the province along class lines. In discussing these matters, Hutchinson found the economic conflict and anti-British sentiments stressed by future historians. But while he did not neglect such elements, he stressed that before 1765 a more personalized, less explosive political controversy which rarely went outside of the General Court itself overshadowed them and waxed and waned in proportion to any governor's political skill.

For Hutchinson, eighteenth century politics presented an administrative rather than a theoretical problem. Since the constitution was sound, specific issues determined when conflict arose. Volume two of the History demonstrated how the intricate interaction of personalities, British provocations of the assembly, and executive prudence determined the scope of controversy at any given time. Hutchinson here erected another pillar of his political thought: the more politics impinged on society, engaged popular interest, and extended beyond an inevitable elite squabble, the greater the threat to social stability and the existing system of government. Hutchinson believed that even where the general populace responded to real grievances -- and he never denied these -- their reaction, if excessive, had to be shaped by demagogues with personal axes to grind who distrusted the prudent attempts of the constitutional authorities to deal with the problems. Ominously, the very provincial constitution Hutchinson so admired contained in embryo the factional ambitions and popular fanaticism which eventually destroyed it. But the constitution's basic soundness, and the traditional limits on conflict worked into it, ensured that generally good laws and an upright population neutralized those incendiaries who would have raised themselves upon the province's ruins. Like his treatment of the seventeenth century, Hutchinson's discussion of the eighteenth came to a heavily qualified conclusion, again positive although for different reasons, and again anticipating diverse interpretations historians have since advanced.

Hutchinson did not follow the efforts of his fellow loyalists and their Whig opponents to show that God was on his side by either indiscriminately tracing the ultimate alignments of 1776 back into the past, or alternatively (as some loyalists did) viewing the eighteenth century as a "golden age" where conflict had yet to appear, and society flourished under the benign aegis of Britain and a loyal elite. Hutchinson rather judged the American Revolution in terms of prerevolutionary politics; seventy-five years of provincial experience served as the norm with which the revolutionary decade could be contrasted, and both change and continuity discerned. Largely because, almost alone of his contemporaries, he began writing before the colonial crisis struck, Hutchinson could treat events of the provincial period as significant even if they did not prefigure the final explosion.(32)

In contrast to scholars before the mid-1960s, Hutchinson characterized the political experience of provincial Massachusetts by the non-ideological competition of small groups for power and privilege, with only intermittent inputs of popular interest. Hutchinson distinguished sharply between the ideological struggles which occurred after 1765 and conflict which had existed previously. He noted that "the terms Whig and Tory had never been used much in America." Consensus existed on the fundamentals of government, as "the people of Massachusetts, in general, were of the principles of the ancient Whigs and attached to the House of Hanover." Only after 1765, and "all on a sudden" at that, were "officers of the crown, and such as were for keeping up their authority, . . . branded with the name of Tories."(33)

Two interrelated causes provoked political conflict before the 1760s. First, Hutchinson blandly observed that "at all times there have been parties, ins and outs"; "there have always been men out of place who wish to be in." Hutchinson neither condemned nor praised such behavior, but merely recognized it as inevitable: people had always disagreed about something, they tended to make common cause against a common enemy, and those who had power were opposed by disgruntled elements. Hutchinson's neutral descriptions of the parties -- modern scholars would say factions -- of the early eighteenth century as "ins" and "outs" implied that he found no important moral distinction between the supporters (court, prerogative) or opponents (country, popular) of the governor. His willingness as a practical politician to accept non-revolutionary political conflict within "the rules of the game" carried over into his political theory. Unlike nearly every eighteenth century thinker except Edmund Burke, Hutchinson did not condemn all political factionalism as inherently disruptive and potentially revolutionary, but recognized the value of some types of association as helpful in airing alternative solutions to problems.(34)

Second, factional strife occurred because the charter of 1691 left some powers of the legislature's three branches vague. Disputes by the house, council, and governor over "different constructions" of these, although endemic, had nothing to do with the new divisions of the revolutionary age. In his "Strictures on the Declaration" of Independence, Hutchinson termed intra-legislative quarrels "mere contests between the governors and assemblies, so light and transient as to have been presently forgotten." By the 1760s, moreover, such disputes were "pretty well settled." However serious it may have seemed to contemporaries, provincial conflict paled into insignificance before the great events yet to come.(35)

No major social or political problems ignited even these generally manageable disputes. Hutchinson repeatedly stressed that "in no independent state in the world could the people have been more happy than they were in the government of Massachusetts Bay." Factionalism did not arise from any complaints with their charter or its new institutions with which "they were so fully satisfied." With the sole exception of "the charges which had been occasioned by Indian wars, they had felt less the burdens of government, than any people who so much enjoyed the benefit of it."(36) Of course, it could also be argued these charges for war were very heavy per capita, and that Hutchinson thereby engaged in a form of special pleading for the government in which he himself played so large a role.

Contention in the General Court, therefore, in the absence of underlying, long-standing grievances, had to be explained as the product of personalities and circumstances. An intermittent phenomenon, Hutchinson accounted for it in historical, rather than structural, terms. Governors William Phips, Joseph Dudley, and Samuel Shute, for example, provoked trouble by refusing to let their personal enemies sit on the council. William Burnet, who "did not know the temper of the people of New England," who "have a strong sense of liberty, and are more easily drawn than driven," proved overly dictatorial. He also went too far in appointing only those who favored his policies to office. Jonathan Belcher went too far to the other extreme, and gave posts to his political enemies indiscriminately in the futile hope of winning them over to his cause. He also possessed an extremely acerbic personality. Thomas Pownall made the mistake of courting the enemies of his predecessor, Governor Shirley, and hoping Shirley's friends would remain loyal out of dedication to government and order. But personalities proved stronger than ideals: when Pownall left the province "he had very few friends left."(37)

Hutchinson considered the governors' personal ability to manage the legislature critical in eighteenth century politics. This demanded, above all, flexibility and the willingness to subordinate their personal convictions and a strict adherence to royal instructions to the practical requirements of a given situation. Burnet's administration, for example, witnessed one long losing battle with the legislature: "a little more caution and conformity to the different usages, manners, customs, and even prejudices of different companies, would have been more politic, but his open undisguised mind could not submit to it." For governors, as for revolutionaries, stressing absolute principles without regard to context could only lead to disaster. Governor William Shirley was more successful. He did not try to redeem the entire provincial debt in 1741 as the Lords of Trade had ordered, because that would have imposed "a burden that the people would never bear." Instead, he realized the intention behind the directive sought to eliminate depreciation, the method being incidental. The "spirit" of the instructions proved more important than the letter.(38)

Hutchinson's approval of political flexibility undoubtedly stemmed from his own long experience in the Massachusetts house and council. He thoroughly knew the political arena of the 1740s and 50s where success came through compromise, persuasion, manipulation, distribution of patronage, and efforts to avoid polarizing issues -- or, as the disgruntled faction termed such methods, "corruption."

Yet the onus of factional strife did not always lie with the governor. Hutchinson described the house of representatives as a fickle, inexperienced, and ignorant body at the mercy of those few members who made governing their major concern. From his own experience, he noted that bills would be referred from one session of the house to the next, only to be suddenly passed by the very same members who had rejected them earlier. The inconsistent attendance of many deputies allowed "any designing person" to pass measures the majority did not favor. (Hutchinson could thank an extremely thin house for approving his own currency plan in 1749.)(39)

Hutchinson blamed the greatest controversies, as in 1720 when "the contests and dissensions in the government rose to a greater height than they had done since the religious feuds in the years 1636 and 1637," on both the executive and the legislature. On this occasion, he took "no pleasure in relating the proceedings of the General Court." Motivated by personal hatred of Governor Shute, leading representatives manipulated the house and carried their case to the public, writing pamphlets and newspaper articles convincing the people "their civil liberties were struck at." But on the other hand, again "apprehensive that some of my readers will be apt to doubt the impartiality of this account," Hutchinson condemned Shute as being "void of art" despite his "great integrity." Determined not to "set the country in an unfavorable light" even if the deputies took steps to undermine the governor with "scarce any attempts" on his part to strike back, Hutchinson still blamed Shute for attaching himself to one of the two factions in the province, making "the other his irreconcilable enemies," and vetoing the assembly's choice of his leading opponent, Elisha Cooke, as its speaker, a power not given to him by the charter. Hutchinson drew the obvious conclusion, perhaps with an eye to the impending colonial crisis, that "when just bounds are exceeded, the second step is as easy as the first," until at length "both sides are drawn to excesses."(40)

Hutchinson went out of his way to be fair to both governors and their opponents. Such impartiality came naturally to a man who had opposed Governor Shirley in the first half of his administration only to become his "prime minister" in the mid-1740s, and who had initially welcomed Governor Thomas Pownall only to become his bitter enemy. For instance, he did not consider Elisha Cooke the "Catiline of that era," which is how Peter Oliver described him, but rather "a fair and open enemy." He respectively praised two of Cooke's principal cohorts, Oliver Noyes and John Clark, as "a person of many valuable qualities" and a man of "a very humane obliging disposition."(41)

Hutchinson applied similar rules to his evaluation of governors. When he could not praise them for their political effectiveness, he usually found something to applaud in their personal characters -- or vice versa. Sir William Phips had been a fine naval captain and was blessed with a "benevolent, friendly disposition." But his humble origins as a mariner and "quick and passionate" temper caused him to break out into unseemly rages against prominent officials, which produced his recall. Joseph Dudley, on the contrary, "applied himself with the greatest diligence to the business of his station" and did an excellent job of managing Queen Anne's War. But he made "ambition" his "ruling passion" and did not hesitate to report "secret insinuations to the disadvantage of his country" to the British ministry to advance his own career.(42)

Hutchinson even passed a mixed verdict on William Shirley, despite their close cooperation in restoring a silver currency and during the French and Indian War. On the one hand, he praised Shirley for resolving the Land Bank crisis of 1741 to the satisfaction of both the Bankers and their opponents, which "rendered his administration easy." In general, he satisfied the populace, and "the prosperous state of the province was very much owing to the success of his vigorous, active measures." But on the other hand, unlike his domestic policy, Shirley's "constantly . . . projecting and prosecuting plans" to strike at the French in Canada earned Hutchinson's criticism. Far from being undertaken for the public good, Shirley wished to advance his "private interest" and possibly obtain a more lucrative post such as commanding a British regiment. The expeditions did not justify their cost in money or lives. After an impartial twelve page narrative presenting reasons for and against undertaking the Louisbourg campaign of 1745, Hutchinson sarcastically concluded that "considerate persons . . . could not . . . avoid gratefully admiring the favor of divine providence in so great a number of remarkable instances which contributed to the expedition's success." Louisbourg should have taught the province not to "depend upon special interpositions of providence" in the future, but to "avoid the like imminent dangers and to weigh the probability and improbability of succeeding in the ordinary course of events."(43)

Only a handful of people received Hutchinson's unqualified praise -- men who, like his father, "regardless of the frowns of a governor or the threats of the people, spoke and voted according to his judgment, attaching himself to no party any further than he found their measures tended to promote the public interest." Such men invariably suffered for their patriotism. Daniel Gookin, the only magistrate who tried to persuade Massachusetts not to vent its anger on friendly and hostile Indians indiscriminately during King Philip's War, "exposed himself . . . to hootings and offensive language from the populace." In the provincial council, chosen annually by the representatives in joint vote with the outgoing council and approved by the governor, members who trimmed their sails to please all parties generally won election without difficulty, whereas those "who have had fortitude enough to resist an undue influence . . . have had violent opposition to their election." In short, Hutchinson praised men like himself who stood apart from their contemporaries and unflinchingly adhered to unpopular courses. It is no wonder that the governors he admired for personal reasons failed politically while those who resorted to devious means succeeded. As he wrote of Lieutenant-Governor William Stoughton: "It is no blemish in his character that he had many enemies. Every man who makes it more his aim to serve than to please the people may expect it."(44)

Hutchinson's insights into Massachusetts provincial society, however personally motivated, have only been explored further by scholars in the past two decades. Like Bernard Bailyn, Jack P. Greene, and Robert Zemsky, Hutchinson observed a factionalism limited largely to an elite, based more on personalities than principles. He would also have agreed with Michael Zuckerman that the people of Massachusetts maintained an orderly, stable, and contented society largely unconcerned with legislative bickerings. He would also have applauded John Murrin's conclusion that a firm loyalty to Britain and increasing "Anglicization" prevailed. Finally, his stress on Dudley's and Shirley's management of military affairs as a key element in the politics of their regimes anticipated my own research.(45)

However, while he emphasized elite in-fighting as the eighteenth century's major political feature, Hutchinson did not ignore occasional direct inputs from the people. Fortunately, from his point of view, most of their contribution appeared on the local level where it did little harm: "from the heats and animosities of popular elections in towns, they judged of the danger to be apprehended from election by all the people in the province." Hutchinson especially censured the Boston town meeting, which had twice removed him as representative for refusing to support paper money. On the second of these occasions he complained to Israel Williams that "we are governed not by weight but by numbers." Boston unwisely rejected a plan by "most of the principal inhabitants" to govern it as a self-selecting corporation "by a great majority" under the influence of a "demagogue."(46)

Provincial government enjoyed more stability than town because "demagogues" only excited the public three times between the Glorious Revolution and the Stamp Act -- in 1714, 1720, and 1741. On each occasion supporters of inflationary currency schemes stirred up the people. In 1714, a faction proposed a private bank to loan bills of credit to anyone mortgaging an estate as security for their value; 1720 marked Elisha Cooke's quarrel with Governor Shute; and the Land Bank of 1741 revived the currency proposal of 1714. Had the monetary schemes or Cooke's machinations succeeded, Hutchinson believed that "the province would have been in the utmost confusion."(47)

Hutchinson condemned paper money as "wretched," a "source of so much iniquity." The mere fact that "the major part of the people, in number, were no sufferers by a depreciating currency" did not justify it. Hutchinson was no populist, nor did the interests of society as a whole coincide with that of the lower orders. Among other calamities, it produced inflation which caused "very great injustice" to creditors, widows, clergymen, and others dependent on fixed incomes. But he not only criticized scrip for its obvious injustices, but also for its profound and subtle social consequences: "the influence a bad currency has on the morals of the people is greater than is generally imagined." The people used their numerical strength to continue inflation to defraud their creditors, an immoral act in itself, and furthermore became the pawns of politicians who from "mistaken principles" or "party's sake and popular applause" devised various means to that end. Hutchinson counted a few wealthy and prominent men among those who would incite the people, but most of these tribunes were "plebians of small estates," "persons in difficult or involved circumstances in trade," or "were possessed of [small] real estates." The possibility of paper currency wooed the people away from "the most sensible, discreet persons" who favored a stable currency -- "men of estates and the principal merchants."(48) Paper money therefore threatened to oust a society's natural and most qualified leaders. Hutchinson blamed bogus leaders for the disturbances of 1714, 1720, and 1741, rather than the population which served them as unwitting dupes. Elisha Cooke, for example, "differed from most who, from time to time, have been recorded in history for popular men." Whereas his predecessors, "to preserve the favor of the people," changed "with the popular air," Cooke "had the art of keeping the people steady in the applause of his measures." "All he found necessary" was "to be careful never to depart from the appearance of maintaining or enlarging their rights."(49)

Inflation thus threatened the very foundations of government by introducing the people as an active force to support unscrupulous leaders trying to erect an entirely different social order. The bank of 1714 "had a universal spread and divided towns, parishes, and particular families" while in 1741 "perhaps the major part, in number, of the inhabitants of the province, openly or secretly" wished the Land Bank well.

Hutchinson deplored nothing so much as the spread of political controversy from the elite to the general public: where "the interest of party prevails over all other considerations, virtue, religion, private friendship, and public good are all sacrificed to it." Such partisanship was especially dangerous in a colony:(50)

> In a colony . . . the people consider the prerogative as an interest without them, separate and distinct from the interior interest of the colony. This takes their attention from the just proportion and weight due to each branch of the constitution and causes a bias in favor of the popular. For the same reason, men fond of popular applause are more sure of success, . . . and consequently men who with unbiased judgments discern and have virtue enough to pursue the real interest of the country are more likely to be reproached and vilified.

Massachusetts' peculiar vulnerability to popular unrest as a colony made "unbiased" men such as Hutchinson himself indispensable and yet rendered their position more precarious. In this light, Hutchinson's ability to persuade the legislature, almost single-handedly, to abolish paper money in 1749 took on tremendous importance. He not only put the people "in a more easy and happy situation than ever before," but he also eliminated the one issue which threatened to unleash the turmoils of popular politics. For in discussing paper money, Hutchinson abandoned his careful weighing of both sides and hurled the sorts of thunderbolts he later reserved for the American revolutionaries. Every time politicians raised the currency issue, the total disruption of Massachusetts' prosperity and the detachment of the inhabitants from their traditional rulers and moral beliefs loomed. By ending this menace, Hutchinson had set a precedent he hoped to repeat in reconciling Massachusetts with Britain during the colonial crisis.

Despite his polemics on paper money, Hutchinson's willingness to admit that class and ideological tensions stressed by modern historians played a role in an otherwise stable political system ensured that unlike most other historians of the period, he did not present the eighteenth century as either a prelude to revolution or a period of harmony totally different from that which followed.(51) If he admired the eighteenth century constitution, he found something to criticize in governors who failed either their duty or their consciences, town meetings which threatened the social order, and demagogues who sought to make political capital of Massachusetts' currency problems by destroying the people's faith in their legitimate rulers. But thanks to the "unbiased" gentlemen such as himself, truly devoted to principle, tradition, and law, the province's sound constitution and the inhabitants' generally high level of morality made it possible to harmonize these pernicious tendencies.

Hutchinson's veneration of pre-revolutionary Massachusetts, therefore, did not arise from personal identification with any particular faction or institution. Governors, councils, assemblies, town meetings, and with rare exceptions individuals alternatively displayed weakness, imprudence, or selfishness. Hutchinson admired the general product of a stable and just society that somehow arose from the interaction of these elements in accordance with traditional rules and limitations. A good constitution, for Hutchinson, did not realize any grand purposes or educate the population to a high morality and idealism. Rather, it brought good out of evil -- by reconciling tensions between England and America, lower classes led by unsavory characters and the natural elite, and the popular and prerogative factions. By implicitly recognizing that a good society can be achieved through a balance of imperfections and diverse interests, Hutchinson established a model for his program during the revolutionary crisis. He did not wish to cramp either parliamentary sovereignty or American rights, but tried to maintain both in an uneasy alliance of opposites which had worked so well in provincial Massachusetts. By discerning this pattern in pre-revolutionary society, he exhibited the sort of mentality James Madison later brought to the Tenth Federalist and Sir Lewis Namier applied to the study of eighteenth century Britain.(52) Limited, self-interested conflict among groups, factions, and individuals, none strong enough to gain total dominance over the others, stabilized a government as effectively as principled, ideological zealotry destroyed it.

* * * * * * *

Hutchinson devoted most of his History to political matters, but his powers did not wane on his excursions into social and economic developments. In dealing with Indian relations, racial prejudice, witchcraft, and the colonial economy he did not permit a general approval of his heritage to blind him to his ancestors' blemishes.

Hutchinson criticized the Puritans' treatment of the Indians severely. Yet he recognized that their behavior could not simply be labelled deplorable without accounting for its changes over time. His discussion struck a good balance between the traditional view that the settlers abused the natives and Alden T. Vaughan's revisionist thesis that the Puritans treated them fairly until King Philip's War. Hutchinson wrote that "at the first arrival of the English the Indians were treated with kindness, to obtain friendship and favor." But their motives were by no means disinterested. Because the tribes constituted a powerful threat for some time, the English at first displayed the respect due to European rulers, as evidenced by the terms of equality in treaties. But this soon ceased, and if the Puritans restrained from open warfare most of the time, they stirred up animosities among the various tribes, thereby avoiding any union against themselves while assuming a superior and supposedly impartial role as arbiters of these disputes. Hutchinson thus recognized both English restraint and professions of friendship while noting the Machiavellian purposes behind such diplomacy.(53)

As the seventeenth century progressed and Massachusetts grew in strength and population, the colony became more aggressive. Following the Pequot War in 1636, no major hostilities occurred for some forty years. In 1656, the Puritans even began a missionary effort, "the long neglect of which," Hutchinson wrote, "cannot be excused." The Indians asked sarcastically "how it happened, if Christianity was of such importance, that for six and twenty years together the English said nothing to them about it." But this episode marked only a brief interruption in a sorry tale. Hutchinson blamed the whites for King Philip's War. The Indians had not understood the treaties ceding their lands: they at most imagined these required them to live in peace with the English and share hunting rights. Hutchinson depicted Philip himself as a tragic figure "who could not bear to see the English of New Plymouth extending their settlements over the dominions of his ancestors." The encroachments had been accompanied by "many abuses offered to particular persons among the Indians by evil-minded Englishmen." But even here, Hutchinson tried to show the other side. He recognized that at least some inhabitants who had "suffered most by Indian cruelties" retained justifiably "strong prejudices against them."(54)

Hutchinson's condemnation of the whites for most Indian troubles did not mean he felt any romantic attachment to the red man as a noble savage. Since he valued stability and tradition as prerequisites of freedom, Hutchinson found little in the natural liberty beloved by Jefferson. He thought the Indians barbarians "who have always shown great savagery to their English captives," and criticized their infidelity to treaties as comparable to Carthage's repeated violations of agreements with Rome. But at the same time, he insisted that the English had no right to retaliate in kind. On practical grounds, this merely "enraged them more." But the moral argument was more compelling: "to destroy women and children for the barbarity of their husbands cannot easily be justified." Hutchinson distinguished civilization from savagery morally as well as technologically. His discussion of Indians demonstrated his belief that no state or individual ought ever to violate the Golden Rule of Christian morality for any purpose whatsoever.(55)

In Indian affairs, as elsewhere, the eighteenth century resolved difficulties the seventeenth could not. Intermittently friendly relations with the tribes became permanent in 1725, when Lieutenant-Governor William Dummer made a treaty with the Maine Indians which "has been applauded as the most judicious ever made." It provided definitive proof of the practical advantages of honorable behavior. A long peace followed this agreement because the General Court strictly adhered to its terms and forbade private persons to trade with the natives and ensured that public truck-houses sold them provisions as cheaply as white men could buy them in Boston. Since this treaty had no major differences from those which preceded it, Hutchinson used it to demonstrate that a solution to this century-old problem had always existed if the province had only adhered to its own professed principles.(56)

In keeping with his belief that a people's history and developing institutions shaped their behavior rather than any innate or "natural" qualities, Hutchinson did not use differences between other cultures and his own to excuse their exploitation. He remarked that "we are too apt to consider the Indians as a race of beings by nature inferior to us, and born to servitude." He extended this belief in man's basic equality to other races and religions as well. The province's acceptance of black slavery shamed him so much that he remarked that "some judicious persons," by which Hutchinson always meant people who agreed with him, thought "that the permission of slavery has been a public mischief." He even took the part of the French Acadians, who suffered "truly deplorable" hardships when exiled to Massachusetts from Nova Scotia during the French and Indian War. He managed to dissociate himself from his own patriotism and a nearly universal hatred of the French by his countrymen to argue that "it was hardly reasonable . . . to charge them with being rebels or traitors," when "for a whole century together, they were once in a few years changing their masters."(57) Hutchinson personally spent much time and money caring for the refugees. Psychologically, of course, one can attribute his concern to the opportunity to take a morally irreproachable stand on yet another unpopular issue.

Hutchinson moved beyond his New England contemporaries, who identified Catholicism or "Popery" with the Anti-Christ and even feared Anglicanism as a close approximation, to espouse toleration of all religions. He used the question of oaths to demonstrate that Christians, Jews, and Moslems should all be sworn on their respective scriptures, as "to have the fear of God before our eyes in all that is essential" and was far more important "than any particular ceremony." Despite his devout Christianity, Hutchinson recognized that social circumstances and traditions rather than personal choice shaped a person's religion, like his culture, and men could not be condemned for adhering to these. But he carried his belief in toleration one step too far. Pleading with the Sons of Liberty during the 1760s, he wrote: "We shall never be all of one mind in our political principles. I desire no more candor from those who differ from me, than I have ever been, and ever shall be ready to show to them."(58) His political opponents, dedicated to a virtuous, undivided society founded on immutable principles of right, could not understand this doctrine, and doubtless considered it incompatible with Hutchinson's demands that they cease their lawless activity. By insisting "Tory" ideas be tolerated, Hutchinson could turn his open-mindedness into a political weapon to demand equal time from his opponents.

In discussing the witch craze which occurred at Salem in 1692, Hutchinson again tried to be both sympathetic and critical toward the perpetrators and thereby dealt intelligently with issues raised by modern scholars. He dismissed theories recently advanced by Chadwick Hansen, that "something preternatural" really was at work in the town, and by Paul Boyer and Stephen Nissenbaum that dissension within Salem itself should be held responsible. Eighteenth century provincials had advanced both theories, but Hutchinson disagreed. He attributed the belief that witches really existed to his contemporaries' refusal to fault their ancestors for the persecution, and refuted the charge blaming Salem's internal problems by noting that the rest of the country joined in readily. Instead, he stressed the collective psychological aspects John Demos and Marion Starkey have emphasized. On one level, "the whole was a scene of fraud and imposture, begun by young girls, who at first perhaps thought of nothing more than

being pitied and indulged." The publication of a
number of books on witchcraft in the 1680s, to whose
details the symptoms of the afflicted conformed,
provoked their imaginations. Once the girls began
behaving in this way, the inhabitants could not help
but interpret their actions as inspired by witchcraft, since all Christendom at the time gave such "a
serious solemn construction, even to common events."
Hutchinson did not hesitate to mention that more
people were "put to death in a single county of
England, in a short space of time, than have suffered
in all New England from the first settlers to the
present times." Once accusations began to fly, adult
persons "afraid of being accused themselves" and others
with "wicked hearts" fingered their personal enemies
and other likely suspects to divert suspicion from
themselves. On the colony-wide as opposed to the
personal level, psychology also operated.
Massachusetts had recently endured "peculiarly great
distress" from the loss of its old charter and the
debacle of the Canadian expedition of 1690, events in
which a religious people could not avoid detecting a
diabolical hand. By correctly calling attention to
the unusual conjuction of circumstances which made
Salem possible, Hutchinson partially exonerated his
ancestors for an admittedly criminal deed which
nevertheless proved an exception rather than (as in
Europe) a rule.(59)

 Hutchinson also had mixed feelings on British
regulation of the colonial economy. He did not doubt
that it injured North America's commerce, and he
concluded volume two of the *History* with as damning an
attack as an American ever penned against the
Navigation Acts, which prohibited trade with the
foreign West Indies. Hutchinson censured the British
sugar planters for having continually tried to
restrain a North American trade with the foreign
islands, which in spite of prohibitions increased
continuously in the eighteenth century. Parliament so
favored the British islands that they proved burdensome both to the northern colonies and to Great
Britain. Their monopoly on sugar production in the
empire raised the prices on rum and molasses, and the
islands obtained supplies and foodstuffs at low rates
because the northern colonies could sell more easily
and legally to them. In addition, in an argument
anticipating Adam Smith's in Book IV of his *Wealth of
Nations*, Hutchinson complained that the islands'
unfair trade advantages and monopoly of the British

market raised profits in that industry disproportionately, thereby attracting capital more beneficially invested in the development of North America. Hutchinson could not understand why the whole empire should suffer merely "to aggrandize the West Indian planters." He was glad Britain enforced its imperial regulations more in the breach than the observance, for a "rigid execution" would have been "unbearable."(60)

Like Benjamin Franklin among his contemporaries, Hutchinson repudiated an empire based on mercantilism in favor of one founded on free trade. Colonial commerce ought to have been unfettered because its value lay less in the goods and specie it supplied directly to Britain or the West Indies, and more in the "amazing addition made to the dominion and wealth of Britain." "The profit of all their trade and of the increase of their substance" permitted the northern provinces "to take so much more of British manufactures." Noting that the mother country suffered from an unfavorable balance of trade with most other nations which only the remittances spent by colonials for manufactured goods enabled it to discharge, Hutchinson suggested that the freer colonial commerce could be made, the greater domestic manufactures would increase. Hutchinson also predicted a decline in British trade with the rest of the world, arguing that "in a short time you will have only your colonies with whom you can carry on any advantageous trade."(61)

Hutchinson's economic ideas paralleled his historical and political theories. The formal, and to the colonies degrading, structure of trade relations of the Acts of Trade and Navigation mattered far less than the mutually beneficial customary pattern that had developed. The colonies ought to have accepted the ample rewards received in practice from lax enforcement as fair compensation for their contribution to British prosperity.

But even if the enforcement of British regulations did become bothersome, Hutchinson thought America had to submit. Like Adam Smith, who defended the Navigation Acts on grounds of imperial defense, Hutchinson insisted that Americans had to accept even the inconveniences of membership in the empire as essential to their prosperity and freedom: "we certainly cannot enjoy and subsist without the

protection of our mother country over our trade at sea, as well as our personal estate. . . . Shall we think much of sharing in the burdens when we have been so great sharers in the benefit"?
Hutchinson had no good words for British commercial policy per se, even though its application proved much less onerous than its intention. It represented a purely negative entry on the ledger of British colonial rule. But since the imperial relation had to be accepted or rejected as a whole, commercial restrictions represented an insufficient motive for embracing the latter alternative.(62)

Hutchinson's theoretical preference for free trade, however, did not always extend to his own activities. His sons, whose business he helped to run, were two of Massachusetts' largest importers of legal English tea during the 1760s. Hutchinson's letters reveal that business was bad as a result of competition with the illegal importers of Dutch tea, who sold their goods duty free. Hutchinson used his leverage as lieutenant-governor to press for some measures to end this smuggling, and once even sent a top-secret letter to England describing a particular vessel which ought to be seized. The only way Hutchinson could have reconciled theory and practice here would have been to argue that if measures restricting trade, to say nothing of injuring his own personal interest, had to continue, why should law-abiding subjects feel their weight exclusively?(63)

Hutchinson's views on British mercantilism epitomized his general outlook on colonial history. In many instances, he objected to British infringements on American liberty, but he also realized that these freedoms themselves could only have existed under the aegis of the Union Jack in the first place. He could distinguish positive and negative effects of the imperial connection analytically, but in practice it had to be accepted or rejected in toto. Furthermore, the effects of British measures, including their lax enforcement, mattered far more as a standard of judgment than the mentality behind them.
Hutchinson applied a similar practical yardstick to both Puritanism and the eighteenth century constitution, and would use the same arguments in opposing the American Revolution. The ultimate question was not whether specific British policies harmed America, or whether Britain violated colonial rights, but whether America would be better off under English

rule or as an independent nation. For a man whose only experience of American self-government consisted of suffering the brunt of mob rule in Boston, the answer could not be in doubt.

FOOTNOTES

1. The discussion in this and the following paragraphs relies principally on J. H. Plumb, *The Death of the Past* (Boston, 1971); Eric Voegelin, *From Enlightenment to Revolution* (Durham, N.C., 1975), 3-34; John Lukacs, *Historical Consciousness* (New York, 1968), 9-21; and Friedrich Meinecke, *Historism* (New York, 1972), Book I. For medieval historiography, the account in Charles Homer Haskins, *The Renaissance of the Twelfth Century* (Cambridge, Mass., 1927), chapter viii, is a good introduction.

2. Lukacs, *Historical Consciousness*, 16; Bolingbroke's famous remark appears in the second letter *On the Study and Use of History*.

3. *Voltaire*, ed., J. H. Brumfitt (New York, 1963), 122, from *The Age of Louis XIV*, "Introduction"; Meinecke, *Historism*, 163; J. H. Hale, *The Evolution of British Historiography* (Cleveland and New York, 1964), 31-34.

4. Ursula Brumm, *American Thought and Religious Typology* (Rutgers, N.J., 1970), 3-101; Sacvan Bercovitch, ed., *The American Puritan Imagination: Essays in Revolution* (Cambridge, 1974), editor's introduction; Robert Middlekauff, *The Mathers: Three Generations of Puritan Intellectuals* (New York, 1971), 320-349.

5. In a book of that title, first published in 1931.

6. H. Trevor Coburn, *The Lamp of Experience: Whig History and the Intellectual Origins of the American Revolution* (Chapel Hill, N.C., 1965); for English antecedents of this view, and how Whig history provoked reactions by both royalists and common lawyers, see J. G. A. Pocock, *The Ancient Constitution and the Feudal Law: English Historical Thought in the Seventeenth Century* (Cambridge, 1957), esp. 148-181.

7. Hale, *British Historiography*, 20, 21; for a sample of loyalist historical writing, see

Lawrence H. Leder, ed., The Colonial Legacy: The Loyalist Historians (New York, 1971).

8. The patriot historians of the American Revolution used history to justify the event in an uncomplicated manner. See especially the discussion of David Ramsay, William Gordon, and Mercy Otis Warren in William Raymond Smith, History as Argument: Three Patriot Historians of the American Revolution (The Hague, 1966), and Arthur H. Shaffer, The Politics of History: Writing the History of the American Revolution: 1783-1815 (Chicago, 1975), for a more complete survey.

9. Meinecke, Historism (original emphasis). The words historism and historicism are used in this sense, and not to mean that history has a morality of its own whereby "whatever is, is right" or, in its revolutionary variant, "whatever is becoming, is right"; Plumb, The Death of the Past, 131-133.

10. Lukacs, Historical Consciousness, 17; Plumb, The Death of the Past, 125; for the "erudites," see Arnaldo Momigliano, "Ancient History and the Antiquarians," in Studies in Historiography (New York and London, 1966), 1-27. Momigliano writes that the "main concern" of these scholars "was to ascertain the truth of each event by the best methods of research." They "aimed at factual truth, not an interpretation of causes or examination of consequences." (ibid., 20, 21); Herbert Butterfield, Man on His Past (Cambridge, 1955), 32-61, 68-70.

11. Lawrence Henry Gipson, The British Empire Before the American Revolution (New York, 1961), XIII, 300; Lawrence Shaw Mayo, Proceedings of the American Antiquarian Society, XLI (1949), 321-339; James Truslow Adams, Revolutionary New England, 1691-1776 (Boston, 1923), 370; Moses Coit Tyler, The Literary History of the American Revolution (New York and London, 1897), II, 394; Michael Kraus, The Writing of American History (Norman, Oklahoma, 1953), 65, all consider Hutchinson the finest American historian of the colonial period. Daniel Boorstin, The Americans: The Colonial Experience (New York, 1958), 382, lauds his "surprisingly comprehensive account";

Esmond Wright's verdict, Causes and Consequences of the American Revolution (New York, 1966), 16, is "cool, accurate, and judicious." Clifford Shipton, in his sketch, in Harvard Graduates, VIII, 119, goes so far as to say that "his fairness, moderation, and courtesy to his political opponents was downright amazing." Dissenters from the consensus which praises Hutchinson include Vernon L. Parrington, Main Currents in American Thought (New York, 1927-1930), I, 196, who calls him a "reactionary" of "narrow partisanship"; Robert E. Brown, Middle-Class Democracy and the Revolution in Massachusetts, 1691-1780 (Ithaca, N.Y., 1955), 205, considers the History "a good example of the way in which a man's interests could shape his interpretation of events"; Bert James Lowenberg, American History in American Thought (New York, 1972), argues that Hutchinson's "knowledge of political theory was severely limited, a limitation fatal to his scholarship and statesmanship alike." Edmund S. Morgan, "The Historians of Early New England," in Ray Allan Billington, ed., The Reinterpretation of Early American History (San Marino, California, 1966), 43, believes that Hutchinson read the conflict between royal authority and colonial liberty back to the Mayflower in a simple-minded way. Harry M. Ward, "The Search for American Identity: Early Historians of New England," in Alden T. Vaughan and George A. Billias, eds., Perspectives on Early American History: Essays in Honor of Richard B. Morris (New York, 1973), 40-62, quotes one of Hutchinson's remarks on a particular issue -- see, for example, pages 52 and 59, respectively, for Indian relations and the causes of the Revolution -- without trying to account for contradictory and modifying opinions.

12. History, I, xxix.

13. History, I, 18, 82; "Stamp Act Essay," 487.

14. History, I, 42.

15. For example, Charles E. Banks, "Religous 'Persecution' as a Factor in Emigration to New England, 1630-1640," favors the economic interpretation, and is criticized by Samuel Eliot Morison in the Proceedings of the Massachusetts

Historical Society, LXIII (1929-1930), 136-154. Favorable verdicts include Perry Miller, The New England Mind: The Seventeenth Century (New York, 1939); Samuel Eliot Morison, The Puritan Pronaos (New York, 1936); Edmund S. Morgan, The Puritan Family (2nd ed., New York, 1966) and The Puritan Dilemma: The Story of John Winthrop (Boston, 1958). Authors who stress the economic motivations and contentiousness of the Puritans include James Truslow Adams, The Founding of New England (Boston, 1921); Darrett Rutman, Winthrop's Boston: Portrait of a Puritan Town, 1630-1649 (Chapel Hill, N.C., 1965); Larzer Ziff, Puritanism in America: New Culture in a New Land (New York, 1973).

16. History, I, 66, 67, 270.

17. Ibid., 3, 27.

18. Ibid., 35, 50, 175, 270.

19. Ibid., 50, 63-65. Emery Battis confirms the upper-class nature of Antinomianism, Saints and Sectaries: Anne Hutchinson and the Antinomian Controversy in the Massachusetts Bay Colony (Chapel Hill, N.C., 1962), 284, 301-348. Lyle Koehler has stressed the participation of women in the movement, "The Case of the American Jezebels: Anne Hutchinson and Female Agitation during the Years of Antinomian Turmoil, 1636-1640," William and Mary Quarterly, XXXI (1974), 55-78.

20. History, I, 33, 55, 58, 106, 66, 175.

21. Ibid., 13, 39, 43, 216, 272, 41, 88, 86, 96.

22. Ibid., 96; "Stamp Act Essay," 487; History, I, xxix, 406.

23. History, I, 81, 263, 214.

24. Ibid., 78, 151, 180, 185-188.

25. Ibid., 216-222.

26. Ibid., 284, 301, 306, 305.

27. *History*, I, 356, 358-359; additions to Volume I of the *History*, *Publications* of the Colonial Society of Massachusetts, XXVIII (1930-1933), 438-446, quote at 443.

28. *History*, I, 274.

29. See, for example, works cited in Leder, ed., *The Colonial Legacy* and Shaffer, *The Politics of History*.

30. See Records of the New Brick Church, in Second Church of Boston Records, Massachusetts Historical Society.

31. *History*, I, 351.

32. A description of the historiography of colonial politics to the early 1960s may be found in Jack P. Greene, "Changing Interpretations of Early American Politics," in Billington, ed., *The Reinterpretation of Early American History*, 151-184; for the idea of a golden age, see works by Hewatt, Proud, and Jones cited in ch. vi, nn. 29-31.

33. *History*, III, 75.

34. *Ibid.*, 184, 74.

35. *Ibid.*, 62; "Strictures," 40.

36. *History*, III, 1, 61.

37. *History*, II, 52, 100, 276, 281; III, 41, 42.

38. *History*, II, 277, 305-306.

39. *History*, II, 336.

40. *Ibid.*, 182, 217, 174, 218.

41. John A. Schutz, *William Shirley: King's Governor of Massachusetts* (Chapel Hill, N.C., 1961), 143. Bailyn, *Hutchinson*, 4-5; *History*, II, 166, 177, 188; Peter Oliver, *Origin and Progress of the American Rebellion*, ed., Douglass Adair and John A. Schutz (San Marino, California, 1961), 25.

42. *History*, II, 56, 160.

43. *Ibid.*, 306, 308, 312; III, 13, 14; II, 321-322.

44. *History*, II, 297; I, 280; II, 7, 91.

45. Bernard Bailyn, *The Origins of American Politics* (New York, 1969); Jack P. Greene, "Changing Interpretations"; Robert Zemsky, *Merchants, Farmers and River Gods* (Boston, 1971); Michael Zuckerman, *Peaceable Kingdoms: The New England Towns in the Eighteenth Century* (New York, 1970); John Murrin, review of New England town studies, *History and Theory*, XI (1972), 226-275; William Pencak, *War, Politics, and Revolution in Provincial Massachusetts* (Boston, 1981).

46. *History*, III, 63; I, 148; Hutchinson to Israel Williams, May 19, 1749, Williams Papers.

47. *History*, II, 156, 30, 174.

48. *Ibid.*, 289, 334, 174, 335, 155, 299-301.

49. *Ibid.*, 286.

50. *Ibid.*, 156, 289, 162, 175.

51. *History*, III, 6; see Robert E. Brown, *Middle-Class Democracy and the Revolution in Massachusetts, 1691-1780* (Ithaca, N.Y., 1951); James T. Adams, *Revolutionary New England, 1691-1776* (New York, 1923); John C. Miller, "Religion, Finance, and Democracy in Massachusetts," *New England Quarterly*, VI (1933), 29-58, for class conflict in the Land Banks; Gary B. Nash, *The Urban Crucible* (Cambridge, 1979); Dirk Hoerder, *People and Mobs: Crowd Action in Revolutionary Massachusetts During the American Revolution, 1765-1780* (Berlin, 1971).

52. Lewis Namier, *England in the Age of the American Revolution* (London, 1930); and *The Structure of Politics at the Accession of George III* (London, 1929).

53. *History*, I, 235; Alden T. Vaughan, *New England Frontier: Puritans and Indians, 1620-1675* (Boston, 1965); (revised New York, 1979); for the traditional view, see Francis Jennings, *The*

Invasion of America: Indians, Colonists, and the Cant of Conquest (Chapel Hill, 1975).

54. History, I, 75, 137, 139, 239, 266, 241.

55. History, II, 108, 70.

56. Ibid., 240-241.

57. History, I, 241, 374; II, 73.

58. History, I, 383; II, xi.

59. Paul Boyer and Stephen Nissenbaum, Salem Possessed: The Social Origins of Witchcraft (Cambridge, Mass., 1974) and Chadwick Hansen, Witchcraft at Salem (New York, 1969); John Demos, "Underlying Themes in the Witchcraft of Seventeenth Century New England," American Historical Review, LXXXV (1971), 1311-1326; Marion Starkey, The Devil in Massachusetts (New York, 1949); History, II, 47, 18, 46; I, 351; II, 9, 12.

60. History, II, 338-343; these pages are the source for the next two paragraphs also. Adam Smith read Hutchinson's History, as the footnotes to The Wealth of Nations indicate, although he did not give him credit for his capital theory.

61. "Stamp Act Essay," 489-491, in addition to ibid. The influence of the American colonial example and colonial theorists such as Franklin and Hutchinson in contributing to free trade and laissez-faire economic thought deserves further study.

62. "Stamp Act Essay," 489-491; Hutchinson's interpretation reconciles the arguments of Lawrence Harper, "The Effect of the Navigation Acts on the Thirteen Colonies," in The Era of the American Revolution, ed. Richard B. Morris, (New York, 1931), who argues that the imperial system was commercially injurious to the colonies, and Robert Paul Thomas, "A Quantitative Approach to the Study of the Effects of British Imperial Policy Upon Colonial Welfare: Some Preliminary Findings," Journal of Economic History, XVIII (1965), 615-638, who disagrees.

63. Hutchinson, like most important Massachusetts merchants, was closely connected with an English house, in his case the Palmer family. Hutchinson's connection with them dates back to the 1730s -- he tried to have Eliakim Palmer named province agent in the early 1740s but failed due to the opposition of Governor Shirley (Shirley to John Thomlinson, January 26, 1742, William Shirley Papers, Massachusetts Historical Society). Hutchinson was pessimistic about business prospects throughout the 1760s and early 1770s, and wrote letters to British officials recommending that the smuggling of Dutch tea be stopped. See letters to Richard Jackson, October 20, 1767, M. XXV, 184; to Lord Hillsborough, September 9, 1771, M. XXVII, 372; to William Palmer, September 24, 1771, M. XXVII, 394.

V. THE CONSTITUTION OF EMPIRE:
A THEORY OF SOVEREIGNTY

Thomas Hutchinson's theory of sovereignty formed an indispensable prerequisite for his interpretation of the American Revolution. It was far more complicated than the charge levelled by his enemies that in the last analysis every nation needed an absolutely unchallengeable sovereign to avoid anarchy. Hutchinson only justified parliamentary sovereignty because, in general, even despite specific measures the colonies considered harmful, Britain in the 1760s and 70s still adhered for the most part to the traditional constitution which had developed over the past two centuries and still proved remarkably responsive to North America's welfare and its demands to redress grievances.

From the first confrontation in 1763 between Britain and America over taxation, Hutchinson not only considered himself a firm opponent of British policy, but he at once anticipated, understood, and condemned the ultimate arguments to which each side drove the other in the next decade. Sovereignty lay at the heart of the colonies' efforts to reduce the scope of British authority. They progressively claimed exemption from certain sorts of laws until they only acknowledged themselves bound to the British Isles by a common king. Parliament, in turn, repealed every objectionable colonial tax except the three penny duty on tea and retained that only as a token of the principle propounded in the Declaratory Act of 1766 -- the power "to bind the colonies in all cases whatsoever." Hutchinson realized that mutually exclusive efforts to define where sovereignty ended and rights began did not work toward a solution, as nearly all his contemporaries on both sides believed, but constituted the problem itself. For the colonies to continue under British rule, the empire had to avoid such a dangerous analytical game like the plague. Only by granting full scope to both American privileges and British authority -- which could be accomplished if each side acknowledged the rights and responsibilities of the other in practice and left matters of theory alone -- could the happy state of affairs established during the eighteenth century be

preserved. Hutchinson thus argued that through
maintenance of traditional and limited sorts of
conflict, which he by no means condemned as they had
led to the freedom and prosperity of both Britain and
America, the empire could survive intact. With both
parties seeking new definitions to accommodate the new
realities of postwar politics, Hutchinson stood almost
alone in insisting that the old empire, with all its
inefficiency and self-contradictions, needed to be
cherished rather than overcome.

Beginning with the Sugar Act of 1764, Hutchinson
realized that Britain had opened the Pandora's Box
of constitutional authority. Even though the law
theoretically reduced the duty on molasses from six
pence per gallon to three, it marked the first tax
(the conveniently forgotten and vastly beneficial post
office duty excepted) imposed by Britain to raise a
colonial revenue rather than serve as a prohibitory
tariff. Hutchinson opposed this measure on both
pecuniary and constitutional grounds. He was upset
that "the distinction between duties on trade and
internal taxes" not only "agreed with the opinion of
the people in England," but also "with the opinion of
most people here." Americans who tolerated the new
duty erroneously supposed it had been levied to
regulate trade, the sort of act "the colonies had at
all times acknowledged to be reasonable."
Hutchinson did not hesitate to express the most
extreme fears being voiced by future revolutionaries
that once Britain levied any sort of tax it became
possible "to find duties enough on trade to drain us
so thoroughly that it will not be possible to pay
internal taxes . . . or even to support government
within ourselves." As early as 1764, he predicted
ominously that "we are in danger of unequal distress-
ing burdens, which finally must affect the nation as
much as the colonies themselves."[1] All taxation
menaced and threatened colonial freedom and
prosperity.

The Sugar Act marked a legal as well as an economic
innovation. Hutchinson thought it would lead to other
duties which "would not consist with the so much
esteemed privilege of English subjects" -- the
"perpetual" right to have "assemblies of their own
choosing to make laws for their government." For
Parliament to raise "monies either by internal or
external taxes from any part of the empire, which is
not represented, can hardly be reconciled to the

constitution of the empire." The Stamp Act, which followed in 1765, also abrogated the privilege of self-taxation, thus violating "the most solemn engagements" England had made with the colonies in their charters. Like many of his opponents, Hutchinson viewed the Stamp Act as a dangerous precedent: "If Parliament begins with internal taxes, I know not where the line can be drawn." The power to tax, once established, could become a power to destroy.(2)

But Hutchinson went even further. Not only did he deny distinctions between internal and external taxes, but he rejected Parliament's right to tax and to pass any laws at all for the colonies of which they did not approve. The colonists in general only awoke to this truth in the 1770s, as non-pecuniary legislation remained their last bastion in trying to salvage some semblance of a tie to Britain. But Hutchinson the loyalist even rejected that. He wrote that "the distinction between acts for taxes, and other acts of legislation seems arbitrary . . . . Have we not a property in them as well as in our estates?"(3)

However, Hutchinson had no sooner made these points, most of them in an essay to protest the impending Stamp Act, than he presented what appeared at first glance a contradictory but equally cogent defense of parliamentary sovereignty. He considered self-taxation a right, not a privilege, but not a natural right common to all mankind, nor an inalienable right which had to be the primary criterion for judging policy, but a right granted by the British Parliament which through long usage had become part of the constitution of the empire. Parliament could abrogate such guarantees, but only "when the safety of the whole shall depend upon it." He maintained:(4)

> It is reasonable British colonies should ever remain subject to the control of Britain and consequently must be bound by the determination of the supreme authority, the British Parliament. You allow that it is possible for such a Parliament to pass acts which may abridge British subjects of what are generally called their natural rights. I am willing to go farther and will suppose that in some cases it is reasonable and even necessary, though such rights should have

been strengthened by the most solemn sanctions and engagements, the right of parts and individuals must be given up when the safety of the whole shall depend upon it.

Hutchinson believed in colonial rights as firmly as anyone, but he could not divorce their preservation from the concrete political situation. That the colonists had any rights at all depended upon their membership in the British Empire, as the quick tour around the world Hutchinson to which treated his readers in the taxation essay demonstrated. Paradoxically, an attack on parliamentary supremacy also struck at colonial liberty, as the latter could not exist without the former. Hence, because he denied any distinction between taxation and legislation, Hutchinson also insisted that "an exception to the authority of Parliament to impose taxes must act as a total independency, for upon the same principle, exception may be taken to all acts whatever."(5) Parliament could abrogate colonial freedom for the greater good, as the French and Indian War had recently shown. To regard the mere interposition of its authority regardless of circumstance as the exercise of a corrupt "power" or "tyranny" which liberty-loving Whigs had to oppose at all costs was simplistic and erroneous.

Hutchinson thus adopted the argument that Parliament, omnipotent in theory, ought not to interfere with the internal policy of the colonies in practice. Supremacy should be "rarely exercised and only when a just and equitable regard to the common interest of the whole empire renders it necessary." A sovereign Parliament possessed the ability to limit itself severely and allow considerable freedom to subordinate bodies. Even then, supremacy had to be exercised "justly" and "equitably": Hutchinson believed that "such is the wisdom and justice of a British Parliament [that] in all cases a tender regard will be had to all rights natural and acquired of any subject."(6) Since sovereignty had been exercised in a benevolent manner in the past, the colonists ought not to allow a few exceptional instances to detract from the whole picture.

Parliament could violate colonial rights with justice in only one instance: "when the safety of the whole shall depend upon it." And Hutchinson thought that in such emergencies, as during the great mid-century wars, the colonies would certainly contribute to the common defense. Massachusetts had to a tremendous extent. But Parliament's right to interpose in emergencies cut two ways -- it also justified extraordinary measures to suppress revolutionary activity. In one of his letters, stolen from his correspondence and published in adulterated form by the Massachusetts assembly, he preferred "some further restraint of liberty" to allowing that the "connection with the parent state should be broken, for I am sure such a breach must prove the ruin of the colony." Logically, therefore "laws of the colonies that may have a tendency to break off this connection," under which "they had been happy for an hundred years past," must be counteracted by Parliament, even at the cost of those liberties whose preservation formed the principal justification of parliamentary sovereignty in the first place. Like Edmund Burke, another traditionalist who admitted that "there are occasions of public necessity so vast, so clear, so evident that they supersede all laws," Hutchinson recognized that in an extreme emergency it might be necessary to violate particular laws or customs to ensure that the authority which guaranteed an entire society be preserved.(7)

Hutchinson's theory of sovereignty thus represented an attempt to balance two forces, each of which had to maintain its proper role to prevent government from degenerating into either anarchy or tyranny. A single, supreme ruling body (such as Parliament) had to exist and maintain emergency powers for a durable government to exist at all. But the hierarchy of traditional institutions (such as colonial legislatures) which accompanied that single power had to be maintained both to counterbalance it and to guarantee popular rights. Hutchinson here anticipated a theory of sovereignty articulated more precisely by Juan Donoso-Cortes, a Spanish statesman who during the Revolutions of 1848 confronted on a world-wide scale the same sort of problem Hutchinson had observed in revolutionary Massachusetts. Donoso insisted that sovereignty had to be "one, perpetual" and yet "limited," with the restriction coming from "resistance encountered in an organized hierarchy." To deny either the supreme power's unity or the social order's diversity would destroy a traditional society. Either a centralizing power which "despised and suppressed all resistances" or the "parliamentary" or representative system "which denied power's unity" by "grounding itself in a contract" led to this destruction.(8)

Like Hutchinson, Donoso saw little continuity between the conflicts of central governments and "constituted bodies" before the revolutionary age and the revolutions themselves. In the former case, both central and local authority sought to maximize their power within the limits of a system that recognized the legitimacy and necessity of the other's existence. But when sovereigns began to violate traditional rights, as parliamentary taxation did after 1763, they provoked a resistance which with a perverse justice denied the sovereign altogether. As Donoso put it, more mystically than Hutchinson, "suppressing the hierarchies which are the natural and hence divine form of variety" on the one hand "and denying to power its indivisibility which is the divine, natural, and necessary condition of its unity," on the other, jointly created unrestrained practices and ideologies where tyrannical governments and Utopian revolutionaries vied to win an absolute triumph over their adversaries.

Unlike Montesquieu and the United States constitutional convention of 1787, both Donoso and Hutchinson denied that the supreme power could be divided within itself. To segment its unity would give birth, as Donoso argued, to a multiple sovereign doomed to "impotency" in emergencies if the "sovereigns" disagreed, or to "tyranny" if they joined together and refused to recognize traditional rights. Hutchinson perceived that the Massachusetts revolutionaries' efforts to reserve certain powers first to Parliament, and then to the king alone, reversed the necessary constitution of both government and society. On the one hand, they divided a supreme authority which had to be united. On the other, they dissolved the traditional structure of government by making the Massachusetts General Court, which had hitherto checked parliamentary power, the sovereign in its own right as representative of the ultimate symbolic rulers, the people. In consequence, no longer did an intermediate institution exist to check the new sovereign as the General Court itself had restrained the old. The denial of traditional, limited sovereignty led to a more absolute and ruthless form. For Hutchinson as for Donoso, not the institutional separation of functions within the sovereign power, but only the tension and yet mutual respect between subordinate and supreme authority, could reconcile the conflicting imperatives of liberty and sovereignty within a framework of tradition and law.

Almost all of Hutchinson's analysis of the American Revolution and political theory came from his efforts to uphold the legitimate requirements of parliamentary rule without sacrificing the blessings of American rights. He tried to educate his contemporaries on both sides of the Atlantic to adopt a grander perspective and support the customary rights of colonial legislatures without denying the need for an ultimate power independent of local institutions. Hutchinson did not view traditional liberty and sovereign power as antithetical, as did both radicals and imperial administrators. Unless both retained their integrity, by the intangible, voluntarily imposed sanctions of custom and self-restraint, liberty under law would cease to exist. And Hutchinson realized how fragile and precarious any such co-existence must be.

With this background in mind, the remark for which Hutchinson has gone down in history as a defender of unlimited parliamentary power can be properly understood. In a message to the General Court on January 6, 1773, he argued that "I know of no line that can be drawn between the supreme authority of Parliament and the total independence of the colonies." But the absence of a rigid line did not render the latter meaningless or permit the former to be arbitrary. Had Hutchinson's opponents thought about the rest of his message, they would have disabused themselves quickly of any such notion. He insisted that as an independent nation, America would be the "prey of the powers of Europe." He hoped that "it will never be our misfortune to know, by experience, the difference between the liberties of an English colonist and those of the Spanish, French, or Dutch." In the _History_, Hutchinson added that, even supposing "after all, a new independent state may be added to the empires of the world, with perhaps the name of a free state" where "a few individuals may attain to greater degrees of power and dignity," nevertheless, the general population "will never enjoy so great a share of natural liberty as they would have done if they had remained a dependent colony."(9) Parliamentary supremacy was defensible because it had always been exercised _in practice_ with restraint and humanity. Given alternative prospects, any change could only be for the worse.

Hutchinson ultimately based his argument for

parliamentary sovereignty on custom, utility, and the comparative observation of political systems. To revolt against it "for an imaginary good, and even that improbable to be obtained, we are parting with real substantial happiness." He did not regard sovereignty as a theoretical concept loosely equated with absolute, unrestrained power, but as a historical fact which explained how "peace and order have been maintained, and the people of the province have experienced as largely the advantages of government as, perhaps, any people upon the globe." Never for an instant did Hutchinson think Parliament had an unrestrained power to do whatever it wanted. When the Massachusetts council insinuated this interpretation in answer to his speech, he rebutted: "for the nature of the supreme authority of Parliament, I have never given you any reason to suppose that I intended a more absolute power in Parliament than what is founded in the nature of government."(10) To say that no line could be drawn between supremacy and independence did not make Parliament omnipotent and reduce the colonists to slaves, as Speaker of the House Thomas Cushing, among others, thought. Hutchinson instead justified the Parliament of the sort that had existed historically and guaranteed American rights and well-being.

To define the privileges and powers of colonists and mother country with canonical precision would have robbed the empire of the very flexibility which was its outstanding virtue. Hutchinson illustrated this point in a message of July 14, 1772. The assembly had insisted that the right of taxation gave it an "acquired and exclusive right of supporting the governor, and therefore, the support of the governor by the crown must be an infringement upon the charter." Hutchinson expostulated with the house to "consider, gentlemen, where this argument will carry you." "The same clause which empowers the assembly to tax the people for the governor's support empowers it also to tax for the defense of government." But did this therefore prevent the crown from helping in time of crisis? To spell out the powers of the supreme and subordinate legislatures in precise detail would be disastrous if a contingency arose -- like the French and Indian War, on the one hand, or the colonial rebellion which followed it, on the other -- requiring Parliament to play a more active role. (11)

British sovereignty provided the great blessing of permitting the legitimate articulation and redress of grievances. As Hutchinson told a grand jury in 1768, "the constitution of government under which we have the happiness to live is the most happy, because we have never yielded up more of the private rights of individuals than was needful to invest the government with power sufficient to protect us as citizens." He continued that it was not only the privilege, but "the duty of every good citizen, who is bound to preserve the laws of the state under which he lives, to apply to the legislative body for the redress of all grievances which arise from the laws."(12)

Historically, Great Britain responded well to colonial petitions, even up to the very eve of the Revolution. In 1776, Hutchinson criticized the Declaration of Independence's contention that the colonials only wished to preserve their violated rights because "if anything short of independence was the redress sought for, all has been granted which could be granted." As he surveyed the situation, he asked a series of rhetorical questions: "Is not the Stamp Act repealed? Have not other duties been wholly taken off, or reduced to the rates proposed or acquiesced in, by the colonies themselves? Have not the strongest assurances been given, that no further duties, or taxes, are intended? Are those that remain such burdens as to make a continuance of disorder advisable?" Referring to Lord North's plan of conciliation, which proposed never to tax the colonies save in times of national emergency, he discovered "a general disposition in government in England, to remove even those burdens." The king told him personally in 1774 that "they are in no danger of further taxes, and nothing hinders the taking off the [one remaining] tea duty, except the denial of the authority that imposed it."(13)

For Hutchinson, British policy after the French and Indian War, while it violated colonial rights, paradoxically did not cause the American Revolution. In the decade between 1765 and 1775, the mother country gave up its ambitious plans for imperial reorganization and colonial taxation. Why then did resistance escalate rather than decline, provoking the ministry to send troops to Boston not to enforce changes but to preserve whatever vestiges of authority remained? Hutchinson had only one answer: "Had our heroes," as he sarcastically referred to the revolutionaries, "conducted [themselves] with tolerable prudence after the repeal of the Stamp Act," the Americans would "have been a happy people." The

presence of soldiers in Boston and the Coercive Acts --
neither of which Hutchinson personally approved on
practical grounds -- could best be understood as "the
acts of a justly incensed sovereign, for suppression
of a most unnatural, unprovoked rebellion."(14) The
Declaration of Independence put the cart before the
horse when it blamed the revolt on Britain's harsh
reaction to colonial protests. The unfortunate
exercise of unconstitutional powers by Parliament
mattered less than the erroneous interpretation of
colonists with ulterior motives who managed to persuade
their countrymen to throw off even a mild overseas
sovereignty.

   Other Americans wrestled with the problem of
reconciling sovereignty with colonial rights. In
Massachusetts, the younger James Otis, Hutchinson's
arch-rival, most closely approximated his effort to
find a solution which did not simply declare for one
of the parties. For all their personal hatred, Otis
and Hutchinson resembled each other in several ways.
Both came from families traditionally active in
politics and had established their careers before the
revolutionary crisis broke out. Unlike most of the
leading patriots, they had experienced the benefits as
well as the burdens of British rule. Both suffered
severe mental crises in the late 1760s, although
Hutchinson's only lasted a few months whereas Otis
became permanently insane in the 1770s. Finally,
because of their efforts to compromise British
sovereignty and American rights, contemporaries
accused both of duplicity, inconsistency, and
hypocrisy. Like Hutchinson, Otis could not imagine an
America bereft of British protection -- even if the
colonists had defended themselves for the most part
in the past. Without a unifying power they would tear
each other apart in the future. But neither could
Otis imagine surrendering colonial rights of self-
taxation and legislation.(15)

   However, unlike Hutchinson, Otis strove for a
definitive solution to these problems. In his four
major pamphlets, he groped toward a sense of a dual
representation in which Parliament retained its
sovereignty, regardless of whether the colonists had
a voice in its proceedings, while at the same time
searching for guarantees that it would not harm
colonial rights. To be sure, both Hutchinson and
Otis regarded the British constitution as an
immemorial web of rights and obligations between

subject and sovereign, but Otis tried to solve the problem of where these began and ended by drawing the very line Hutchinson had tried to avoid. In England, the common law courts had declared acts passed by Parliament to be in violation of the fundamental principles of English law. Colonial courts and legislatures could do the same. Hutchinson abhorred such a notion, as it would deprive the sovereign of flexibility in emergencies and would grant a dangerous autonomy to the courts. He also found little merit in Otis' theory that people possessed rights apart from a particular historical context. Instead, he believed attempts to erect powers of judicial review and define a dual representation simply reflected the doctrinaire position into which each party had forced the other. Mutual good-will and self-restraint had held the empire together for over a century. If they could do so no longer, rigid definitions would not help. In the past, Britain had tolerated American violation of the Navigation Acts, and the colonies had borne such outrages as impressment. Such problems had proven exceptions to the rule, and to create a scheme to eliminate theoretically jurisdictional quarrels for all time manifested a futile Utopianism.

Hutchinson and Otis disagreed on practical matters too. To be sure, both thought that as long as Parliament generally wished well to the colonies and regarded their welfare as vital to the empire's own, resistance could not be justified because of specifically harmful acts. But by 1765, Otis had come to regard Parliament as the organ of a hopelessly corrupt British ruling class, totally unworthy of the empire it had inherited. It had therefore forfeited its mandate to rule. Hutchinson, on the contrary, believed parliamentary malevolence much exaggerated by men like Otis himself, and that colonial incendiarism posed a far greater danger to both the empire and provincial rights.

FOOTNOTES

1. H to Ebenezer Silliman, November 9, 1764, M. XXVI, 223, 224; H to William Bollan, November 17, 1764, M. XXVI, 221; History, III, 254.

2. H to ?, August 3, 1763, M. XXVI, 127; "Stamp Act Essay," 482-483; H to Richard Jackson, October 20, 1767, M. XXV, 185.

3. "Additions, III," 51; H to William Bollan, November 17, 1764, M. XXVI, 221.

4. "Stamp Act Essay," 481.

5. "Additions, III," 51.

6. H to Richard Jackson, October 20, 1767, M. XXV, 185; "Stamp Act Essay," 481, 489.

7. "Additions, III," 63; Burke, "Speech on the Plan for Economical Reform (1780)," II, 239.

8. The quotations and information about Donoso-Cortes in this and the following paragraphs appear in Frederick D. Wilhelmsen, "Donoso-Cortes and the Meaning of Political Power," Intercollegiate Review, III (1967), 109-127. Donoso rested his "law of variety and unity" between hierarchy and power on the analogous relationship of God and the universe in Catholic theology. Hutchinson did not utilize Donoso's religious language.

9. Bradford, 339-340; History, III, 255.

10. "Strictures," 39; History, III, 255; Bradford, 368; H to John Pownall, April 19, 1773, M. XXVII, 885.

11. Bradford, 333.

12. Quincy, 307.

13. "Strictures," 41; Diary, I, 181.

14. H to William Bollan, November 10, 1769, M. XXVI, 869; "Strictures," 39.

15. For information on Otis, I am indebted to James R. Ferguson, "Reason in Madness: The Political Theory of James Otis," <u>William and Mary Quarterly</u>, 3rd ser., XXXVI (1979), <u>194-214</u>.

VI. THE AMERICAN REVOLUTION:
CAUSES AND REMEDIES

While as a loyalist Hutchinson attributed primary blame for the American Revolution to the ambitions and resentments of demagogues and propagandists, he did not have a simple explanation for the event. He knew full well such types had always plagued societies, yet revolutions had occurred intermittently rather than frequently. The obvious criticism of the rebels, then, only formed one element in Hutchinson's complex interpretation in which he tried to account for their success in terms of the unusual setting which emerged after 1763. Hutchinson's analysis not only anticipated his fellow loyalists' monocausal concentration on factional resentment in America. He also hinted at the Imperial historians' notion of an unfortunate war; the Nationalists' idea of inevitable independence; the Progressives' emphasis on class conflict; Lawrence Henry Gipson's stress on the importance of the French and Indian War; Bernard Bailyn's ideological interpretation; the contentions of students of British domestic politics that weakness and division in England and encouragement by English radicals played an instrumental role; Perry Miller's linking of Calvinism and revolution; Carl Bridenbaugh's and Gary Nash's emphasis on the Revolution's urban impetus; and Robert E. Brown's and Michael Zuckerman's analysis of the democracy and autonomy of local governments as major underlying causes. Hutchinson could synthesize in advance much future scholarship because as a nonprofessional, his own sense of identity and personal success did not depend on advancing an "interpretation." Instead, because he staked his self-worth and career on reconciling the contending parties, he had to show them how apparently contradictory perceptions of the crisis were in fact reasonable responses for particular people and groups, but fell short of the comprehensive understanding needed to end their quarrel. By seeking to provide a panoramic overview of the Revolution's causes and especially by stressing the American position when addressing Britons and vice versa, Hutchinson hoped to establish a niche for himself as one of history's great peacemakers. Let us examine the various elements of his interpretation in turn.

While recognizing the onerousness of colonial taxation, Hutchinson did not consider it the proximate cause of the revolt or sufficiently burdensome to justify the revolutionaries' response that Britain had schemed to enslave them. (Having been charged as the mastermind of this plot, Hutchinson knew it did not exist.) Here he agreed with George Louis Beer and other scholars of his school that the British side of the story had much merit. He knew the money to be raised by the Stamp Act would go "to keep up forces for the defense of the southern colonies, then harassed by Indians, still directed by the French, and for preventing the revolt of the Canadians." Britain planned to use the money to defend the colonies in the future, not to pay its own war expenses. However much Hutchinson condemned taxation from an American perspective, he nevertheless also appreciated the counter-argument that the "immense" sums Britain had contributed to American defense during the French and Indian War made some colonial contribution for the future eminently reasonable. The taxes in some way met Hutchinson's criterion that violations of traditional rights could be allowed when "the safety of the whole" was at stake.(1)

Hutchinson's ambivalence in weighing defense against liberty also appeared in his mixed verdict on whether the colonials owed Britain compliance with taxation for assistance during the wars of the 1740s and 50s. In his essay written to thwart the Stamp Act, he argued the negative. The provincials had contributed more per capita to the common fund than the inhabitants of Britain. Even more important, Virginia's expeditions to the Ohio Valley did not cause the French and Indian War but Britain's foolish return of Louisbourg, a French fortress guarding the mouth of the St. Lawrence and captured by Massachusetts on its own initiative in 1745. This campaign made the colonies "the object of French resentment." And whatever the merits of taxing other colonies, Massachusetts' own war effort had been of such proportions that Britain could never doubt its willingness to contribute voluntarily.(2)

But with his penchant for trying to maintain both horns of a dilemma simultaneously, Hutchinson considered British aid to have been absolutely essential, regardless of the colonists' own efforts. Without England, the French would have marched down the Hudson and caused unspeakable havoc. Even at

Louisbourg, the British fleet proved the deciding
factor. Hutchinson agreed with John Adams, among
others, that Britain had no altruistic motives for
aiding the colonies -- "fear of losing that
advantageous trade" rather than "paternal affections"
inspired the ministry to send thousands of redcoats
to the New World. But regardless of motivation, the
undeniable fact remained that Britain had "expended a
far greater sum" in the "Great War for Empire" "than
the whole property, real and personal, in all the
colonies would amount to." Even if the colonists
protested taxation, their opposition had to be
circumspect, as "in a moral view," North America could
not separate from an empire which had been weakened in
saving it.(3)

Hutchinson viewed the relationship between England
and America as symbiotic. Like Beer, he regarded the
Revolution as a tragic "separation of two kindred
people" linked both commercially and defensively. He
dreaded that America would lose its liberty without
British protection just as he feared that England would
"lose, not the thirteen states only, but every part of
its possessions in the West Indies" if America became
independent.(4) If these fears were not realized, it
was largely because from the War of 1812 to World War
II, again despite periodic crises, Britain continued to
supply America with manufactures and capital investment
while raw materials such as cotton and foodstuffs
flowed in the other direction. The British fleet's
"enforcement" of the Monroe Doctrine and American aid
to the Allies during the world wars have confirmed
Hutchinson's diagnosis that American and British
interests were indeed indissolubly linked, although he
could not, like his contemporaries, have imagined that
such a relationship could have continued following
American independence.

Just as one aspect of Hutchinson's interpretation
foreshadowed Beer, another anticipated Lawrence Henry
Gipson's thesis that the conquest of Canada proved
more important as a cause of Revolution than long-
range trends in colonial society. He not only agreed
with Gipson's assertion that the ouster of the French
removed the immediate need for British protection and
thereby made independence thinkable, but he also
discussed victory's psychological implications on the
American mind. The outcome of the war "produced a
higher sense of the grandeur and importance of the
colonies." With the signing of the peace, "a new

scene opened" and "there was nothing to obstruct a gradual progress of settlements, through a vast continent, from the Atlantic to the Pacific Ocean." "Speculative men" began to dream of a purely "American empire" with its capital in Philadelphia. Calculating colonial population increase, they predicted America would soon eclipse Britain. Hutchinson here referred implicitly to Benjamin Franklin's <u>Observations Concerning the Increase of Mankind, Peopling of Countries, etc.</u>, as well as a spate of other publications (discussed by Richard Koebner in his study of the idea of <u>Empire</u>) which heralded an altered American consciousness. Thus, the cession of Canada "prepared [men] to think more favorably of independency, before any measures were taken with a professed design of attaining to it."(5)

But while Hutchinson agreed with Gipson that the "Great War for Empire" made a revolution immediately possible, he also thought that the increasing wealth and population of the colonies made independence inevitable sooner or later. As he wrote to British historian William Robertson in 1773, "the prevalence of a spirit of opposition to government in the plantations is the natural consequence of the great growth of colonies so remote from the present state and not the effect of oppression." Like both nationalist and imperial historians a century later, he sensed a fatality in the course of events, although he dreaded rather than welcomed the separation. In 1772, he expressed the thought that the colonies would not remain under the Union Jack another century. Three years later, he informed Lord Hardwicke that "America is now in such a state as I imagined that one time or other it would be, but I did not expect to live to see it." Hutchinson had even gone so far as to admit privately that "perhaps it is better both for the nation" and the colonies "that these commotions should happen now than a half a century hence."(6) How remarkable that a man could struggle so valiantly to maintain a regime which by his own admission had violated colonial rights and was doomed to extinction!

But in the last analysis, Hutchinson sided with those loyalists who simply condemned the Revolution as the product of a number of unscrupulous men -- James Otis, the Adamses, John Hancock, etc. -- who skillfully misrepresented British measures and the intentions of the province's royal officials in order to rise to power and vent their personal malice. These propagandists turned the colonies' thoughts from peaceful remonstrance to rebellion. Hutchinson observed that "the exception to the constitutional authority of Parliament was first taken, and principally supported by men who were before discontented." "To keep up a spirit of discontent," they resorted to "evils merely imaginary, or to such as were at a distance and feared rather than felt. . . . Groundless fears were artfully raised by men whose views were their own advancement and the ruin of the present easy model of government."(7)

Hutchinson took great pains to blame a handful of individuals for the Revolution. He never confounded "the faction" with the populace. He agreed with his opponents that the colonists had the real grievances of taxation and interference with their traditional institutions which could serve as a basis for popular resentment. He therefore had to explain how he could blame the Revolution on a handful of men if the people in fact became incensed over legitimate issues. He did this by denying that colonial complaints were directly linked with the decision of certain politicians to strike out for independence. While "the acts for imposing duties and taxes may have accelerated the rebellion," even without them, "other pretences would have been found for exception to the authority of Parliament."(8)

Independence must have been the aim of the revolutionary leadership because Britain conceded almost every substantive point demanded by the colonists after 1765. Hutchinson always divorced the motivation of the leaders, who misused injurious but not malevolent British measures, from the general population's, who took their protestations of defending colonial rights at face value. He repeatedly exonerated the general body of the colonists from any guilt: "a judgment ought not to be made of the body of the council, much less the representatives, and still less of the body of the people . . . the votes and messages . . . were the composition of a very few." In fact, considering the propaganda barrage to which they had been subjected and Britain's hopeless mishandling of the situation, it was amazing it took ten years following the Stamp Act before armed resistance began: "it must be said in favor of the people of Massachusetts Bay that these arts [of deception] had been used with them for many years together, with very slow success." In short, "the people agreed with their leaders in the means" used to redress grievances, but "they did not agree in the end," for "not one in fifty wished to be independent."(9)

In the last analysis, Hutchinson's explanation of the Revolution's psychological roots resembled that put forward by Bernard Bailyn. Hutchinson concluded that "the people had been persuaded that all their liberties were in danger. It was immaterial whether they had been deceived or not, the persuasion was the same, and this was what would cause them to go to all lengths." But he differed from Bailyn, who attributed this fear of despotism to a collective perception of British policy common to both leaders and followers. Hutchinson blamed it on the conscious efforts of specific individuals. He therefore considered the people's desire to preserve liberty conservative whereas the radical leaders made no secret of their aims:(10)

> The controversy between America and the mother country has occupied volumes of writings, and has enlisted the persistence, the endeavors, and the ingenuity of many literary writers in order to explain its elaborate intricacies and party claims. All this is only wasting time and puzzling a very simple case. . . . The English asserted the power of Parliament over the colonies; the Americans denied it. There -- that is the whole of the dispute. Strange, however, as the best and plainest argument stated to the case was used by Dr. [Joseph] Warren and Samuel Adams. The first spoke of the Americans as "a people determined to be free" and Adams exclaimed:- "Independent we are, and independent we will be." There is no mystification there. The time had come, the English government saw it not. The whole of the American controversy is comprised in the above remarks.

Hutchinson thereby excused the province he loved, to whose service he had devoted much of his life, from producing a revolt he abhorred. The people acted rationally based on the (gross mis-) information provided by the incendiaries. By separating leaders and followers he unconsciously laid the groundwork for resolving the historiographical controversy whether the Revolution marked a conservative resistance to tyranny (true for the followers) or a radical desire for home rule (applicable to the leaders). He also pre-empted the argument whether the concrete assaults of British measures (honest sentiment of followers) on colonial liberties or "fears for the future" (propaganda of leaders) provoked resistance. Conflicting interpretations of the event could be reconciled by not insisting that all the revolutionaries shared a common mentality. Hutchinson argued in vain to British administrators that by taking advantage of the dichotomy between followers and leaders and isolating the former for punishment they could stop the march of revolution.

None of the points advanced so far, however, explains the social composition of the revolutionary movement, but only describes its ideas and the protesters' motivation. Hutchinson went on to explain which classes of people participated in or rejected the Revolution. The patriot incendiaries were a new sort of faction to appear on the stage of Massachusetts politics. They lacked the familial and social prominence which had previously characterized the province's governing elite. Hutchinson described them as a "few desperate men," some of whom "can never be in worse circumstances than they are at present." He argued that because "very few of them will ever be left executors to any will or entrusted with the guardianship of any children or have the care of any private affairs," they might have a chance of better prospects "if they could reduce all to a chaos" and establish a government "upon a new creation." Hutchinson generalized with considerable accuracy that "the greatest revolutions" were instigated by men who "owed all their popularity to the cause in which they were engaged." The Massachusetts Revolution was thus a social as well as a political upheaval. Whatever may be true of the other colonies, biographical information about loyalist and patriot leaders reveals that in general during the 1760s younger men, who held no standing in society apart from their political activity, replaced those who had held office because they and their families had been "deferred" to by their communities.(11)

These "desperate" characters, men such as John and Samuel Adams, Ebenezer Mackintosh (head of the South End mob), William Molineux, Thomas Young, and John Hancock -- a wealthy heir whose "estate was lost with much greater rapidity than it had been acquired" by his sensible uncle, Thomas -- found their ranks augmented by a few people of prominence, notably the Otis and Bowdoin families. These clans abandoned the restraints of traditional elite politics and devoted themselves wholeheartedly to ambition. The younger James Otis "swore revenge" on Hutchinson and promised that he would "set the province in a flame though he perished in the attempt" when Hutchinson became Chief Justice of the Superior Court instead of James Otis, Sr. The elder Otis, for his part, hated Hutchinson so much that he declared his willingness "not only [to] renounce my share in the government, but also his whole estate, which was not a small one," rather than sit on the council with Hutchinson. Hutchinson attributed the council's own reluctance to support law and order to "a family of large property and high resentment" -- the Bowdoins. Sons of Liberty James Pitts and councillor George Erving were related to family head James Bowdoin, and John Temple, the one customs commissioner who sided with patriots, married his daughter. But while the personal spite of some wealthy and established families may have given the revolutionaries a sorely needed aura of respectability, and even more sorely needed funds to keep some of the lower orders in the streets, "the principal demagogues" were "men of desperate fortune."(12)

Hutchinson assigned a role to the Boston mercantile community and the lower orders not unlike that described by Arthur M. Schlesinger, Dirk Hoerder, and other Progressive and New Left historians. Many merchants exhibited far more hostility to British authority from 1760 to 1770 than they did afterwards, when they perceived the movement threatened to engulf them as well. "Many of the principal merchants," Hutchinson noted, "had been very active in opposing the Stamp Act," and had prevented the ringleaders among the rioters from being arrested and punished out of fear they too would be implicated. Commercial men also took the lead in framing the non-importation agreements of 1768-1770 and "called the lowest class of the people to their assistance" to "threaten all who import with some form of coercion." However, the people soon mastered their masters. By the time Hutchinson succeeded Francis Bernard as governor, he noticed that "the better sort who see the terrible effects of anarchy seem to increase." Upon taking the chair, he wrote to Lord Hillsborough that "I have received every mark of civility and respect from every order of men, a few only excepted whose neglect rather does me honor." And when he left the province in 1774, over 120 gentlemen and merchants and all the province's lawyers, except three or four, signed documents praising his administration. A study of who became loyalists in Massachusetts confirms Hutchinson here: many of the merchants who protested the Writs of Assistance in 1761 or supported non-importation ultimately followed him into exile.(13)

Yet while many of the "better sort" eventually abandoned the revolutionary movement, they nevertheless did little or nothing to aid the government when it still might have made a difference. Hutchinson consistently and vainly tried to obtain some form of tangible assistance from the loyalist community. In 1770, he informed ex-Governor Bernard that there was "not a single person in government who will join with me" in supporting royal authority. He believed that "nothing [was] wanted but resolution enough in the merchants to shake their minds to overcome the democratic tyranny in this town." He complained that he was "absolutely alone" and three months before leaving for England, wrote desperately to Israel Williams: "I don't know where to find another to join me to put ten thousand to flight for everybody gives way . . . except the chief justice [Peter Oliver] and they forbid him to appear." Williams and other friends of government in western Massachusetts received Hutchinson's repeated entreaties to use their influence in the General Court to counteract that of Boston's representatives. But the numerically insignificant, elderly, peace-loving, family-oriented loyalist leadership could not fight a mass movement.(14)

Hutchinson attributed the loyalists' reluctance to become involved counter-revolutionaries to Britain's refusal to back them up by suppressing the inciters of disorder. He complained in 1770 that "if Parliament rises and provision is not made for punishing these people I will never depend on any measures for that purpose again." Without British support, he could not motivate the other loyal merchants, whose inactivity belied the governor's remonstrances that "they are enough if they would exert themselves." As late as January 1775, even after the Coercive Acts had been passed and implemented, Hutchinson could tell Lord Hardwicke "that the true reason why the people go to such lengths without terror is because never anything which has yet been threatened from England has yet been executed."(15)

Hutchinson could regard a British garrison and the Coercive Acts as provocative rather than punitive since resentment fell on the whole population rather than the handful of radical leaders. The soldiers who arrived in 1768 could not be used because the province charter required the authorization of a justice of the peace to employ them, and none would. This legalism exasperated General Thomas Gage, but Hutchinson defended adherence to the letter of the law on the grounds that "if they are at all to act without a civil magistrate this will be changing civil government into a military, which ought to be the last remedy and never continued a moment longer than a cure is effected." Having never desired the troops in the first place, Hutchinson found an excuse for not employing them. Military force was no solution; it rather demonstrated that Britain had despaired of one.(16)

Hutchinson and the loyal justices of the peace, of whom he appointed a considerable number, found themselves more handicapped than helped by a mere six to twelve hundred redcoats. To be effective, their commanders had to deploy European troops in one of the two open areas of town, thereby leaving "all the obnoxious people in town," the loyalists themselves, at the mercy of their enemies. Even though Hutchinson remained less certain than other "gentlemen of persuasion and good judgment" that the mob could easily have overpowered the troops, he considered it "a moral certainty that the people of this town would have taken to their arms" had he drawn upon them, which would have instantly destroyed a chance for peaceful accommodation. In fact, Hutchinson used the Boston Massacre as an excuse to persuade the regiments' commander to order them out of town.(17)

Aside from needlessly provoking Boston by sending troops who could act neither legally nor expediently, Britain contributed in other ways to the internal authority of Massachusetts being "miserably weak," "a mere form." To paraphrase Theodore Roosevelt, the mother country spoke loudly but carried no stick at all. Violence went unpunished. Parliament repealed laws the colonists opposed with enough ill grace to ensure they felt no gratitude. Hutchinson considered it "dangerous for a minister of state of the Parliament to propose or threaten anything relative to America which they do not perform or execute." "The frequent changes of administration" in the 1760s, which saw no fewer than six ministries, each dedicated to reversing its predecessor's policies, caused "the people in America [to] neither hope nor fear anything which can pass concerning them in England as they used to do."(18) The American incendiaries' boldness found its perfect complement in the British administration's weakness and inconsistency.

To compound the difficulties created by the mother country for loyalists trying to maintain its authority against all odds, discontented factions in British politics directly encouraged the radicals and caused them to think Parliament would soon install a ministry favorable to their designs. As early as 1763, Hutchinson found Otis and his supporters capitalizing on the "licentiousness" at home and rationalizing their behavior by arguing "they do not go as far as Wilkes does." Three years later, following the Stamp Act riots, the "six words of Mr. [William] Pitt when he said, 'I am glad America has resisted,' gave a deeper wound to the peace of America than all the tumults, mobs, and rebellious acts which preceded." The revolutionaries only had to wait for the Great Commoner's inevitable reassumption of power to be fully vindicated, or so they thought. Even other ministries countenanced Hutchinson's opponents. In 1766, James Otis Sr. received a letter from Lord Shelburne warmly approving his opposition to the Stamp Act, a message Otis circulated in the Massachusetts legislature while Hutchinson fumed: "it is known I have never received a like notwithstanding my repeated applications. I alone seem to be neglected by the ministry and left to the mercy of wild men when a little countenance and support would have enabled me to . . . defeat all their schemes."(19) Even if Hutchinson indulged in a bit of self-pity and glorying in his martyrdom, one can pardon his exasperation at being passed over for his fidelity to his superiors.

Hutchinson understood full well the derivative nature of American radicalism. Not only did the revolutionaries base their ideas on the Old Whig principles of Locke and the New Whig thought of The Independent Reflector, but on a more practical level they followed "the opposition in England in everything they do." As late as 1774, House Speaker Thomas Cushing showed Hutchinson a letter from Province Agent Benjamin Franklin advising "the people to persist and continue" because "their friends [were] increasing" and there was "the greatest probability that there would be a great majority in favor of America at the next Parliament." Hutchinson informed Governor William Tryon of New York that "agents and correspondents" directed the rebellion from England, exclaiming "what a situation is a Massachusetts governor in from a constant conspiracy on both sides of the water to distress him." No wonder, given the combination of provocative but unenforced parliamentary legislation, lack of support for those officials who tried vainly to uphold it, and unpunished traitors in England corresponding with those in America, that Hutchinson could write an English correspondent: "You have brought all this trouble upon yourself and upon us by your imprudence."(20)

Not only did the weakness of post-Stamp Act ministries demoralize the Massachusetts loyalists, but active and unchecked intimidation by the populace of Boston destroyed whatever resilience lingered. In 1770, after years of urging from Hutchinson, "the well affected merchants presumed to attempt an active association and a number of them met at the Coffee House." No sooner did the meeting get under way, however, than Dr. Thomas Young appeared, refused to leave or be silent, and "threatened to call the mob to oppose them." The patriots wantonly forbade their rivals to form associations, and prevented them from exercising their legitimate political rights: "Men of weight and value, although they wished to suppress the disorders, could not be induced to attend the town meetings," for fear "not only of being outvoted, but offended and insulted." Hutchinson's dislike of the town meeting, strong during the provincial period, reached new heights during the Revolution. He attacked it as "no parliamentary sort of government, at best a corruption of it. The majority which conduct all affairs, if met together upon another occasion, would properly be called a mob."(21)

Hutchinson repeatedly identified the rank-and-file support for the Revolution with "the plebian party in Boston," "all the inferior people," or "the people of the lowest class." They formed a most appropriate following for their ne'er-do-well leaders. As he wrote in 1768, "many of the common people have been in a frenzy and talked of dying in defense of their liberties" when the British troops arrived. Most of the "merchants" enforcing non-importation "had no connections in trade or any property, but said if they had no property they had liberty and their posterity might have property." At the same time, the lower orders had no independent role but merely served as the mouthpieces and strong arms of their leaders. They were "under the influence of a few of a higher class," men "of intemperate dispositions and desperate factious men of property." While many important citizens remained loyal or repented their early support of the resistance, nevertheless Hutchinson complained that "too many of rank above the vulgar have countenanced and encouraged" those at the base of the social structure. My own research and Philip Swain's has confirmed Hutchinson's analysis here: membership in formal organizations continued to be dominated by men of considerable wealth even as late as 1775, but participants in actual mobs, such as the Tea Party, and especially the men who enlisted in the Continental Army from Boston once the war began, tended to be young and propertyless. Literally thousands of men in Boston too poor to be listed as taxpayers, many because of their youth, still fought against taxation without representation.(22)

Hutchinson just as carefully distinguished Boston's behavior from Massachusetts' in blaming leading patriots rather than their gullible but honest followers for the Revolution. Only gradually did the tumultuous spirit spread beyond the metropolis. In 1766, he confidently asserted that "if the spirit in the town of Boston should subside, I think the other parts of the province so sensible of the miserable state we are in, that from a mere internal principle of virtue we should return to our former state of order." The Convention of 1768 -- called by the representatives and town of Boston to prepare resistance to the arriving British troops as the house had been dissolved -- proved a failure. "A great part of the country members declared they were sent to keep the rest from doing mischief." But by 1770, in one of his many "secret and confidential" letters, Hutchinson admitted that the situation had changed once the troops landed. His friends in the hinterland told him "that the town [of Boston] has the entire control of the province, and even if some towns could be rallied" to send "a few good men" to the legislature, "the entire province must give way to the town." Still, this trend only set in because British weakness and futile displays of strength lent an air of plausibility to the radicals' cries of tyranny. Hutchinson realized from the start that "had our confusion . . . proceeded from an internal cause we have good men enough in the country to have restored peace and order."(23) Both external and internal disruptive forces had to collaborate to destroy traditional Massachusetts society.

The province's social and institutional framework made it peculiarly sensitive to overseas attacks on its traditional rights, making it fertile soil for the radicals. Only with difficulty had men such as Hutchinson himself held off the forces of disorder throughout the century. In particular -- anticipating the work of Robert E. Brown and Michael Zuckerman -- he stressed the relative equality of economic conditions and the democracy and autonomy of the towns as the most important characteristics of provincial society. He noted that "property is more equally distributed in the colonies, especially those to the north of Maryland, than in any nation in Europe." "In some towns, you scarce see a man destitute of a competence to make him easy." Widespread distribution of wealth ensured that the population would normally be conservative, "tender of their property and see[ing] the importance of enjoying it in quiet." But when any threat appeared, the people would be more suspicious than most populations because they had more to lose and had higher "notions of liberty" than "any part of the globe." In addition, the proverbial New England town meeting had assumed so many of the functions of government during the eighteenth century that it would regard any intrusion from the outside as an assault on its traditional rights. Hutchinson explained:(24)

> Every town is of course a distinct corporation with powers of making by-laws, raising money, etc. and they hold their meetings when and as often as they please. All meetings are determined by the majority of voices and although the province law provides that a man who does not pay a small tax shall not be deemed a qualified voter yet it is not one time in twenty that any scrutiny is made. . . . Every man in the government being a legislator in his town thinks it hard to be obliged to submit to laws which he does not choose and which were made by a house of representatives consisting of one hundred men, for one or two only of whom he could give his vote; and it is harder that a council who are still in a more distant relation to him should have a share in the laws, and harder still that a governor in whose appointment he has no voice should

control or restrain the council or house; and it is infinitely unreasonable that this whole legislature should have an external power or authority to which it must be subject. In short, they are taught by the constant use of this sort of town government to think any other form unreasonable.

During the Revolution, "every town" in Massachusetts became an "absolute democracy," which for Hutchinson meant it had no "form of government" at all.(25) Precisely because these local republics so resented incursions on their liberty he urged Britain to avoid provoking the province and thereby lending an air of plausibility to the patriots' charges it planned to enslave the colonies. Hutchinson's admiration for the provincial, not the town, constitution and favorable attitude toward the population's behavior illustrated that he could tolerate even such distasteful bodies as town meetings within a generally beneficial framework as long as they retained their traditional places.

The democratic structure of local society ensured that "the three professions" -- lawyers, physicians, and clergy -- depended for their livelihood and influence on conformity with popular prejudices. During the revolutionary years, the people received the law from the faction, after which they laid it down for their erstwhile superiors. Hutchinson specifically called attention to the role of religion in the Revolution. An intimate connection existed between town meeting government and Congregational church polity. The populace elected ministers as well as town officials, and the meeting house had both secular and sacred functions. Hutchinson blamed the "lax government -- or rather no government -- among the several professions of dissenters" for their loyalty to the patriot cause, rather than their dislike of the Church of England, which he placed a distinct second. Still, they believed Anglicanism threatened town autonomy by stressing loyalty to an extra-local hierarchy. And as Alice M. Baldwin and Perry Miller, among others, have pointed out, Hutchinson noted that the "prayers and preachings of many of the clergy" won numerous converts for the revolutionary crusade.(26)

Despite his dislike of the dissenting religions' political implications, Hutchinson remained a bulwark of the "New Light" New Brick Church of Boston until he left for England. In fact, he adhered to the Puritans' traditional faith even though he admitted, while in England, that he found Anglicanism more congenial.(27) Hutchinson's apparent inconsistency can only be explained by his political theory. If the potential for revolution had been checked for a century, the town meeting and church had to be included in the bundle of institutions which comprised Massachusetts' heritage.

Hutchinson's many-faceted interpretation of the Revolution has not been recognized because he scattered his conclusions as random insights throughout his History, letters, and pamphlets. Yet it cannot be doubted that he always retained a balanced perspective, as his one purely theoretical exercise, the "Dialogue Between an American and a European Englishman," clearly demonstrated. Rather than presenting his ideas as a coherent system, he always tried to show his audience the other side of the story. He frequently blamed the people he addressed, whether imperial officials or the Massachusetts assembly, for the crisis, thereby obtaining the sort of vilification from both sides which convinced him he was right. But neither the form in which Hutchinson presented his ideas nor his personal motivations for doing so ought to obscure their significance.

Methodology as well as motive accounted for differences between Hutchinson's treatment of the Revolution and that of other contemporaneous scholars, both loyalist and patriot. With few exceptions, loyalists adopted a "devil" theory of the rebellion. Hutchinson's kinsman Peter Oliver did this so literally that he suggested a painter looking to sketch the devil search out Samuel Adams. In particular, historians such as Thomas Jones of New York, Joseph Galloway of Pennsylvania, Jonathan Boucher of Maryland, and Alexander Hewatt of South Carolina blamed the New England "independents" or "Presbyterians" for spreading republican principles. Galloway and Hewatt were so obsessed by this connection that they respectively saw seeds of rebellion planted by the Presbyterian intercolonial synod of 1764 and George Whitefield's preaching. (Hewatt conveniently ignored Whitefield's Anglicanism.) Hutchinson, while recognizing autonomous predispositions in New England local government, lived there and remembered Massachusetts' loyalty throughout the eighteenth century.(28)

Most of Hutchinson's fellow loyalists failed to take the colonial period seriously or, on the contrary, never got around to talking about the Revolution. Alexander Hewatt, Pennsylvania's Robert Proud, and George Chalmers, who lived in Maryland and later became a member of Britain's Board of Trade, respectively stopped their major works in 1765, 1742, and 1763. For Hewatt and Proud, these dates ushered in a new era of politics where rowdy, disreputable elements overthrew the loyal elites which had hitherto maintained social order and popular confidence. There was no point in cataloging the events after 1765 because the forces bent on revolution had already won, and simply awaited a convenient excuse to complete their triumph. Chalmers, on the other hand, traced the colonies' desire for independence back to Plymouth Rock. Assuming everyone in Britain knew the disasters of the 60s and 70s only too well, he concentrated on proving the colonists had been recalcitrant and determined to be independent all along. He hoped to show that had Britain applied a firm hand in time, the conflict might have been avoided.(29)

On the other hand, Massachusetts' Peter Oliver, Joseph Galloway, and Thomas Jones had almost no interest in the colonial period. Oliver and Galloway, like Chalmers, simply set it up as a prologue (or "porch," as Oliver called it) for the Revolution to show how the ungrateful Americans had behaved despicably toward their tender mother from the first. Jones, on the other hand, found a "Golden Age" in New York politics before 1752, at which time Presbyterian Whig leaders planned a series of confrontations with royal power and its loyal native supporters that undermined respectable opposition to the Stamp, Townshend, and Coercive Acts and diverted resistance toward independence.(30)

Only Hutchinson managed to present a sophisticated account of how latent colonial tensions, combined with British innovations, managed to fuse under the complicated circumstances which arose after 1763. By devoting two volumes to the colonial period and one to the Revolution, and also in having begun his study of colonial history before the Revolution broke out, Hutchinson could do justice to both changes and continuities between the two, whereas his contemporaries argued for one or the other. Finally, because he wrote much of his work before and during the Revolution rather than as an exile in England, he wrote history to support his policy of reconciliation instead of using it as a weapon to damn the Revolution uncritically.

Hutchinson's narrative also differed from the nationalist historians of the late eighteenth and early nineteenth centuries who justified the Revolution. Two of the most recent studies of these historians are entitled History as Argument and The Politics of History, and that just about sums it up. Creating a heritage to serve as the basis of national unity and to promote public spirit in the troubled years from 1780 to 1800, first generation American historians presented the Revolution as the effort of a united people, rarely if ever considering the loyalists save to dismiss them as both morally corrupt and numerically insignificant. Differences between sections, personal characteristics of leaders, and class and religious division went by the boards. Not all, to be sure, adopted a devil theory of George III or Thomas Hutchinson, although most did, but without exception they forced the complexity of historical events into the old Whig straight jacket of corruption and power versus virtue and liberty. So eager were they to trace a love of freedom back into the colonial past that they wrote of Pilgrims and Puritans who came to America for political rather than religious freedom, conveniently forgetting their religious intolerance or brushing it away as comparatively mild given the general tone of the seventeenth century. The historians of the young nation also found a special meaning in American history, and looked upon the Revolution as the first step in mankind's universal liberation from the tyranny of what John Adams had called "the canon and feudal law." Providence had invisibly shepherded the creation of the United States as a key element in the political, even the spiritual, redemption of mankind. Even with David Ramsay, whose account is by far the most nuanced and subtle of the patriot historians, one misses Hutchinson's restraint and effort both to criticize and appreciate opposite sides of the question.(31)

Unlike his contemporaries, Hutchinson's greatest strength rested in his search for diversity and complexity where they sought unity and clear-cut causal patterns. To some extent, his own unique position in the pre-revolutionary decade, caught squarely between America's most intransigent radicals and Britain's most extreme efforts at colonial reform, dictated the moderation of his case. Other loyalists and patriots experienced the Revolution as partisans, not conciliators. Also, Hutchinson, a New England Congregationalist whose ancestors had done much to shape the province's history, could not allow his church and forbears to shoulder the blame for the crisis. He had to affix it to other elements both at home and abroad. But if Hutchinson wrote prejudiced history, as he undoubtedly did, his biases, unlike those of other eighteenth century writers, dictated the sort of historical understanding and balance prized by professionals today. He examined the different motivations of leaders and followers, prominent and lower-class citizens, and town and country. He looked at sociological, psychological, constitutional, and ideological aspects of the struggle without collapsing them into a monocausal interpretation, and he could sympathize with both outraged colonists and outraged Britons. Hutchinson provided not so much an interpretation of the Revolution in the traditional sense as an array of insights, each of which scholars have subsequently elevated into an explanation of the whole event.

* * * * * * * * * *

Hutchinson's remedy for the disease of rebellion conformed to his diagnosis. In general, he argued that England should take advantage of the different motivations of the leaders and the populace, separate the two groups, reward the inhabitants for their good intentions, and punish the instigators for their treasonable ambition. As long as British taxation and regiments affected only the entire province the incendiaries had nothing to fear, as the people found their criticisms of Britain reasonable and protected them from criminal prosecution. Hutchinson also realized that because many of the leaders had little wealth to lose, they had a small stake in a conflict disrupting social and economic life. In fact, they needed to provoke disorder because "the moment tranquility shall be restored the importance of these people is at an end and the country will be restored to its normal state." He therefore urged Britain to abandon its policy toward Massachusetts. After his pleas to local juries to prosecute specific individuals for rioting, libels, and perjury fell on deaf ears, he suggested that the most prominent rebels be tried before the House of Lords. But even here he wished to see no man hanged or severely punished. Rather, he simply wanted to frighten them into revealing their true aims or recanting their challenge to Parliamentary supremacy. By such a public humiliation and conviction, the people would be "convinced of their obligation to continue subject to the supreme authority." Hutchinson thought punishment confined to "three or four of the most active." rebels would suffice, and he only suggested they be disabled from voting or holding government office. Far from returning his opponents' malice in kind, Hutchinson only wished them punished to show the people that Britain's disfavor fell exclusively on the ringleaders. He thought such an example would persuade the rank-and-file to abandon them.(32)

By concentrating so heavily on the chief propagandists, Hutchinson refused, unlike many loyalists and imperial administrators, to attribute the Revolution to the excessive freedom the colonists enjoyed. He gloried in this liberty and even hoped Britain might extend it. He insisted that "disorders in the colonies do not seem to have been caused by the defects in the forms of a constitution of government," since "they have not prevailed in the several colonies in proportion as one colony has been under a more popular form of government than another." If such were the case, Rhode Island and Connecticut, under no British supervision at all, would have been more obstreperous than Massachusetts or Virginia. Hutchinson repeatedly begged his English connections that "the more favor you show the colonies in freeing them from taxes of every sort and indulging them in such forms of constitution civil and ecclesiastical as they have been used to, the more agreeable it will be to me." He realized that further burdens played right into the radicals' hands. It was "impracticable" to make the Americans "easy while they were apprehensive of an intention to raise a revenue amongst them." Once "discontent should fill the minds of the people" and "their legislative power should be taken away" by either taxation or through the imposition of military rule, "they would no longer consider submission to the government essential to their interest."(33) And unlike some of the more belligerent loyalists, Hutchinson knew any new regime imposed through force would not only cost more than it could collect, but it could not keep its power in the face of colonial unrest. Britain had to rule through colonial consent whether it wished to or not.

Hutchinson therefore never wanted any troops sent to Boston, although his enemies published one of his letters of 1767 which could be so misinterpreted. Hutchinson wrote that "three or four hundred troops would be sufficient to prevent riots and tumults," but only if the people as a whole voluntarily supported the government. "Once they were fixed in the contrary sentiment," Hutchinson refused even to estimate "what number would be necessary." Troops were worse than useless in such a situation, as a letter to William Bollan written about the same time made perfectly clear: "force which could be supposed to be sent to keep the colonies in subjection would alienate them to such a degree that nothing but the last extremity could make it advisable."(34) However, British authorities determined to give the colonists a taste of power distorted his letters as effectively as the Boston radicals did later.

Hutchinson similarly abhorred any British efforts to tinker with the provincial constitution. True, in letters written in 1770 and 1771 to the Earl of Hillsborough, he did advise and recommend such changes. But he only did so because His Lordship ordered that he make such suggestions, and refused to allow Hutchinson to continue to procrastinate. Hillsborough enlisted Francis Bernard's aid in their mutual scheme to obtain a royally appointed council for Massachusetts. Bernard severely rebuked Hutchinson's efforts to dissuade them: It was not a question of whether the charter would be altered, but how. Bernard complained that "Lord Hillsborough wants your opinion what is necessary for reforming the government," but Hutchinson's advice read "like a lawyer's opinion, in which doubts and difficulties are stated but no conclusion is drawn." He also added, which must have made Hutchinson smile because that was precisely his intention, that Hillsborough thought that Hutchinson "had no desire that there should be an alteration of your government." In former letters, Hutchinson had written that he "expected . . . such an alteration." But expectation is not synonymous with approval. Hutchinson's "friends" distorted him as artfully as his opponents. They read into his complaints that the council had failed to support him their own desires to alter that body's composition. For instance, in 1769 Hutchinson had written that "I do not think the people in Boston would have run into extravagances if the council had expressed their disapproval." But in the very next sentence he added "I have never proposed an alteration of the constitution."(35)

Under pressure from Bernard and Hillsborough, Hutchinson gave in. He did so only because he sensed the inevitability of change, and tried to make it as innocuous as possible. His recommendations were a far cry from their elaborate schemes. He only proposed a triennially elected council instead of an annual one, and gratuitously threw in the suggestion that Maine be separated from Massachusetts, since squatters were flouting the property rights to the country -- claimed by Hutchinson and a number of loyalists, among others -- with the complicity of the General Court. Even so, Hutchinson responded unenthusiastically. He stressed the "great difficulty" required to alter the council in the face of popular disapproval, added that even the "judicious people" -- e.g. the loyalists -- "doubt [that] royal appointed councils are good," and feared "the consequences would more than contravene the advantage." He blamed the council's populistic behavior in recent years on "a particular family," "false" and "absurd notions of government," and "artful and designing men." The leading men of Massachusetts had been duped by a handful of ambitious partisans as effectively as the general population, and knew not what they did. The institution itself, Hutchinson argued, was sound. Two years earlier he had written that "for eighty years past they were in general well behaved." Hutchinson's defense of the council illustrated perfectly his maxim that "the best institutions are liable to abuse."(36) Therefore the abusers, rather than the institution itself, ought to bear any punishment.

But if Hillsborough and Parliament determined to go ahead in the face of all his reasons to the contrary, Hutchinson advised them how to proceed with a minimum of social disruption. First, to maintain royal authority, they should alter the charter "when the people were in tolerably good order" rather than when they were incensed. The two years after the Boston Massacre, when the province had calmed down considerably, would have been an excellent time to proceed. Second, he suggested that the king be empowered by Parliament to make any of a number of possible alterations, but only after Massachusetts had been heard in its own defense. This would not only ensure that any change proceeded from negotiation rather than unilaterally, but that generosity demonstrated by the king would increase loyalty to him in the future.

By actually offering changes against his better
judgment, Hutchinson hoped to reach the best practical
settlement for his beleaguered government. As with
naval impressment, he understood that sometimes
Massachusetts could not avoid an evil entirely, and so
had to handle the problem as best it could.
Revolution, the third alternative to acquiescence and
compromise, did not exist for Hutchinson.(37)

In addition to preserving the constitution intact,
Governor Hutchinson sought to avoid confrontations
with his opponents. He made it his rule "to avoid
whatever might occasion this discontent, and to indulge
even every prejudice, so far as was consistent with his
trust." He advised the Earl of Dartmouth, who
succeeded Hillsborough in 1772, "where any unnecessary
change or innovation has been made which has not a real
tendency to strengthen government, or where there . . .
is room to doubt whether a measure has been consistent
with the charter or other rights; or where the thing
desired is immaterial in itself but improved to be of
importance -- I wish to see the people satisfied."
Hutchinson urged that existing privileges be extended,
advocated the abolition of the vice-admiralty courts
-- which would make convictions for customs violations
virtually impossible, and realize Hutchinson's dream
of free trade -- and favored the appointment of judges
during good behavior rather than at the pleasure of
the governor and council. He even came up with the
imaginative idea of sending a parliamentary commission
to America to investigate the crisis at first hand. By
extending American liberties at precisely the moment
the radicals claimed Britain had imperiled them,
Parliament could easily prove their charges were mere
lies.(38)

However, Hillsborough's insensitive instructions,
which required Hutchinson to confront the assembly
with a variety of provocative measures, hampered his
plans. He had to veto bills subjecting the customs
commissioners to provincial and local taxes. With a
fine sense of irony these officials had complained
that the Massachusetts legislature taxed them without
representation, although the sums involved were
minuscule. Hillsborough also forced Hutchinson to
transfer the command of Castle William in Boston
Harbor from a provincial to a royal officer, and to
remove the General Court to Salem, which he claimed
prevented him from socializing and talking
extensively with the representatives as he spent much

time in Boston. It was no coincidence that
Hutchinson's recommendations to Dartmouth advocated
the reversal of all Hillsborough's policies.(39)

Despite his provocative instructions, Hutchinson's
policies paid handsome dividends between the Boston
Massacre and the Tea Act of 1773. His willingness to
do "everything in my power consistent with the trust
of government to reconcile civil and military, Whig and
Tory" caused a favorable change in the "temper of the
people" to be brought about "sooner and to a greater
degree than anyone could expect." Hutchinson managed
to ingratiate himself with the representatives, and
claimed that even his political opponents, aside from
the handful of die-hards, had "no objection to me
except that I stop them in their course and the only
chance they have is worrying me out of the government."
The Bostonians only disliked his "bad principles." The
house even selected their governor to head a commission
to adjudicate the province's boundary with New York,
a vote of confidence in an executive unmatched in
provincial history. Hutchinson may well have been
deluding himself that Massachusetts distinguished so
sharply between his political stand and his personal
qualities, but he at least overcame the opposition to
the extent that few quarrels occurred from 1770 to
1773.(40)

If Hutchinson sought to conciliate the colonists,
he also thought Britain would do well to incite
divisions among the different provinces. By emphasiz-
ing that all the colonies needed the mother country's
protection from each other's unfriendly behavior,
Britain could weaken the intercolonial resistance
movement and strengthen loyalty. In 1770, when the
New York boundary dispute surfaced again, Hutchinson
insinuated that "with a little manipulation [it] may
be increased." Unfortunately, this plan conflicted
with his other scheme to ingratiate himself with
Massachusetts by settling its outstanding boundary
dispute. Hutchinson believed the colonies had little
in common, and even hoped a foreign war might occur to
impress upon them their "dependence on the kingdom to
save" them. Any government could function in the
absence of threats to its survival; the revolutionaries would see their weakness only in an emergency.
Hutchinson's efforts to divide the colonies among
themselves or his desire for a mutual enemy may appear
Machiavellian, but he justified these thoughts as
providing a painless alternative to the evils of social

war, and keeping the "colonies from measures which must be their destruction."(41)

Hutchinson also worked to sow dissension among leading revolutionaries. He urged former Governor Bernard to wean Benjamin Franklin, who remained in England until 1774, from the faction in America. He himself encouraged a breach between John Hancock and Samuel Adams, hoping "it will be easy enough to manage them" when "they are divided." He promised Admiral James Gambier he would also take every chance to woo another likely candidate, James Bowdoin. Patronage and flattery proved of limited value, however, although Hancock convinced Hutchinson of his friendship long enough to be appointed commander of the Corps of Cadets, the executive bodyguard. As Hutchinson realized later, when Lord Dartmouth suggested that if Samuel Adams were responsible for most of the trouble he should be bought off, "such an appointment would increase his abilities if not his disposition to do mischief." The Massachusetts charter had been framed so officeholders could be removed only by the governor with the council's approval even if he appointed them solely on his own. By the 1770s the council was firmly in the patriot camp and would never have removed Adams.(42)

Hutchinson's ideas to manipulate and conciliate his opponents failed. In fact, retrospectively he found them counter-productive. As the revolutionaries sought "to be independent," once "he waived all disputes with them upon specific points," they resorted "to personalities and things of a general nature." Hutchinson's success ensured that they employed wilder exaggerations and personal slanders to stir up the people. Moreover, they objected to British sovereignty in theory once Parliament repealed the tax acts which had provoked the controversy in practice. Hutchinson avoided "engaging with them in a dispute upon the authority of Parliament" for two years, but finally felt compelled when in 1772 the radicals created the Committees of Correspondence. Hutchinson regarded them as totally illegal. His exchange of messages with the General Court in 1773 caused Lord Dartmouth to censure him, even though he had been primarily responsible for two relatively peaceful years, for initiating the controversy. The rebuke "mortified" Hutchinson, who testily replied that "I had been formerly instructed to endeavor to bring the assembly from their excesses by argument and persuasion."(43)

Hutchinson's personal popularity, undoubtedly a residue of his career as a judge and opponent of impressment, functioned much as his conciliatory policies by driving the patriots to new heights to overcome it. Samuel Adams frankly admitted that he showed the house some letters of Hutchinson pilfered by Benjamin Franklin because "a great part of the people were still attached to the governor." Adams designed "to make him odious," and to ensure his removal through the same tactics that had undone Francis Bernard and would forever serve as an object lesson to "all governors who had not kept on good terms with the people." The letters' publication also ended all chance of reconciling John Hancock, whom Hutchinson had freely criticized in some of them.(44)

When Parliament passed the Coercive Acts in response to the Boston Tea Party, Hutchinson recognized that Britain and the Massachusetts radicals had together undone everything he had tried to accomplish. Learning of these measures, he prepared immediately to resign, claiming that a governor "of a firmer constitution of both mind and body" would have to carry them into execution. Hutchinson roundly attacked the acts as "excessively severe," certain "to bring the greatest distress upon many of the tradesmen." Most disastrously, they fell equally on rebels and non-rebels . The latter, whom Hutchinson termed "the best subjects the king had in America" because they had resisted the threats of the mob despite England's unconcern, now had no incentive to remain true to their principles. Hutchinson "dreaded" the "alteration of the charter," finally decided upon over his protests, with good reason. Its annihilation immediately ended British rule as the people formed an independent legislature rather than submit to the changes. Hutchinson saw no point in continuing his History of the Colony and Province of Massachusetts Bay once news of the "Intolerable Acts" arrived: the province of Massachusetts Bay had ceased to exist. His last words in volume three lamented that "from that time all pacific measures for restoring the former dependence upon the supreme authority of the British dominions were in vain and to no purpose."(41) When Britain repudiated his own plan of reconciliation and avoidance of force, it ensured an outcome so far removed from the traditional Massachusetts with which he identified that it no longer mattered much what happened.

If Hutchinson could have been expected to sympathize with any of the Coercive Acts, it would have been the act limiting town meetings to one a year to elect officials and for no other purpose. But he did not. True, Hutchinson had suggested to Hillsborough that "the powers given to the towns were never intended by law to extend further than the management of the inmost concern of each town," and "every other meeting for any other purpose" constituted an "unlawful assembly." For this reason, he had been so alarmed by the Committees of Correspondence. Towns communicating on affairs beyond their ken repudiated their century-long tradition of adherence to their proper powers. Except for Boston, "there has scarce ever been any instance of any other town meddling with any affair but what immediately concerns them." Before the Revolution, "tumults, riots, and other marks of discontent were hardly known, except in an instance, now and then, in some of the maritime towns." Hutchinson placed the onus not on town meetings but on the peculiarly volatile situation in Boston and the handful of individuals responsible. He condemned the Massachusetts Government Act changing the town meeting, and only wished for a law subjecting persons concerned in "illegal meetings to incapacities for civil privileges."(46)

When Hutchinson resigned as governor, he went immediately to England, supported by addresses from the most respectable people in Massachusetts, to persuade Britain to repeal the Coercive Acts. But the conduct of the ministry soon convinced him the real trouble lay in Massachusetts. George III personally assured Hutchinson that the colonists faced "no danger of further taxes," and he "expressed his intention and desire to grant relief when they could put it in his power." Inquiring as to what that meant precisely, Hutchinson discovered that the king did not even insist on the colonists' "explicit acknowledgement of the right of taxation." Hutchinson himself had long warned that "violent measures to require an explicit acknowledgement of right" would "set all the people in America in a perfect frenzy." George III only asked for "orderly behavior." He told Hutchinson that "actions speak louder than words."(47) Like the American Civil War, according to some scholars, fought over the status of an imaginary Negro in an uninhabited territory, the Americans rebelled because they would not submit to taxes Britain promised not to levy. Behind both taxation and slavery lay the question of sovereignty.

But conciliation and the preservation of American institutions constituted only half of Hutchinson's plan. Just as he defended both parliamentary supremacy and colonial tradition as a judge, or refused to challenge Parliament even where it illegally and unlawfully condoned impressment, he somehow hoped the colonists would recognize that parliamentary rule was a good not an evil. As he wrote in 1774, "I have never had but one plan for the government of America." On the one hand, he "wished the legislatures of the colonies the full enjoyment, and especially in matters of taxation, of every privilege." But on the other, "the supremacy of Parliament must never be given up." Hutchinson fervently hoped that "the colonies would return to their former state of submission to this authority by lenient measures, without discussing points of right." But if Britain determined to pass taxes and reform legislation, these had to be effectively enforced. Once the colonies began to violate law with impunity, Britain would play straight into the hands of those seeking independence. Hutchinson pleaded with successive ministries to "repeal any laws now in force as you please but what remains take some effectual method to carry into execution." Hutchinson thought the colonists could recognize the benefits of Parliament's rule if laws were passed "evidently calculated for their benefit" instead of taxes or trade restrictions. He especially suggested Britain establish chancery courts and open up some desirable but prohibited trade which it could then tax unobjectionably.(48)

Hutchinson knew the extraordinary difficulties involved in implementation of his plan. He seemed to glory in the impossible task he had set himself. He wrote in 1767 that "there never was more occasion for a mixture of resolution and moderation," although exactly who should be moderate or resolute and where he failed to say. Complaining later than an appointed council would cause "a terrible convulsion" but that the elected one had become a terrible nuisance, he exclaimed: "It seems as if we can bear neither the cause of our malady nor the cure of it." Hutchinson feared that without the preservation of traditional colonial institutions and the suppression of those who persisted in challenging the imperial authority guaranteeing these privileges, "the kingdom and the colonies" would be "no longer one empire." British measures, however, with what struck him as a perverse fatality, invariably undermined the autonomy of colonial government while doing nothing to stop treason. Hutchinson hoped that Britain could do better than presenting America with a choice between the Scylla of arbitrary rule and the Charybdis of democracy run wild.(49)

In his efforts to avert the American Revolution, Hutchinson stood alone once again. His every effort at reconciliation provoked either the ministry or the radicals to even greater excesses: he had only to point to a problem and Britain sent troops or planned to alter the government; he had only to achieve a fragile harmony in Massachusetts and his rivals began to calculate new methods of disrupting it. Caught between or above two worlds bent on collision, Hutchinson's ideas and programs simply became obstacles to parties seeking total victory over each other.

Other voices besides Hutchinson's counselled moderation and compromise. But almost without exception, they suggested sharper definition of colonial rights and the power of Parliament. Plans appeared such as the American Parliament which Joseph Galloway and nearly half the First Continental Congress hoped for, or Francis Bernard's proposal of an American nobility to promote loyalty among important colonists to England. But Hutchinson's principle was that "no line can be drawn." Rather than limiting both colonial liberty and parliamentary authority, which he knew would only enrage both sides all the more, he pleaded that the traditional system which retained both be kept intact. Maximum liberty was compatible with the fullest extent of parliamentary rule -- if not in the mind of theorists, in the reality of eighteenth century history. Colonial freedom had helped make Britain the world's greatest power, and in turn Britain had preserved its provinces from foreign conquest. Only if the colonists kept the substance and Parliament the form, as in the past, could the empire be preserved. To restructure it, to use force, would destroy it.

When Hutchinson arrived in England in 1774, he hoped that "there never was an administration more disposed to adopt both parts of his plan," to revoke obnoxious legislation and exercise sovereignty through benevolent acts, than Lord North's regime. One other voice had been urging the same program for a decade. Many of Edmund Burke's speeches and letters on colonial affairs echoed Hutchinson's. Burke spoke for the Rockingham Whigs, a faction which in many ways resembled Hutchinson and the small band of prominent Massachusetts loyalists. Champions of the "Whig supremacy," a coalition of wealthy landowners and commercial men which had dominated English politics from the Glorious Revolution until the reign of George III, they appeared almost as the mirror image of the similar group which ruled Massachusetts over the same period. During the 1760s, both elites faced challenges to their traditional positions from the royal prerogative on the one hand and urban radicals, such as John Wilkes in England and Samuel Adams in Massachusetts, on the other.(50)

Burke, like Hutchinson, refused to recognize challenges to parliamentary supremacy: "general reasonings which were employed against that power went directly to our whole legislative right, and one part of it could not be yielded, to such arguments, without a virtual surrender of the rest." He, too, knew that "if Great Britain were stripped of this [supreme legislative] right, every principle of unity and subordination in the empire was gone forever."(51) The Rockinghams put such rhetoric into practice by sponsoring the Declaratory Act of 1766, reserving Parliament's right to bind the colonies in all cases whatsoever.

But the Rockinghams repealed the Stamp Act. If, like Hutchinson, they insisted on parliamentary supremacy checked only by self-restraint, morality, and custom, they also agreed with him that these limitations, at least in the North American colonies, guaranteed nearly total autonomy. Burke insisted that "the authority of which I was so jealous could not under the actual circumstances of our plantations be preserved in any of its members, but by the greatest reserve in its applications." Both Burke and Hutchinson believed that popular indignation would destroy a parliamentary authority exercised beyond customary bounds. For the momentary satisfaction of flexing its prerogative, a belligerent ministry could easily bring down the empire. Just as Hutchinson urged that Parliament only exercise its sovereignty in obviously benevolent cases, Burke pleaded to "let the colonies always keep the idea of their civil rights associated with your government." Then "they will cling and grapple to you, and no force under Heaven will be of power to tear them from their allegience. .

. . as long as you have the wisdom to keep the sovereign authority as the sanctuary of liberty."(52) Burke and Hutchinson understood intuitively what so few men in the eighteenth century could comprehend: in any real, functioning state, the power which upheld liberty also supported authority. The conflict between "liberty" and "power" stressed by English and American radicals only represented an extreme and rare occurrence when a state had broken down. In such circumstances, restoration of the balance would produce less general unhappiness than revolutionary war.

Hutchinson's and Burke's conceptions of Anglo-American relations differed analytically, not theoretically. While aware of the threats to imperial unity on the other side of the Atlantic, each placed primary blame for the disruption on those individuals he confronted personally. Burke put a different interpretation on Hutchinson's insight that the Massachusetts radicals took their cue from England. Far from imitating such extremists as Wilkes, they were assuming "to themselves, as their birthright, some part of the very pride which oppresses them." The Massachusetts radicals truly defended liberty and represented real popular feeling, rather than distorting it, as Hutchinson claimed. If they went too far, Parliament had done so first. Instead, Burke's denunciations of the English ministry for risking a revolution resembled Hutchinson's attacks on his Bostonian opponents for inquiring into the natural rights of man. Burke argued that "if intemperately, unwisely, fatally, you sophisticate upon the very source of government, by urging subtle deductions and consequences odious to those you govern, from the unlimited and illimitable nature of supremacy . . . they will cast your sovereignty in your face."(53) But despite their penchants for focusing their exasperation on the most immediate culprits, both Hutchinson and Burke shared a mistrust of the rationalizing, systematizing ideology which sought to "fix" principles of government and worked its poison throughout the English-speaking world.

Burke, like Hutchinson, ultimately admonished his contemporaries to moderation and prudence. "Those who would put an end to such quarrels by declaring roundly in favor of the whole demands of either party have mistaken . . . the office of a mediator."(54) But one of the tragedies of revolution is that men with a sophisticated understanding of the situation must, in the last analysis, support a cause grossly oversimplifying their position and join a set of zealots defining their roles for them. Burke and Hutchinson thus placed ultimate responsibility for the colonial crisis, which they diagnosed in nearly identical terms, on opposite sides.

FOOTNOTES

1. *History*, III, 254.

2. "Stamp Act Essay," 488, 489; H to William Bollan, July 14, 1760, M. XXV, 14, 17.

3. *History*, III, 253; "Stamp Act Essay," 489.

4. Hardwicke, August 31, 1778, 148; George Louis Beer, *British Colonial Policy, 1754-1765* (New York, 1900), as quoted by Jack P. Greene in the "Introduction" to *The Reinterpretation of the American Revolution* (New York, 1968), 5.

5. *History*, III, 61. Richard Koebner, *Empire* (Cambridge, 1961), 105-113; Lawrence Henry Gipson, "The American Revolution as an Aftermath of the Great War for Empire, 1754-1763," *Political Science Quarterly*, LXX (1950), 86-104.

6. H to William Robertson, December 28, 1773, M. XXVII, 1155; H to John Hely Hutchinson, February 14, 1772, M. XXVII, 324; Hardwicke, June 17, 1775, 23; H to Charlton Palmer, March 26, 1766, M. XXVI, 473.

7. *History*, III, 184.

8. "Strictures," 26; *History*, III, 294.

9. *History*, III, 220; "Additions, III," 41, 37.

10. Bernard Bailyn, *The Ideological Origins of the American Revolution* (Cambridge, 1967); *History*, III, 326; *Diary*, I, 234.

11. "Dialogue," M. XXVIII, 101-109, "Addition, III," 26; see William Pencak, "The Revolt Against Gerontocracy: Genealogy and the Massachusetts Revolution," *National Genealogical Society Quarterly*, LXVI (1978), 291-304, for evidence confirming the interpretations in the following paragraphs.

12. *History*, III, 215; H to Israel Williams, January 21, 1761, Williams Papers; H to Thomas Gage, January 10, 1771, M. XXVII, 449; H to ?, June 4, 1768, M. XXVI, 640; H to ?, February 16,

1769, M. XXVI, 725; H to Thomas Whately,
April 30, 1770, XXV, 414. In the letter to Gage,
referring to the younger Otis' madness,
Hutchinson wrote ironically: "Otis was carried
off today in a postchaise. He was as good as his
word: set the province in a flame and perished
in the attempt."

13. Arthur M. Schlesinger, The Colonial Merchants and the American Revolution (New York, 1918); Dirk Hoerder, Mobs and People: Crowd Action in Revolutionary Massachusetts, 1765-1780 (Boston, 1971); History, III, 107; "Hutchinson in America," 81; H to Lord Hillsborough, June 8, 1770, M. XXVI, 1093; H to Francis Bernard, July 2, 1770, M. XXVI, 1122; H to Lord Hillsborough, April 21, 1771, M. XXVII, 246; History, III, 329.

14. H to Francis Bernard, March 18, 1770, M. XXVI, 993; H to Francis Bernard, June 26, 1770, M. XXVI, 1117; History, III, 184; H to Israel Williams, February 23, 1774 and September 14, 1770, Williams Papers; H to John Worthington, January 31, 1771, M. XXVII, 175.

15. H to Francis Bernard, April 28, 1770, M. XXV, 405; Hardwicke, January 4, 1775, 6.

16. General Thomas Gage to Lord Hillsborough, October 31, 1768, C.O. 124/433; found in Frederick Lewis Gay Transcripts of State Papers, XI, 106-118, esp. 116, Massachusetts Historical Society; H to Richard Jackson, August 18, 1769, M. XXVI, 779.

17. H to ? (fragment), March 19, 1770, M. XXV, 375; H to Lord Hillsborough, March 12, 1770, M. XXV, 386.

18. H to William Bollan, October 31, 1769, M. XXV, 189; H to William Bollan, December 27, 1765, M. XXVI, 336; H to ?, July 25, 1769, M. XXV, 320.

19. H to ?, August 3, 1763, M. XXVI, 127; H to John Hely Hutchinson, February 14, 1772, M. XXVII, 524; H to Thomas Hutchinson Jr., April 29, 1766, M. XXVI, 448.

20. H to Francis Bernard, December 3, 1771, M. XXVII, 453; Hardwicke, January 4, 1775, 7; H to William Tryon, July 6, 1773, M. XXVII, 930; H to Robert Wilson, March 11, 1770, M. XXVI, 1044.

21. H to Francis Bernard, May 30, 1770, M. XXV, 417; H to Thomas Whally, May 24, 1771, M. XXVII, 294.

22. H to Richard Jackson, April 21, 1766, M. XXVI, 436; H to John Pownall, March 21, 1771, M. XXVI, 1008; H to Lord Hillsborough, July 26, 1770, M. XXVI, 1135; H to Thomas Whately, October 5, 1768, M. XXV, 277; H to Francis Bernard, May 22, 1770, M. XXVI, 1073; H to Lord Hillsborough, May 29, 1771, M. XXVII, 609. Philip Swain Jr., B.A. thesis on Boston soldiers, "Who Fought?", Tufts University, 1980; summarized in William Pencak, War, Politics, and Revolution in Provincial Massachusetts (Boston, 1981).

23. H to Richard Jackson, April 21, 1766, M. XXVI, 436; H to Israel Mauduit, December 5, 1768, M. XXVI, 693; H to Francis Bernard, March 25, 1770, M. XXVI, 1023.

24. H to Richard Jackson, October 20, 1767, M. XXV, 185; Zuckerman and Brown, cited ch. vi, nn. 45, 51.

25. H to Richard Jackson, November 9, 1767, M. XXV, 215.

26. H to Richard Jackson, November 9, 1767, M. XXV, 215; H to Francis Bernard, August 8, 1769, M. XXVI, 764; H to ?, December 24, 1771, M. XXVII, 465; H to John Pownall, June 8, 1770, M. XXVI, 1094; Alice M. Baldwin, The New England Clergy and the American Revolution (Durham, 1928); Perry Miller, "The Moral and Psychological Roots of American Resistance," in James Ward Smith and A. Leland Jamison, eds., The Shaping of American Religion (Princeton, N.J., 1961), I, 322-350. See also Edmund S. Morgan, "The Puritan Ethic and the Coming of the American Revolution," William and Mary Quarterly, 3rd. ser., XXIV (1967), 3-18; Alan Heimert, Religion and the American Mind (Cambridge, 1966).

27. Bernard Bailyn, The Ordeal of Thomas Hutchinson

(Cambridge, 1974), 22-23.

28. Peter Oliver, The Origin and Progress of the American Rebellion, ed. Douglass Adair and John A. Schutz (San Marino, California, 1961), esp. ch. i and 39-45, and works cited in nn. 29 to 31 below.

29. Alexander Hewatt, An Account of the Rise and Progress of the Colonies of South Carolina and Georgia (2 vols: London, 1779); Robert Proud, The History of Pennsylvania in North America (2 vols: Philadelphia, 1797-1798); George Chalmers, Political Annals of the Present United Colonies from their Settlement to the Peace of 1763 (London, 1780).

30. Oliver, Origin and Progress; Thomas Jones, The History of New York During the Revolutionary War and of the Leading Events in other Colonies in that Period (2 vols: New York, 1879).

31. See various works cited in Arthur H. Shaffer, The Politics of History: Writing the History of the American Revolution, 1783-1815 (Chicago, 1975), esp. ch. iii and iv, and William Raymond Smith, History as Argument: Three Patriot Historians of the American Revolution (The Hague, 1966).

32. H to ?, [c. June, 1770], M. XXVI, 1103; H to William Bollan, February 18, 1769, M. XXVI, 723; "Additions, III," 31; H to Lord Dartmouth, December 2, 1773, M. XXVII, 1093; H to ?, n.d., M. XXVII, 489.

33. H to Lord Hillsborough, January 22, 1771, M. XXVII, 169; H to Richard Jackson, August 18, 1769, M. XXVI, 774; (See also H to Lord Shelburne, January 18, 1768, M. XXVI, 584; H to Richard Jackson, October 20, 1767, M. XXV, 183); H to ?, [not sent, c. February, 1770], M. XXVI, 961.

34. H to Richard Jackson, October 20, 1767, M. XXV, 183; H to William Bollan, October 31, 1767, M. XXV, 189.

35. Francis Bernard to Thomas Hutchinson, November 7, 1769, Bernard Papers, VIII, 23, Sparks Manuscripts,

Harvard College Library; H to ?, February 16, 1769, M. XXVI, 722.

36. H to Israel Williams, September 29, 1774, Williams Papers; H to Lord Hillsborough, October, 1770, M. XXVII, 32; H to Lord Hillsborough, January 22, 1771, M. XXVII, 171, 173; H to ?, February 16, 1769, M. XXVI, 725; Quincy, 312. For ownership of Maine land, see James Stark, Loyalists of Massachusetts (Boston, 1903), and Lists of Muscongus Proprietors (January 1, 1773) and Lincolnshire Proprietors (July 12, 1768) and letter of Francis Bernard to Thomas Flucker, February 1, 1774, all in Henry Knox Papers, LI, Massachusetts Historical Society.

37. H to Lord Hillsborough, January 22, 1771, M. XXVII, 173; H to Francis Bernard, October 20, 1770, M. XXVII, 55.

38. History, III, 208; H to Lord Dartmouth, October 9, 1773, M. XXVII, 1026; "Additions, III," 64-66, 74; History, III, 285.

39. History, III, 247; Bradford, 306; H to John Pownall, July 17, 1771, M. XXVII, 333, complained that the Commissioners were ruining his chances for an accommodation with the legislature; H to ?, June 4, 1771, M. XXVII, 300.

40. H to Lord Hillsborough, January 22, 1771, M. XXVII, 174, 171; H to ?, June 28, 1773, M. XXVII, 928; H to Lord Hillsborough, March 9, 1771, M. XXVII, 223; H to William Tryon, April 26, 1772, M. XXVII, 565.

41. H to Lord Hillsborough, October 9, 1770, M. XXV, 473; H to ?, [early 1769], M. XXV, 376.

42. H to Francis Bernard, October 8, 1771, M. XXVII, 408; H to Thomas Gage, November, 1771, M. XXVII, 449; H to James Gambier, May 7, 1772, M. XXVII, 589; H to Lord Dartmouth, October 9, 1773, M. XXVII, 1026, 1027.

43. H to Thomas Whately, May 24, 1771, M. XXVII, 292; History, III, 246, 247; H to ?, June 14, 1773, M. XXVII, 912, 913; H to ?, June 21, 1773, M. XXVII, 916.

44. H to ?, June 14, 1773, M. XXVII, 912; H to Francis Bernard, October 16, 1773, M. XXVII, 1039.

45. H to John Pownall, April 25, 1773, M. XXVII, 905; Diary, 174; Hardwicke, October 18, 1775, 65; History, III, 329.

46. H to Lord Hillsborough, October 9, 1770, M. XXV, 470; H to Lord Dartmouth, December 21, 1773, M. XXVII, 1093; History, III, 208.

47. Diary, 181, 176; H to ?, n.d., M. XXVI, 750.

48. Diary, 188, 189; History, III, 266; H to Richard Jackson, October 20, 1767, M. XXV, 189.

49. H to William Bollan [?], October 31, 1767, M. XXV, 188; H to ?, February 14, 1767, M. XXVI, 543; Diary, 189.

50. Diary, 189. Accounts of the Rockingham Whigs may be found in Charles Ritcheson, British Politics and the American Revolution (Norman, Oklahoma, 1954); G.H. Gutteridge, English Whiggism and the American Revolution (Los Angeles, 1942).

51. Burke, "Observations on a Late Publication on the Present State of the Nation," (1769), I, 398; "Letter to the Sheriffs of Bristol," (1777), ibid., II, 224, 231.

52. Burke, "Speech on Conciliation with America" (1775), II, 179. (Hutchinson objected vehemently to the British tendency to "consider the colonies as your property to improve in the best way you can for your advantage." "Stamp Act Essay," 486.) Burke similarly condemned the "pride, perverseness, and insolence" which caused Britons to speak of "Our subjects in America; Our colonies; Our dependents." ("Speech at Bristol Previous to the Election" (1780), II, 417.)

53. Burke, "Letter to the Sheriffs of Bristol" (1777), II, 234; "Speech on American Taxation" (1774), II, 73.

54. Burke, "Letter to the Sheriffs of Bristol" (1777), II, 99.

PART III: THE POLITICAL THEORIST

VII. NATURAL LAW AND NATURAL RIGHT

Thomas Hutchinson's political thought flowed from his historical inquiries. He had observed a good society at work in eighteenth century Massachusetts, and sought to apply the lessons he absorbed to fight the American Revolution. In forging an intimate alliance between history and political philosophy, Hutchinson followed in a tradition as old as western thought, if not a general human phenomenon.

Political theory has always reflected changing conceptions of man's role in history. Pre-reformation Christian thought, epitomized by St. Augustine, held that human efforts could not alter the structure of history. In this context, government was either a necessary evil or a limited good which provided the context in which Christians could individually and as communities work out their salvation. A virtuous or vicious state could not help or hinder significantly the pursuit of goodness, truth, and salvation -- in fact, the faith sometimes flourished under persecution. Because even the worst state did preserve a modicum of order, Christians had to obey their rulers as long as they did not compel behavior which contradicted the tenets of the faith. Then the individual had no alternative except to submit to whatever punishment the authorities inflicted. (Some thinkers, such as Thomas Aquinas, granted a right of resistance in these cases.)

A good state adhered to natural law, a shorthand expression for the immutable standards of right and wrong which have governed all civilized society: not to murder, not to steal, to honor parents and legal authority, not to lie, etc. No "raison d'etat" or special morality existed exempting a state from standards applicable to individuals. Under no circumstances could rulers, upon peril of their souls, demand that their subjects violate this fundamental precept which defined man's nobility and humanity. In short, as John Morrall has written: "Medieval Europe offers for the first time in history the somewhat paradoxical spectacle of a society trying to organize itself politically upon the basis of a spiritual framework. . . . Instead of religion, as heretofore, forming the buttress for a communal political tradition, it was now elevated essentially above the political sphere and from this position of transcendence it bestowed on political authority whatever limited justification the latter possessed." If the reality of medieval life belied such exalted norms, one can only shudder to think what the "Dark Ages" would have been like had not many thinkers and ordinary people believed them.(1)

The Renaissance and Reformation, by opposing traditional Catholicism, had to endow political activity with a new significance. Renaissance theorists sought to resurrect the past glories of Greece and Rome, when the state had been regarded as a positive good and the primary focus of civic, spiritual, and intellectual life, the inevitable fruit of man's true nature rather than a means of protecting him following his fall from grace. The Florentine theorists Machiavelli and Guicciardini, much like the American Revolutionaries, extravagantly praised "republican virtue" which required the citizen to subordinate his individuality and pursuit of private gain to the general good to derive a true sense of purpose. Religion, as manipulated by The Prince, retained the purely instrumental function of bolstering the state. For the Reformation's leaders the primitive Christian community played a role analogous to the ancient state for contemporary secular intellectuals, only here the state protected a reborn church instead of vice versa. Though Lutheranism retained inhibitions about accepting political authority as a positive good, the Calvinists and Puritan sects identified the political and Christian communities for worldly purposes. They used the state to enforce conformity to Utopian Christian ideals which they believed would soon conquer the world.(2)

Various movements and thinkers had anticipated the sixteenth century upheavals. Since Joachim of Fiore in the twelfth century they had sought to define the vocation of Christian man as participation in politically and religiously oriented movements rather than personal adherence to unchanging values. When such theories were put into practice, they revolutionized human behavior and consciousness. Christendom split into armed ranks of states, each claiming a monopoly of the true religion. Being a good Christian now meant not only behaving in a morally acceptable way, but also adhering to a particular creed and effectively working for its victory. Neither Protestants nor Catholics could admit the holiness of states or individuals adhering to the other camp. Similarly, defenders of "republican virtue," royal absolutism, or the traditional privileges of towns and nobles each claimed a monopoly of knowledge as to the correct organization of the state. The birth of modern Europe marked the substitution of the form, ideology, or self-proclaimed purpose of a state to judge its legitimacy in place of the traditional Christian standard of natural law.

After justifying political action as conducive to greater, millennial purposes, thinkers next began to view it as an end in itself. The transition can be traced in one mind, that of Machiavelli. He not only defended Roman republican principles in the <u>Discourses on Livy</u>, but wrote a handbook on the acquisition of political power for its own sake in <u>The Prince</u>. But it remained for the Englishmen Thomas Hobbes and John Locke to justify the state not because it pursued an ideal order but rather because it preserved those secular, limited principles which had motivated its formation in the first place. Government existed to secure the natural rights of man -- life for Hobbes, life, liberty, and property for Locke. To demonstrate that government existed only for the purposes they maintained -- as opposed to both contemporary and historical theory and reality -- Hobbes and Locke constructed their symbols: "the state of nature," "the social compact," and "natural rights." They argued that man only left a state of nature voluntarily, entered into a social compact, and thereby joined his fellows to preserve his natural rights.

Substituting natural rights for natural law replaced a restrictive political system where men ought to aspire to be virtuous with a permissive one designed to facilitate the pursuit of self-interest or the self-satisfied enjoyment of personal blessings. Natural rights theory also opened the door for a defense of revolutionary political activity in the modern age. Revolution could be justified not because a state behaved iniquitously from a moral point of view, but because certain individuals and groups believed the government interfered with their natural rights. The respective rights and powers of subject and government could no longer be adjudicated before the tribunal of a higher morality, but became a question of political power. Locke himself realized this: disgruntled groups had the right to appeal to the people. By supporting their actions, the majority affirmed the soundness of their interpretation of a society's fundamental law. If revolts or protests failed, they were wrong. As a consequence, the inhabitants of a Lockean country existed not only as moral but as political beings who had to accept a formulation of natural rights philosophy and either vote or act upon it. A population aware of its political rights formed both a prerequisite and a result of a government based upon the rights of man.

The first modern revolutions combined the Utopian political ideals of the Renaissance and Reformation with Locke's philosophy. For the American and French revolutionaries, the state existed to establish a superior political regime founded on virtue, the major benefit thereof being the preservation of man's natural rights. American historians have recently debated whether "New Whig" ideology -- which stressed the moral degeneracy of British and American society and sought to replace it with a "Christian Sparta," to use Samuel Adams' words -- or the "Old Whig" thought of Locke -- which emphasized the natural rights violated by British legislation -- constituted the primary element of revolutionary thought. Here scholars have put asunder what ought to be joined. Both forms of Whiggery were absolutely essential to justify revolution. New Whig thought explained why the violations perceived by Old occurred, and predicted further exactions from a depraved Britain. The appeal to the traditional rights of Englishmen similarly worked hand-in-glove with those of man. As Hutchinson remarked, Americans frequently "confounded the general principles of government with the principles of the particular constitution of the English Government."(3)

The American Revolution may be distinguished from its predecessors since it sought to bring into being certain political principles held to be universally valid, such as liberty, equality, and sovereignty through representation, as the revolutionaries defined these terms. Previous upheavals such as the Revolt of the Netherlands which began in the 1580s, the English Revolution of the 1640s, and the Glorious Revolution of 1688, justified themselves upon the conservative principle that a monarch had deviated from the true structure of the constitution and had acted tyrannically. Except for a few fringe groups in the Puritan Revolution such as the Levellers, Diggers, and Fifth Monarchy Men, previous revolutions did not claim to set an example for all mankind or insist that only governments which institutionalized republicanism and virtue did not enslave or degrade their people. Those who would term the American Revolution conservative should consider that it initially denied the moral legitimacy of nearly every regime on earth.

Demonstration that the American Revolution marked the first of a new species explains why Thomas Hutchinson, a man of a traditional, conservative temperament, felt compelled to create a political theory new to America to counter it. Before a state emerged founded on natural rights, no need existed to stress history and tradition so strongly.(4) Hutchinson could not simply satirize or dismiss popular and revolutionary politics, as did Jonathan Swift and Samuel Johnson; he had to convince an excited people that its true interest lay in abandoning the bogus freedom the revolutionaries offered.

Hutchinson responded to the American Revolution with a political theory which tried to reconcile the moral absolutism of pre-Reformation Christianity with a concern for the development of social institutions which had emerged in the late and post-Medieval period. He regarded the state as a positive but limited good, designed not to produce the earthly millennium and/or secure the rights of man, but simply to provide a secure existence for its inhabitants in accordance with traditional practices. Enduring political and social arrangements conferred legitimacy upon a state regardless of its form of government or self-proclaimed purposes. Hutchinson did not, however, subordinate morality and justice to a pragmatic or materialistic theory of politics. A state could not last without respecting traditional guarantees of popular customs and liberties and conforming in some measure to the doctrines of natural law. Hutchinson thus made historical experience the measure of political theory, not in the sense of an idealized past serving as the model for an imaginary future, but in the form of a government's ability to preserve itself from internal disruption. By de-universalizing the state, by not endowing it with a mission it could not possibly fulfill, Hutchinson provided a means for non-revolutionary states to attain a theoretical legitimacy to challenge the ideas propounded by "the

Age of Democratic Revolution." In fact, given Hutchinson's criteria, the revolutionary state alone could not achieve legitimacy, for it had to ride roughshod over both moral and positive law in its misguided idealism.

Hutchinson's theory of politics stood at odds not only with the Founding Fathers', who after a brief spurt of millennialism acquired a great respect for experience and history thanks to the tribulations of the Critical Period, but even from his fellow loyalists'. The framers of the Constitution ransacked history for general rules to create institutions most appropriate to the preservation of republican government. The ancient world especially contained numerous lessons which could help establish the new nation upon a firm foundation. Similarly, with the exception of a few eccentrics such as Jonathan Boucher, who espoused the divine right of kings, American loyalists and even British statesmen accepted John Locke's theories of sovereignty, resistance, representation, and the social contract wholeheartedly, but drew different practical conclusions from them than the revolutionaries. They argued that Britain had simply not behaved tyrannically, and in disputed cases the majority of the empire (embodied in Parliament) could bind the colonial minority. Similarly, loyalists and British administrators drew up their own plans of reform which had more in common with the constitutional innovations of the patriots than with Hutchinson's conservatism. His rejection of both Lockean thought and institutional change set him apart from nearly everyone of importance in the revolutionary age, most of whom regarded the irrationalities of the first British Empire as the cause, rather than the solution, of the crisis.(5)

Hutchinson therefore defined an enterprise which has since characterized counter-revolutionary thought. Many of the defenses of Christianity, political stability, and tradition, and many of the criticisms of revolutionary thought and action which have appeared in the writings of far better known theorists may be found in Hutchinson's. His ideas strikingly resembled those of Edmund Burke, who used many of the same arguments to oppose the French Revolution and bolster the ancien regime of traditional Europe in the decade following Hutchinson's death.

* * * * * * * *

At first glance, Hutchinson's political thought may appear primitive and naive, especially by eighteenth century standards. Basically, all he hoped to show is that governments best preserved themselves by doing justice according to principles universally accepted as valid by civilized men and incorporated into national custom and law. Hutchinson identified these with Christian morality and natural law much as C. S. Lewis, in The Abolition of Man, has referred to them as the "Tao," and shown how every major civilization in the world has adopted similar moral commandments.(6) A society fulfilling these principles instilled them in its inhabitants through religion and education, passed laws that conformed to them, and executed these statutes in the courts. Hutchinson had little interest in the questions which so vexed his contemporaries -- what rights does man possess by nature?; which should be left to the individual and which delegated to the state?; which race, class, or religion is best suited for freedom?; what is the grand pattern of history and a particular nation's special role in it?; what procedures, such as representation, validate legislation?; what sort and degree of equality is desirable? Hutchinson was not ignorant of these questions. He had thought them through and refuted not merely the revolutionaries' solutions, but even the relevance of such issues to the more crucial matters of personal happiness and social welfare. Hutchinson believed that each state worked out problems of right and obedience one way or another, and the content of what institutional arrangement developed mattered less than the fact that it emerged peaceably, traditionally. Only men who had moved beyond, or beneath, a proper interest in the great moral foundation of society would think of making other criteria the test of a political system, and would do so for ulterior purposes at that. By-passing the true issues, Lockean revolutionaries justified breaches of absolute morality to implement their own principles when they threatened to overthrow a state which failed to adhere to their maxims.

The most fundamental tenet of Hutchinson's political philosophy is that "natural law" -- "that is, the law which every man has implanted within him" -- is universally and irrevocably binding on both states and individuals and can never be justifiably violated under any circumstances whatsoever.(7) Hutchinson completely agreed with Burke's aphorism that "political problems do not primarily concern truth or falsehood. They relate to good or evil." Hutchinson judged many practical examples by this standard in his History. For instance, he criticized an act of seventeenth century Massachusetts which violated a treaty with Connecticut by taxing its commerce on the grounds that "in all ages and countries, by bodies or communities of men, such deeds have been done," of which "most of the individuals of which such communities consisted, acting separately, would have been ashamed." Individual and collective morality were the same; governments could not claim expediency or necessity to exempt them from rules they enjoined on their subjects. Similarly, it was always "highly criminal . . . for persons under pretence of rectifying public wrongs, to invade private rights." If innocent people had to suffer to free a people from its chains, then the actions should not be undertaken as oppression would merely shift focus. Hutchinson would have heartily concurred with Burke's dictum that "power . . . to be legitimate must be according to that eternal, immutable law in which will and reason are the same."(8) Hutchinson thus linked political and moral obligation because the well-ordered state existed primarily to do justice. There could be no right to do wrong.

A society with moral laws, however, could exist only where a belief in God prevailed. Because everyone possessed an innate knowledge of natural law, it derived its authority from the God who gave man his conscience. Hutchinson's repeated denunciation of blasphemy from the bench in the late 1760s attested to his conviction that religious indifference had preceded political upheaval and produced a decline of morality in Massachusetts. He found blasphemy intimately linked with the unrest. In August 1766 he termed blasphemy "a very high crime . . . of the most dangerous nature" which "tends to the dissolution of all ties of government, and saps the very foundation of society." The previous October he had ordered a grand jury to inquire into offences "such as denying the existence of God, blasphemy, or attributing to God what is inconsistent with God, or denying what belongs and is due to Him, a denial of the established religion, all profaneness, lewdness, and those crimes which a chaste mind cannot bear the recall of."(9) Given that most of the revolutionaries considered themselves religious men who called upon God and the Scriptures to support their cause, Hutchinson clearly hoped his orations would compel the people to think more seriously about the true moral implications of such utterances.

Hutchinson also expressed his distaste for contemporary law insofar as it "punished crimes, only as they affect society" instead of treating offences as they accorded with absolute standards of good and evil. The consequences of substituting sociological jurisprudence for adherence to natural law were devastating. Hutchinson particularly regretted that "we have departed so far from the spirit of our fathers under the old charter," when "a refractory, disobedient child" who "continued obstinate . . . was put to death" that such a child "has become so common among us as scarcely to be noticed." Hutchinson blamed adults' own immorality for the children's sorry state. When people unthinkingly committed perjury by refusing to testify against smugglers and rioters, it demonstrated godlessness since "a man must be abandoned to all sense of religion, who can call his God to witness a falsehood." In keeping with his belief in a universal moral conscience, Hutchinson argued that "the lightest punishment" a perjurer could expect would be "to be perpetually goaded with the stirrings of his own conscience" and "to live in horror [of Hell] all his days."(10) Hutchinson recognized disobedience in children and blasphemy as signs that the social order was falling apart even if these crimes did little physical harm to private individuals. If children failed to respect authority or people flaunted their irreligion and immorality with impunity in court, the preconditions for social revolution already existed. But if Hutchinson could persuade inhabitants to discipline their children -- many of the rioters in Boston were young men and boys -- or testify against the radicals, he could restore Massachusetts' traditional order.

Perpetuating the religious and moral sense to make crimes such as perjury impossible demanded an established, protected church, as Hutchinson believed many people behaved morally only out of fear of eternal damnation. He testily claimed that the Boston clergy had attacked him without cause because he had "in many instances endeavored to raise the dignity of the clergy." When the Baptists in Massachusetts complained of being oppressed in the 1770s, Hutchinson retorted that "in general they have all the liberty which can consist with a legal establishment for maintaining public worship." Without a church supported by law, even one as republican as the Congregational, Hutchinson thought the situation in Massachusetts would have been much worse. As his attack on perjury indicated, he agreed with Burke's reason for defending an English establishment; it was "of infinite importance" that all who took part in public affairs "should not be suffered to imagine that their will . . . is the standard of right and wrong." Instead, they must "act in trust and . . . are to account for their conduct in that trust to the one great Master, Author, and Founder of Society." Hutchinson echoed these sentiments when he repeatedly warned grand juries that "all of us [are] accountable to the Supreme Governor of the universe" and prayed for "the Great God [to] bless and direct" their efforts.(11)

While Hutchinson staunchly defended an established church, he opposed religious persecution with equal vehemence. Not only did he find Puritan intolerance uncongenial if unavoidable, he shared none of the contemporary English prejudices against Roman Catholics. His "European" spokesman criticized the "American" in their dialogue for accusing the Catholics of holding treasonable principles through allegiance to the Pope which few adhered to any longer. The "European" insisted that Catholics had become scapegoats for a variety of ills in Britain and accused of crimes and principles they had to deny strenuously.

The only time I have been able to discover when Hutchinson approved explicitly of John Locke occurred in a letter where he recalled that while at college he had read Locke's *Essay on Toleration* "with attention" and "was astonished that anybody who had thought at all should have thought differently upon the subject, and yet all the world" had previously "received the absurdities of a contrary doctrine." Hutchinson followed Locke's theory in his *History* by insisting that "experience" showed that no government could legitimately restrain its inhabitants from "liberty of conscience," which "can never be supposed . . . by any compact whatsoever, to be submitted to the supreme authority." This sentence also marked the only time Hutchinson ever acknowledged the existence of any sort of social compact, and he only applied it to ensure maximum freedom on the most important question of all, the state of an individual's soul. He did not acknowledge that it possessed any validity as a criterion to judge other actions of governments and individuals. Hutchinson's passionate defense of religious freedom resembled Burke's, who urged Catholic emancipation on the grounds that "crimes are acts of individuals, and not of denominations." To "arbitrarily class men under general descriptions in order to proscribe and punish them in a lump" for their sincerity would be "an act of unnatural rebellion against the legal dominion of reason and justice."(12) A society should be grateful that its inhabitants held to their religion so tenaciously. The idea that only one form of church was legitimate struck Hutchinson and Burke with the same absurdity as the notion that all governments had to conform to a specific structure.

Hutchinson realized that given a religious, morally sensitive population, he could use oaths for witnesses, jurors, and office-holders to link a state's laws with natural law itself. Oaths rendered obedience to the former as obligatory as conformity to the latter. Hutchinson became almost fanatical during the 1760s in his insistence that oaths never be violated regardless of the practical consequences, as he realized full well the effects once men who had sworn to obey laws began to disregard them. When he refused to allow the famous tea ships to depart from Boston harbor without a customs pass, which he could only have granted legally if their cargoes had been landed, even British administrators accused him of provoking a needless showdown, to say nothing of risking the peace to protect his own mercantile investments. Hutchinson retorted that he had no moral choice. Had he granted a pass "he would have been guilty of a direct violation of his oath, by making himself an accessory in the breach of those laws which he had sworn to observe." And while Hutchinson developed a theory of free trade, he also tried conscientiously to enforce the mercantilist trade acts. As he wrote his friend Samuel Swift, "I have taken a solemn oath as governor to do everything in my power that the Acts of Trade may be observed." Even though he considered the Stamp Act "unconstitutional" he also thought it "legally right," and therefore insisted that "the oaths I had taken bound me in discharge of my public trust."(13) Hence, Hutchinson opposed his colleagues on the Superior Court who would gladly and illegally have done business without the stamps. His behavior in these three instances could be cited as inconsistent with his contention that he truly cared for colonial rights or maintaining harmony, but only strict adherence to his philosophy of law explains why he could argue so strenuously for American liberty and try to reconcile England and the colonies while still enforcing laws he did not believe in.

Hutchinson also used the oath, with extraordinary rhetorical effectiveness, the day after a mob destroyed his house in 1765. Defending his refusal to speak to the crowd concerning his involvement with the Stamp Act, he expostulated:(14)

> I am not obliged to give an answer to all the questions that may be put to me by every lawless person -- yet I call God to witness -- and I would not for a thousand worlds call my Maker to witness to a falsehood -- I say, I call my Maker to witness, that I have never in New England or in Old, in Great Britain or America, neither directly nor indirectly, was aiding, assisting, or in the least promoting or encouraging what is commonly called the Stamp Act.

By linking moral law with both the content and execution by government officers of statutory law, Hutchinson's remark that the sovereignty of Parliament could not be "more absolute . . . than what is founded in the nature of government" can now be fully understood. It meant that he considered the modern idea of sovereignty -- defined by Bertrand de Jouvenel as "a will capable of exercise on every subject matter whatsoever without limitation . . . a command from on high which its form validates whatever its substance, and which has neither limits nor rules governing its subject matter" -- to be "the most criminal [principle] that can be devised." Burke proved equally vehement on this point: any law "against the principle of a superior law, which it is not in the power of any community, or of the whole race of man, to alter -- I mean the will of Him who gave us our nature, and in giving impressed an invariable law upon us," was *ipso facto* "null and void."(15) Hutchinson and Burke went to such incredible lengths to extend parliamentary sovereignty in theory precisely because they so carefully circumscribed it in practice. It was a rare government indeed which had so closely approximated traditional and moral limits in practice.

Like Burke, Hutchinson believed that his political opponents denied that human law must be judged by divine law. Instead, the radicals insisted that governments existed to preserve "rights" rather than execute justice. Hutchinson charged that "it has been publicly asserted by some of the heads of the party, who call themselves sober men, that the good of the public is above all considerations, and that morality can be dispensed with and immorality is excusable, when this great good [a society based on natural rights doctrine] can be obtained by such measures." Once they had altered the state's goal, people would insensibly grow to believe that rioting against and slandering non-revolutionary public officials could indeed be justified as a means of acquiring inalienable rights. On the contrary, Hutchinson would only allow specific positive laws and customary institutions to be superseded, and then only when "the safety of the whole" made it indispensable. Natural law had to be preserved immaculate. Those individuals who separated the ends and means of government were "lawyers for putting an end to the law" and "divines to religion and virtue." By attacking the fundamental basis of their authority they undermined their professions. Burke agreed with Hutchinson that "no arguments of policy, reason of state, or preservation of the constitution" could in and of themselves justify an immoral law, and he joined Hutchinson in condemning the idea that "any body of men have a right to make what law they please -- or that laws can derive any authority from their institution merely, and independent of the quality of the subject matter." Hutchinson and Burke found their opponents substituting the process by which laws were passed -- through representative institutions of a sovereign people -- for the substantive content of the law itself and the tradition behind the sovereign as the criterion as to whether it ought to be obeyed. By such reasoning, no act of a monarch, however salutary, could be approved and no law of a properly constituted republic, however pernicious, could be condemned. The same John Adams who roundly castigated mankind's slavery under the tyranny of the "canon and feudal law" also insisted that "a democratical despotism is a contradiction in terms." Vox populi, vox dei.(16)

Hutchinson thus discovered in the American Revolution not merely a political upheaval, but an immoral and irreligious rebellion against the norms which had traditionally guided the behavior of Christendom. A population believing in Christianity and moral law could not have perjured themselves or committed violence against law-abiding people such as Hutchinson himself. His numerous remarks about blasphemy, perjury, and morality indicate that he viewed the American Revolution as the same sort of cataclysmic event which Edmund Burke considered the French. Burke defined the three principles of the French revolutionary government, even from the first when it maintained a low level of violence (as did Hutchinson's Boston, where no one was killed before Lexington and Concord except in the Boston Massacre) as "Regicide" -- "which lays it down as a fixed law of nature and a fundamental right of man, that all government not being a democracy is an usurpation" -- "Jacobinism" -- "the revolt of the enterprising talents of a country against its property" -- and "Atheism" -- "when in place of religion and social benevolence and of individual self-denial they institute impious, blasphemous, indecent theatric rites in honor of their vitiated perverted reason, and erect altars to the personification of their own bloody and corrupted republic." Hutchinson clearly spoke of the same tendencies even if he did not use identical words. In Burke's "Regicide" he would have recognized the denial of parliamentary sovereignty and the substitution of popular rule -- "taxation without representation is tyranny." In "Jacobinism" he would have seen the persecution and eventual exile of Massachusetts' ruling elite by men of no previous importance who seized control of the revolutionary state. And "Atheism" existed in the popular disregard of moral law and the prostitution of the Congregational Church to the level of a "stalking horse" for the Revolution. "Too many of the clergy" condoned political violence and became celebrants of vice instead of guardians of virtue. If Massachusetts did not destroy its churches as did the French, it had no need to: they had destroyed themselves when they condoned political insurrection.(17)

By stressing so strongly that both states and persons had to conform to the moral law of Christianity, Hutchinson had to face the problem of how an individual confronted with an unjust state ought to behave. He ruled out revolution, for that would harm innocent individuals. Revolt also implied any given aggrieved individual possessed the right to decide for himself which acts of government were moral and which were not. If any substantial number of people acted upon this principle, it would topple any state. Once the population questioned royal government Hutchinson saw nothing to prevent the fragmentation of

Massachusetts into various warring factions. He predicted it would be split into "innumerable divisions; every town, every parish, and every particular club and connexion will meet and vote and execute just as they please." Once revolution began, it would follow its own principles with remorseless logic until every man became a law unto himself, or until a unifying tyranny provided welcome relief from such anarchy.(18)

Hutchinson believed he saw signs of total social collapse after 1765, and indeed these tendencies alarmed the revolutionaries themselves until Shays' Rebellion and other signs of internal disorder provoked the Constitutional Convention. To deny effectively the sovereignty of Parliament, the revolutionaries had to stir up "disorder, riot, breaches of the peace, and what are commonly called mobs." Illegal action here led to "other irregularities which are the consequence of them." The trouble could not be "confined to one point." Hutchinson contrasted "the contentment and order, the happy effects of a constitution [eighteenth century institutions] strengthened by universal assent and approbation," with the "disorder and discontent" that were "the deplorable effects of a constitution enfeebled by contest and opinion." He found "divisions and animosities" disturbing towns and families; robberies occurred frequently in daytime for the first time in provincial history. Squatters invaded land belonging to loyalists in Maine, and land rioters roamed Berkshire County. The students at Harvard College took a leaf from their elders and complained of an "unconstitutional" educational system which violated their "natural rights." Class conflict appeared which denied the respect traditionally shown to prominent inhabitants. Revolutionary politics "gave the lower sort of people such a sense of their importance that a gentleman did not meet with what would be called common civility any longer." "Levelling principles" eliminated "the principal men" from any role in the government. The denial of parliamentary supremacy translated itself into general lawlessness because "if individuals or particular parts of government may resist whenever they shall apprehend themselves aggrieved, instead of order and peace and a state of security," "the great ends of government, we may expect tumults, wars, and a general state of danger."(19) Paradoxically, the very natural rights philosophy which claimed to protect life, liberty, and property could not even hope to realize its own slippery and deceptive goals.

Hutchinson used the words "anarchy" and "tyranny" alternatively to describe the government of revolutionary Massachusetts once this "perfect barbarism" had arrived. He detected little difference between the two because both represented arbitrary power without law. In 1767 he predicted that "if such an unlimited liberty is indulged and carried on, we shall soon approach nearly to the state of licentiousness which is worse than tyranny." He described the coercion of peaceable merchants and the destruction of their tea in two ways: "in times of anarchy there is no kind of outrage which is not to be feared," and "there is never greater tyranny in Constantinople than has lately been in Boston."(20)

Hutchinson detected in the government of the partisans of liberty a despotism unrivaled by the bashaws of Persia and sultans of Turkey with whom the revolutionaries, ironically enough, had also compared the loyalists and their British masters. Hutchinson found reasons to assert that "a democratic tyranny" was the worst. When an entire society chose to suppress dissent, it would weigh far more heavily on the minority than when a government without mass support tried to govern a recalcitrant populace. By virtue of his own experiences as a member of a persecuted minority, but also thanks to tolerationist principles he had advanced in his History years before, Hutchinson was extremely sensitive to personal liberty and the setbacks it suffered when popular protest made community freedom its primary goal.

The common denominator of anarchy and tyranny was the absence of law, whereas "the established authority have the law for their rule." The "corruption of a democracy" which succeeded it in Massachusetts "have no law but sic volus" (what we want, or, to bring it up to date, power to the people). Burke made a similar comment on popular rule unrestrained by moral or traditional considerations:(21)

> The right of the people is almost always
> confounded with their power. The body of
> a community, whenever it can come to act,
> can meet with no effectual resistance;
> but till power and right are the same,
> the whole body of them has no right

inconsistent with virtue.

Hutchinson thus argued that even where government appeared to violate natural law or inalienable rights, the individual could not oppose statutes which violated the most sacred principles. Such behavior would demonstrate arrogance rather than courage. Hutchinson believed men ought to suppose the collective will of society correct and their personal consciences at fault; to set individual belief above the wisdom of an entire people or government would be the height of presumption. In instances of conflict, a disgruntled person simply had to make the best of the situation. As Hutchinson wrote to Israel Williams, "the men you talk of and wish for are only to be found in Plato's Commonwealth. We that fancy we are most like them . . . see things happening many times through a false medium and are biased though insensibly by one prejudice and another. Perhaps the case is the same with some who are opposed to us." The lesson was obvious: "this consideration should tend to keep us from discontent . . . in our minds when measures are pursued contrary to what appears to us to be right."(22) Hutchinson's extraordinary sensitivity to different perspectives on the same issue, combined with his willingness to suffer for his principles, undoubtedly explains why he would be far more passive in the face of laws he disliked than most men. On the other hand, however, his insistence that men should bear their unhappy lot in silence or at best protest through traditional channels was good counter-revolutionary strategy.

In ultimate cases, where a government violated the highest morality or compelled a man to commit an act his conscience could not allow, Hutchinson believed that if he were indeed sincere, he would endure martyrdom rather than try to enforce his personal ideals against society's will. Hutchinson argued that if as a judge he had to execute a law "on its nature immoral or contrary to the Supreme Legislator of the World," he could see no alternative except to "quit my post and subject myself to any penalty rather than to obey it." Self-sacrifice represented the only option for a man devoted to tradition, social stability, and the rule of law when these conflicted with a higher morality. As he told a grand jury which he hoped would indict some rioters: "if it should unfortunately happen, that any one individual should be injured, or greatly wronged by those appointed to rule over him, and the laws of the land afford him no remedy, he ought patiently to bear his unhappy lot, and it is incumbent upon him to have recourse to that maxim, that vengeance belongeth only to the Most High."(23) Few men ever bore their lot more patiently than Hutchinson himself. However the revolutionaries must have angered him, he never ventured beyond the strictest limits of legality to counter them. Such restraint was wise strategy, as plotting violence would have turned the population against him and undone the very system of law his authority depended upon. But his theory of non-resistance also flowed logically from other aspects of his thought.

To be sure, the requirement that individuals obey the law or suffer in silence did not mean no legitimate remedy for grievances existed. People had the right to call the government's attention to their miseries. "The manner . . . of redress," however, had to be "in such ways and forms as the established rules of the constitution prescribe." Each society would develop its own rules, some affording the inhabitants more, others less opportunity to obtain relief. But if the constituted authorities themselves did not pass judgment on such petitions, there would be no way of ascertaining whether "such matters, alleged to be grievances," simply represented the unreasonable demands of private persons. Hutchinson had no qualms about exercising this right of petition with the same conscientiousness that he performed his other duties. His opposition to impressment, the quartering of British troops in Boston without provincial consent during the French and Indian War, and British policy after 1765 attested to his willingness to employ legal protest to its fullest extent.(24)

In addition to allowing for peaceable, traditional remedies, Hutchinson permitted resistance to established authority in certain limited and carefully circumscribed instances. He defined despotism, which indeed ought to be opposed by any means that did no harm to innocent people, as "a freedom in those who are vested with executive and judiciary powers, from the restraint of known established laws." While this was acceptable in Asiatic societies which had developed that form of government, the English constitution "abhorred" such tyranny and no subject had to obey an official who acted contrary to law. In such cases, "mobs, a sort of them at least, were constitutional," and Hutchinson regarded most popular

violence in Massachusetts prior to the Stamp Act as
the legitimate response to outrageous and illegal
behavior by unfaithful officials who had violated
their trusts. He especially condoned resistance to
naval impressment, cooperated with the Knowles rioters
in 1747, and in 1769 ensured Michael Corbet would be
freed for killing the members of an unauthorized
British press gang. In short, Hutchinson held that
"passive obedience and non-resistance, from the
application of them in the last century," "where they
meant that the power of the king [was] above the law"
were indeed "deservedly odious" violations of
parliamentary sovereignty and traditional English law.
Obedience to law necessarily encompassed those
entrusted with its execution, and insofar as they did
not comport with their statutorily defined functions
they were simply murderers, robbers, or (like press
gangs) kidnappers. But the Boston revolutionaries
misinterpreted Hutchinson's arguments. They
twisted them to imply that he authorized violent
opposition to laws themselves which in theory harmed
the subject although he failed to act on this principle
out of a corrupt desire to ingratiate himself with the
British government.(25)

    Hutchinson believed that the best way to remedy
social evils and restore harmony in time of crisis was
to appeal to human decency and alter men's hearts and
minds rather than tamper with the institutional
structure of government or enforce one's principles
through violence. His reluctance to recommend changes
in Massachusetts' constitution or even to call for the
radicals' severe punishment bears this out. He only
appealed, throughout the 1760s and 70s, for ration-
ality and moderation on both sides. As he concluded
his speech the day after a mob had destroyed his
house in the Stamp Act riot, "May God give us better
hearts."(26)

    Hutchinson's theory of moral and political
obligation can best be understood as a three-tiered
level of reality of God, the state, and the person.
The two lower orders ought to govern themselves by the
same norm as the highest, and in turn the person had
to obey the state's laws except when it, in turn,
violated the law of God. Each level possessed a means
of communicating and executing its authority. God
gave man natural law both through conscience and
culture, the state passed laws of its own, and the
individual could exercise his liberties and was held

liable for obedience to positive and moral law in the courts. Disobedience of a lower level to the demands of a higher could never be justified. On the one hand, this implied government officials especially had to comply with the laws upon pain of legitimate popular resistance. To be sure, Hutchinson assumed the law would be clear enough for citizens to know when such behavior took place, and in many instances it undoubtedly would be (if a public official attacked someone, for instance). By violently resisting a despotic ruler, the subject did not so much violate the law as become its enforcer. On the other hand, conscience could not be opposed to law, unlike despotism, except as non-resistance willing to suffer martyrdom. The individual could exist as a civilized person only if he appropriated the moral and traditional laws and customs of his society.

Precisely because Hutchinson so firmly refused to compromise his devotion to law and morality, he refused to concern himself with those matters of politics and ideology which preoccupied his political opponents and which radicals and liberals ever since, as opposed to conservatives, have made the touchstones of their philosophy. He denied that the form of a government, the manner in which it represented the popular voice, the social compact, or natural rights, had any validity as standards. These could indeed be part of a society's traditional arrangements, as they were in America and Britain to some extent. But they did not constitute the yardstick by which even these states could be measured.

First, Hutchinson maintained that the form of a government did not assure or deny its legitimacy. He began a speech to a grand jury on the nature of the state by explaining "the fundamental principles which all . . . rights stand upon," rather than assuming that the preservation of these rights themselves constituted the fundamental principles. The "end of government" was "the happiness of every individual, so far as it is consistent with the safety of the whole." Happiness did not simply imply material comfort but the enjoyment of "that security in our persons and property which we cannot have in a state of nature." This in turn required the preservation of moral and statute law and custom. Government did not exist to guarantee the natural rights of the individual, as it did for the revolutionaries, but to establish a situation under which some of these rights could develop. Unlike Locke and his followers, Hutchinson conceived of society as existing before the person and shaping him, rather than imagining it to be a rational choice arrived at by individuals who already possessed reason and rights. Government existed to limit, as well as sanction, the pursuit of life, liberty, property, and happiness by private individuals.(27)

Hutchinson insisted that "in order to achieve this state of security which is the purpose of government," "we are under a necessity of giving up some of our original rights in order to have a full enjoyment of the remainder." He did not argue that man surrendered his rights once and for all through a social compact when he left a state of nature to live under government. Rather, men constantly surrendered rights under the customary and legal arrangements of their respective societies. The American revolutionaries, on the other hand, believed in "inalienable rights," as the Declaration of Independence proclaimed. Hutchinson countered that no right was absolute, but all were surrendered in varying degrees depending on the state. Hutchinson here made the same point Edmund Burke would reiterate in his Reflections on the Revolution in France: "the moment you abate anything from the full rights of men each to govern himself and suffer any artificial, positive limitation upon these rights, from that moment the whole organization of government becomes a consideration of convenience."(28)

For Hutchinson, as for Burke, any government which passed laws not contradicting the laws of God was legitimate. Hutchinson remarked with indifference that "in Asia the climate or some other cause inclines to despotism. No prince in Asia has a right to deprive me of my natural liberties by compelling me to become his subject, but if for the sake of his protection I become and continue his subject, I have as much submitted my natural rights to his government there although I have parted with more of them than I should have done in Europe." It was "immaterial" in whom "the sovereign power" was lodged, because "no one form of government can be said peculiarly to be of divine authority or moral obligation than another." "Such power must be lodged somewhere or other or there is no government." Burke agreed. He wrote that "the happiness or misery of mankind, estimated by their feelings and sentiments, and not by theories of their rights" always "ought to be the standard for the conduct of legislators towards the people." As such, the "first question a good statesman" should "ask himself" is what is the "peculiar and characteristic situation of a people," and what are the "opinions, prejudices, habits, and all the circumstances that diversify and color life."(29)

"The form most stable for any government and people" did not depend upon the conscious choice of the inhabitants or their "republican virtue," but rather, Hutchinson wrote, "upon such a variety of circumstances that it seems impossible to determine it with certainty except by trial only." Why is there despotism in Asia -- because of the "climate or some other cause." Unlike Montesquieu, neither Hutchinson nor Burke expressed interest in systematizing the "principles" or causes which would tend to produce particular forms of state. Every nation simply had to be accepted for what it was. Hutchinson believed it impossible to determine why a state developed certain institutions except "by trial" -- that is, by working these out in its own particular, unique way.(30)

Hutchinson thus accepted the world for what it was, which implied a greater toleration of diversity and refusal to pass judgment on other states and nations as inferior because they differed from certain supposed fundamentals. He refused to indulge in the speculation of his contemporaries over which races and nations were best suited for liberty, modes of thought which easily turned into an excuse for subjugating and exploiting non-Europeans. Hutchinson not only regarded such prejudices as fallacious, they also contradicted Christian belief in the moral equality of mankind. Killing two of his favorite birds with one stone, Hutchinson argued that "because we differ in our several opinions, let us not slander or traduce one another's characters. We might as well quarrel, and destroy men, for their different looks or complexions." Even though he detested the Indians' culture as barbaric and fairly low on the scale of providing its subjects with happiness and security, he refused to transfer cultural distaste into racism. He lamented the distinction made in colonial wars and courts "between the guilt of killing an Indian, and that of killing an Englishman, as if God had not made of one blood all the nations of men upon the face of the earth." He likewise went beyond a mere condemnation of slavery and condemned all racial prejudice against blacks. He doubted a story that when the Indians saw a black man for the first time, they thought he was "Abamocho," or the devil. Hutchinson reasoned that they ought therefore to have considered the first white man they saw the devil as well, "their color being a median between both." Unlike most Europeans, Hutchinson found nothing innately repulsive in blacks. To be sure, his toleration of diversity may be attributed to his need to mediate between opposite political movements and thereby retain a major role for himself in Massachusetts. But his willingness to carry toleration and a respect for diversity to its humane and logical conclusions suggests that his ideas shaped his behavior instead of merely serving as an excuse for it.(31)

Hutchinson only described the development of traditions and customs in detail once -- in his discussion of his own society in the History. To determine the fundamental principles of any state, his theory would require him to write a historical account of its development instead of arguing whether it conformed to a priori standards. When Massachusetts was first settled, the country's underdeveloped economy and perilous frontier existence required "the utmost industry, economy, and frugality" to build up wealth and ensure security. This demanded "laws with heavy penalties to enforce the observance of them." Dissension and idleness could perhaps be afforded in a secure and prosperous state, but not in an isolated outpost. Since the settlers came mostly from the same social class and were "very near upon a level, more than common provisions were necessary to enforce a due obedience." Men do not easily follow orders of those they perceive as no better than they. Hutchinson thus made the interesting observation that a state does not develop its laws and an ideology of social control to reflect its social structure but rather to compensate for its inadequacies. Thus, the relatively egalitarian society of colonial New England had to create a hierarchical order.(32) One could apply Hutchinson's insight to the present and note without praise or blame how a modern America criss-crossed by hierarchies of wealth, ethnicity, race, and education vehemently asserts its commitment to equality and permits limited social mobility in order to preserve the loyalty of the lower orders.

When the strength of Massachusetts' religious ideals and the fact of its isolation from England were added to its equality and precariousness,

Hutchinson thought that "all these circumstances may pretty well account for the laws of the colony." Nowhere did he generalize from the case of Massachusetts to explain the configuration of institutions and laws in any other state. Given his careful exposition of the unique, interrelated circumstances which shaped the Bay Colony's development, he probably considered such generalizations impossible and, at any rate, irrelevant. History determined political theory.

Hutchinson and Burke therefore directly challenged the revolutionary notion that man automatically retained natural rights in any good society. Samuel Adams expressed the contrary view as well as anyone, arguing that it was "the greatest absurdity to suppose it in the power of any one or any number of men at the entering into society, to renounce any of their essential rights . . . the principal of which are life, liberty, and property." Hutchinson, on the contrary, insisted that "acts affecting property . . . must always be submitted to the supreme authority, for public use and benefit, or the ends of government cannot be answered." Adams, however, thought that men would only surrender "any essential right . . . through fear, fraud, or mistake," and under such circumstances could do whatever would be necessary to recover it, as "the eternal law of reason and the great end of society would absolutely vacate such renunciations." No man could "voluntarily become a slave."(33) The men who made the American Revolution found giving up innate rights to a sovereign power an intolerable state of slavery. For Hutchinson this surrender was a universal fact of human history.

Adams' argument had obvious inconsistencies. People did pay taxes and give up property, could be tried in courts of law where they could lose their liberty, or could be compelled to fight for their country. Natural rights theory circumvented these difficulties through the concept of representation, which enabled the people (who remained their own sovereigns) to surrender those natural rights essential for the purposes of government. Adams argued that "the supreme power cannot justly take from any man, any part of his property without his consent, except in person or by his representative." Only a government in which legislation depended on representation could claim legitimacy. Adams and his fellow patriots were not alone in holding this view. The very British administrators who planned and justified colonial taxation governed their behavior by the same Lockean fundamentals. They developed the idea of "virtual representation" to satisfy their consciences that Parliament indeed represented the colonies even as Adams tacitly admitted that the General Court represented women, children, and disfranchised people who did not meet the property qualification. The Lords of Trade, in a letter to Hutchinson's predecessor Francis Bernard, qualified his instruction to forbid new towns empowered to send representatives to the legislature by informing him it applied only to subdivisions of existing towns. Even the most zealous imperial bureaucrats admitted that recently settled parts of the province possessed "a clear, indisputable right to be represented in the assembly . . . by those principles of reason and justice which require that they should have some share in the formation of those laws by which they are to be bound and governed."(34) Except for Hutchinson and a few others, the idea that "taxation without representation is tyranny" held sway throughout the English-speaking world.

Hutchinson, however, set himself against his age by arguing that representation in the Whig sense, like natural rights, possessed no charismatic magic conferring legitimacy on governments. The very idea of representation as used by his opponents was a fiction. "Even in case of representation by election," he queried, "do not the people give up part of their natural rights when they consent to be represented by such persons as shall be chosen by the majority of the electors, although their own voices may be for some other person?" It also contradicted a man's natural rights to choose representatives only every seven years in England, or even every year in Massachusetts, as he might well disagree with his deputy's vote on a given issue and wish to remove him. To function at all, representation had to subordinate itself to majority rule, in which case the colonists' argument against parliamentary sovereignty collapsed. (They got around this by arguing that Britain and America were two separate communities, so different in interest as to require separate representations. Hutchinson did not answer this argument, except implicitly -- America and Britain had developed symbiotically.) Any contention that representation justified law, Hutchinson concluded, became "an objection against a state of government" per se "rather than any particular form," as no government founded on representation ever had or ever could exist.(35)

Yet in a very different sense, Hutchinson accepted the argument that "there should be a representation of some sort in order to legitimate government of every kind." But by "should," he only meant that "the supreme authority of every government under Heaven, is in fact the representation of its people." Any nation, as it appeared to the world and in history, presented itself in the form of whatever political institutions it had developed; without these, it could not exist at all. Moving from the general to the specific, Hutchinson argued that "what share the people have in the election of the representatives or supreme authority of Great Britain, depends not upon any established rules or maxims, but is to be collected only from practice, which has been different in different periods." In his "Dialogue Between an American and a European Englishman," Hutchinson argued that the despotic Great Khan represented Mongolia just as the democratic New England town meeting represented its towns.(36)

For Hutchinson, as for the twentieth century theorist Joseph Schumpeter, popular elections simply constituted one method among many of choosing leaders. As long as the people recognized them as such, they remained a good way to assemble a law-making body in certain instances. But Hutchinson went on to insist that when representation became elevated from a convenience into a "natural right," an absolute good which enabled each man to govern himself and became the sole criterion of sovereignty, all sorts of mischief resulted. Hutchinson thought nothing could be more pernicious than a society beating its head against a wall trying to realize impossible principles, for it could only have gotten such notions in the first place if demagogues perverted the popular will and disrupted traditional arrangements. Hutchinson explained that:(37)

> The perfection of a popular government seems to consist in the benefits supposed to arise from the free, unbiased judgment of delegates frequently elected by the unbiased voice of the people upon measures for promoting the public interest. So far as this free judgment is thrown away, and men are induced, instead of acting according to their

own judgment, to act according to the judgment of others, whether the motive be bribery, corruption, misrepresentation, or undue influence of a demagogue, so far there must be a departure from the perfection of this form of government.

Hutchinson here equated what popular governments normally consider an illegitimate form of political influence (corruption) with persuasion by politicians, which is usually acceptable. Hutchinson, however, labelled such persuasion as demagoguery and misrepresentation. Once voters were persuaded to approve measures they would not have if left to their independent judgment, the same effect was produced as if they had been bribed with money. Under such conditions, elections became vehicles through which a not-so-select group of individuals could perpetrate their schemes. To do this they have to persuade the people that they really are representing the public will, which implies that the irrelevant and pernicious principles of natural rights and representation had to have been introduced into the political debate in the first place. Paradoxically, therefore, when a "representative" government claimed to be based on "popular sovereignty," it was sufficient proof that it did not truly represent the people's wishes.

Hutchinson's critique of political representation can be made clearer by means of an analogy to John Kenneth Galbraith's idea of "artificial demand" in a mature capitalist economy.(38) Galbraith maintained that the market mechanism of supply and demand functions only if people demand goods and services they really need. Once the supplier begins to stimulate demand artificially through advertisement, the whole conception of a market price arrived at through the free interaction of producers and consumers can no longer function -- the market and the consumers are at the mercy of the producer. Similarly, Hutchinson demonstrated that when politicians began to influence the populace, the mere form of representative elections no longer guaranteed a government responsive to genuine popular interests. He refused to admit the possibility that such incendiaries may truly represent genuine popular resentment, rather than manufacture it.

Hutchinson reached the conclusion that genuinely representative government could only function in the absence of the sort of democratic politics he saw emerging in Massachusetts. He tolerated eighteenth century town government if it respected its proper limits, but not once the people ceased to act in their true interest. Conversely, the difficulties of popular government could be minimized by limiting the penetration of politics into society, the best way being to ensure the personal independence of those elected to office. Hutchinson did not mean by this independence from attachment to the royal prerogative as his opponents did, but rather independence of their constituents. He insisted that for "each representative to vote according to the opinion of his town is unconstitutional and contradicts the very idea of a Parliament," and had opposed Boston's right to instruct him on currency matters. Gentlemen in politics ought to be elected because they could disinterestedly perceive the common good, not because they adhered to particular political platforms. Similarly, Burke too argued that "authoritative instructions from people which their legislators are bound blindly and implicitly to obey . . . are things utterly unknown to the laws of the land, and which arise from a fundamental mistake of the whole order and tenor of our constitution." Popular government could work only if it remained unpolluted by the evils of mass politics.(39)

Hutchinson undoubtedly derived his notion of the legislator's role from his own experience with the Massachusetts General Court, where deputies decided matters of provincial concern after debate and persuasion. Most legislators lacked any factional ties, which were usual in the British Parliament, to hinder them from making up their minds free of influence. This uncorrupted system endured because towns did not usually elect assemblymen for their opinions on either the principles of government or particular issues, but because they trusted their judgment. That this ceased to be true after the 1760s exemplified the discontinuity between revolutionary and provincial politics. For Hutchinson to be able to write that "<u>merely</u> a difference in opinion upon the principles of government had caused many of the best men in the province to be denominated tyrants" illustrates how much his conceptions of legislation and representation differed from those of his opponents.(40) Prudence, personal morality, and service to the community determined fitness for public office.

Precisely because Hutchinson tolerated "mere" differences in political principles, he opposed nearly everyone else in eighteenth century Anglo-America and agreed with Burke in not censuring all political associations or parties out of hand. He realized that "it is impossible for men in any society to be of the same mind." "Doubts and disagreements" were "not only necessary, but useful, for by this means the good of the country is often attained, the most salutary means of government adopted, and the whole business of the public weal better executed." Hutchinson found unanimity neither useful nor desirable in public affairs, much as he did not think all nations ought to conform to the same principles. Like Burke, he considered "party divisions . . . inseparable from free government."(41)

But Hutchinson by no means approved of the modern mass parties to which the "Age of Democratic Revolution" gave birth. Such views have been erroneously attributed to Burke, who explicitly defined a legitimate party as "a body of men united for promoting by their joint endeavors the national interest upon some particular <u>principle</u> in which they are all agreed." The key word is principle. Neither Burke nor Hutchinson had any use for parties based on ambition or which threatened the fundamentals of a sound constitution. Burke condemned factions held together by "leaders [who] choose to make themselves bidders at an auction of popularity" and "become flatterers instead of legislators, the instruments, not the guides of the people," just as Hutchinson found no virtue in associations where men "have not a spark of public spirit and see the public interest rise or fall with no other pleasure or than as their own particular interest is concerned." Both men also abhorred parties which threatened the legitimacy of the state. Hutchinson declared that "confederacies to limit the supreme authority can never be admitted under any government." Burke condemned the French revolutionary parties as such confederacies, and even considered the "king's friends" in Britain "private inclinations of a court, against the general sense of the people" to be "a scheme for undermining all the foundations of our freedom" Hutchinson took the same attitude toward his opponents in Massachusetts.(42)

While far more permissive than their contemporaries, Burke and Hutchinson severely circumscribed their attitude toward parties. They did not accept parties based upon ideology, self-interest, or mere self-perpetuation. By a legitimate association, they understood a group of disinterested men who would be members of the legislature itself or people of similar social prominence. They only recognized the sort of divisions which had divided the respective governing aristocracies of England and Massachusetts during the relatively stable first half of the eighteenth century.

Hutchinson especially feared the results when ideologically-based platforms of factious politicians extended themselves to the population at large. Throughout the History, he recorded the deplorable effects of politics on manners and morals, especially in connection with currency disputes. Hutchinson's generalizations on the politicization of life would not be out of place in Gustave Le Bon's The Crowd or Ortega y Gasset's The Revolt of the Masses. He noted that "no subject affords a larger freedom, not only for mere cavils, but for plausibility of exception, than that of government." "Resentment is never stronger than when it proceeds from party," for politics caused "all sense of guilt incurred by groundless imputations upon character" to be "easily lost." In addition, "truth and right were more frequently, in a higher degree, violated in political contests and animosities than upon any other occasion." Groups of like-minded men mutually reinforced such deplorable conduct, and were "capable jointly of such acts as being the act of any one would cause them to be ashamed." Hutchinson frequently expressed a desire to leave politics, and his belief that those who could not make amends for their political activity might well be damned souls is explained by such remarks. Such a theory of party also fitted well with his counter-revolutionary activities; by approving the sort of political association to which he belonged, he could rule out most others as insurrectionary or corrupt.(43)

Hutchinson was not only extremely far removed from approving of any conception of natural rights, representation, or political activity such as his contemporaries, he also denied the idea of a social compact, arguing "that all that is said of natural contracts is merely ideal." A written constitution restricting the rights of government would render the state a "mere rope of sand" as it would imply that "every individual has a right to judge when the acts of government are just and unjust and to submit or not to submit" according to his own interpretation of the restrictions which the contract placed upon him. Trotting out his acid test of history and custom, Hutchinson found no "instance of any government from the creation of the world established upon such fundamentals which has continued for a long period of time without alteration." He challenged his opponents to study British history since the days of Julius Caesar and asked, "Have the people ever assembled together in one body so as that we may suppose these fundamental" rights "to have been settled by the majority of individuals?"(44) How could anyone be so misled as to believe in the sincerity of politicians who made criteria which the world had never seen the only test of a legitimate government?

But while Hutchinson dismissed the idea of "natural contracts," he clearly had a notion, similar to Edmund Burke's that "society is indeed a contract." But far from being a conditional document which bestowed legitimacy on a government, it was, Burke noted, an ongoing "partnership in all science, a partnership in all art, a partnership in every virtue and perfection . . . between those who are living, those who are dead, and those who are to be born." Hutchinson similarly thought than an individual could not place himself outside his society's customs and pass judgment upon them, as his knowledge of natural law and whatever blessings of civilization he enjoyed came from his state. Consider Hutchinson's example of the Asiatic despot. Everyone living under his rule continuously contracted his allegiance to him by accepting his protection. The social contract was unconditional: the subject accepted the social and political system, faults and benefits, under which he lived. True, some governments were clearly better than others because they granted more liberty to the subject. Hutchinson agreed with his opponents that "the best constitution of government must most certainly be that in which we have parted with the fewest of our natural rights -- that is, where we part with no more than absolutely necessary to attain the very ends of society and government." He even took great pride in demonstrating that "the government under which we have the happiness to live is therefore the most happy, because we have never yielded up more of the private rights of individuals than was needful to invest the government with power sufficient to protect us." But the key difference remained that he refused to make a uniquely fortunate circumstance the basis of a universal judgment: if the Pilgrims and Puritans had removed to Tartary, they would "have been subject to the Great Khan."(45) If rights only existed in a customary and developmental perspective, they could not be made the basis of political revolution or constitutional change.

Because Hutchinson considered contracts which effected the passage from a state of nature to a state of society as fictional, it did not follow that he thought a state of nature itself to be an imaginary concept. In fact, he had a far more vivid image of it than those of his contemporaries who used natural man to define political obligation. Hutchinson's studies of the American Indians convinced him that the aborigines were "averse to human society" and "as near to a state of nature as any people upon the globe."(46) They had no government to speak of, because without an "idea of property, but few laws are necessary." If there were any "personal injuries or affronts, every man was his own avenger."

Hutchinson's discussion of the Indians stands out most curiously in his History. For the first and only time, he abandoned his careful weighing of pros and cons and launched a tirade describing the pathetic condition of men obliged to live outside civilized society. This unique chapter makes it possible to argue that Hutchinson cared less about accurately describing Indian society and more about using it as a vehicle to demonstrate the irrelevance of any argument that man's benefits in the state of nature could serve as a standard to judge the law of a civilized society. It is also possible he wished to deflate the "noble savage" idealization of the Indian as free and more virtuous than over-civilized man.

Immorality in nearly every respect characterized natural society. Having "as little as can well be imagined of religion," the Indians were "false, malicious," "infinitely cruel to their enemies," and lazy and idle as well -- "never employing themselves about any other business than what was absolutely necessary." Hutchinson continued his tirade to mention their "indifferent" intelligence and to describe their hygiene as "more dirty, foul, and sordid than swine." He saved his choicest epithets for the Indians' sexual mores, or rather their lack of them. "Husbands and wives, parents and children lived always in one room or wigwam" and "made no privacy of those actions which nature teaches even some irrational animals to be ashamed of," such as "the elephant, the deer, etc. who never copulate but in secret." Man without society lived at a level beneath the beasts themselves. The term "state of nature" was actually a euphemism. Hutchinson was even more scornful of the unfaithfulness of husbands and wives, and observed that "a young woman was not less esteemed for having accompanied with a man, their usual practice being to live together upon trial, before they took one another for husband and wife." Even when married, Indians made no scruple to "run from one wigwam to another and" -- as Hutchinson delicately phrased it -- "take what they like." In conclusion, it may be safely asserted that Hutchinson posed a purely rhetorical question at the conclusion of his analysis -- "did ever any other people, in this respect, approach nearer to the brutal part of the creation?" A hardworking, churchgoing Puritan who remained faithful to his wife for a quarter century after her death must have considered these among the worst crimes a people could commit.

The image of a virtual Hell upon earth, then, appeared in Hutchinson's mind whenever his opponents invoked a state of nature. Natural man possessed only the unenviable right to be fouler than a pig and more brutal than an elephant. When Hutchinson told the General Court that "I would not urge [the instructions in] my commission" to justify "an encroachment upon your natural or constitutional rights," he linked rather than separated the two categories. The crucial test of a right was not that it was "natural," but rather that it was "constitutional" according to the particular arrangements of a given society.(47)

In short, Hutchinson allowed the legitimacy of any government except one based upon the inalienable transfer of natural rights into a state of society, the most exceptionable of these being the supposed right of all individuals to consent conditionally to the laws of the state that governed them. The one state which his political enemies considered free and not an excuse for slavery was the one, in his opinion, which constituted no legitimate government at all. In his discussion of the Indians, as in his treatment of societies in revolution, Hutchinson joined tradition with morality. Revolutionary and natural societies possessed neither. Morality, justice, and the benefits of an orderly society only developed if people had enough self-discipline to restrain their temptation to degenerate morally or espouse fatuous Utopian schemes in politics. Hutchinson knew enough history to realize the precariousness of "rights" of any sort. He believed that to tamper with their foundations by raising irrelevant questions about the social order marked the unspeakable folly he witnessed in his own time.

FOOTNOTES

1. John B. Morrall, *Political Thought in Medieval Times* (London, 1958, New York, 1962), 10.

2. See especially J. G. A. Pocock, *The Machiavellian Moment: Florentine Political Thought and the Atlantic Republic Tradition* (Princeton, N.J., 1975), 83-330. The following paragraphs are indebted to Leo Strauss, *Natural Right and History* (Chicago, 1953) and Eric Voegelin, *The New Science of Politics* (Chicago, 1952). Strauss draws attention to the distinction between natural rights and natural law, and Voegelin has traced the development of Gnostic and Utopian thought from the Middle Ages to modern times.

3. See in particular the contrast between Bailyn, *The Ideological Origins of the American Revolution* (Cambridge, 1967); and Randolph G. Adams, *Political Ideas of the American Revolution* (New York, 1939; first published 1922). "Dialogue," M. XXVIII, 106.

4. Christopher Dawson, *The Gods of Revolution* (New York, 1972), 45, finds in the American Revolution "two features which were to become characteristic of the revolutionary movements of the future. One was the conception of political revolution as part of a universal and almost cosmic change which far transcended the local and historical circumstances of any particular state. The other, which is closely related, was the note of messianic idealism, which looked forward to a social millennium and the birth of a new humanity." Conservative scholars who see a conservative American Revolution can profit much from Dawson's analysis of the revolution; *ibid.*, 38-47. See in particular Russell Kirk, *The Roots of American Order* (La Salle, Illinois, 1974), ch. xi; Robert Brown, *Middle-Class Democracy*; Willmoore Kendall and George Carey, *The Basic Symbols of the American Political Tradition* (Baton Rouge, La., 1971). Useful correctives are Richard B. Morris, *The Emerging Nations and the American Revolution* (New York, 1970); Robert R. Palmer, *The Age of the Democratic Revolution* (Princeton, N.J., 1959), I, 213-235; Cecilia M. Kenyon, "Republicanism and Radicalism in the American

Revolution: An Old-Fashioned Interpretation," *William and Mary Quarterly*, 3rd. ser. XIX (1962), 153-182; Bernard Bailyn, "Political Experience and Enlightenment Ideas in Eighteenth Century America," *American Historical Review*, LXVII (1962), 339-351. As late as the 1820s, Prince Clemens von Metternich understood America's world-wide revolutionary threat very well, if allowances are made for his prejudice: "They have distinctly and clearly announced their intention to set not only power against power, but to express it more exactly, altar against altar. In their indecent declarations they have cast blame and scorn on the instituions of Europe most worthy of respect, on the principles of its greatest sovereigns, on the whole of those measures which a sacred duty no less than an evident necessity has forced our governments to adopt to frustrate plans most criminal. . . . If this flood of evil doctrines and pernicious examples should extend over the whole of America, what would become of our religious and political institutions, of the moral force of our governments, and of that conservative system which has saved Europe from complete dissolution?" Quoted in Richard B. Morris, *Emerging Nations*, 157.

5. Mary Beth Norton, "The Loyalist Critique of the American Revolution," in *The Development of a Revolutionary Mentality: Library of Congress Symposium* (Washington, D.C., 1972), 130, 132. For the Founding Fathers, see Douglass Adair, *Fame and the Founding Fathers* (New York, 1974).

6. The content -- though not the application -- of Christian morality and natural law were considered perfectly evident until modern times; see C. S. Lewis, *The Abolition of Man* (New York, 1947). Hutchinson's religious convictions were genuine. He was pleased to find a religious bent in one of his sons, and deplored the fact that "want of religion is no blemish in the present age." The preface to his last will and testament summarized these sentiments best: "my body I commend to the earth, to be buried at as small expense as can consist with decency; my soul I commend to the mercy of God, through the merits of Christ, humbly imploring the forgiveness of the innumerable sins of my long life." *Diary*, II, 342, 326, 366 [third person altered to first in

final quotation].

7. Quincy, 113.

8. Burke, "Appeal from the Old to the New Whigs" (1791), IV, 169. History, I, 133; Quincy, 219; Burke, "Reflections on the Revolution in France" (1790), III, 356.

9. Quincy, 222, 176.

10. Ibid., 259-261.

11. History, III, 240; Burke, "Reflections" (1790), III, 355; Quincy, 312, 224.

12. "Dialogue," M. XXVIII, 107; H to ?, August 27, 1772, M. XXVII, 678; Burke, "Speech at Bristol Previous to the Election" (1780), II, 417; Bernard Mason, ed., The American Colonial Crisis: The Daniel Leonard-John Adams Letters to the Press, 1774-1775 (New York, 1972), 120.

13. History, III, 313; H to Samuel Swift, January 4, 1774, M. XXVII, 1166; H to John Pownall, August 31, 1765, M. XXVI, 305.

14. Quincy, 173.

15. Bertrand de Jouvenel, Sovereignty (Chicago, 1957), 169; H to Lord Dartmouth, October 9, 1773, M. XXVII, 1025. Burke, "Tract on the Popery Laws" (?), VI, 322.

16. H to Israel Williams, February 23, 1774, Williams Papers; Diary, I, 174; Burke, "Tract on the Popery Laws," VI, 322.

17. Burke, "First Letter on a Regicide Peace" (1796), V, 308-314; "Additions III," 31, 29.

18. "Dialogue," M. XXVIII, 106; H to Francis Bernard, October 19, 1769, M. XXVI, 830.

19. Quincy, 220; Bradford, 341; Quincy, 175, 223, 261; H to Thomas Goldthwait, January 29, 1771, M. XXV, 498; H to Lord Hillsborough [October, 1770?], M. XXVII, 32; History, III, 135; H to John Pownall, March 21, 1771, M. XXVI, 1008; H to Thomas Whately, October 3, 1770, M. XXVII,

19; "Dialogue," M. XXVIII, 107.

20. Quincy, 246; H to ?, December 30, 1773, M. XXVII, 1158; H to ?, December 23, 1773, Massachusetts Historical Society; H to Israel Mauduit [December, 1773], M. XXVII, 1150.

21. H to Thomas Pownall, May 1, 1770, M. XXVI, 1040; Burke, "Reflections" (1790), III, 311.

22. H to Israel Williams, August 8, 1759, Williams Papers.

23. "Dialogue," M. XXVIII, 107; Quincy, 268.

24. Bradford, 341.

25. Ibid., 334; H to Richard Jackson, July 27, 1768, M. XXVI, 659; Bradford, 203; History, III, 234.

26. Quincy, 173.

27. Quincy, 234, 307.

28. Ibid., 307; Burke, "Reflections" (1790), III, 311.

29. "Dialogue," M. XXVIII, 108, 106; History, I, 181; Burke, "Speech on the Petition of the Unitarians" (1792), VII, 45.

30. H to Francis Bernard, December 10, 1770, M. XXVII, 127.

31. Ibid., 237; History, III, 6; "Dialogue," M. XXVIII, 107; History, I, 400. Most colonials did consider blacks innately inferior; see Winthrop Jordan, White Over Black (Chapel Hill, N.C., 1968).

32. History, I, 369-370 is also source for the next paragraph.

33. [Samuel Adams], "A State of the Rights of the Colonies" (1772), in Merrill Jensen, ed., Tracts of The American Revolution, 1763-1776 (Indianapolis, New York, and Kansas City, 1967), 237; History, III, 131.

34. [Samuel Adams], "Rights of the Colonies," 239;

Board of Trade to Francis Bernard, Bernard Papers, IX, 310, Sparks Manuscripts, Harvard College Library.

35. Bradford, 339; Jean-Jacques Rousseau shared Hutchinson's contempt for the concept of representation. He wrote "sovereignty cannot be represented, for the same reason that it cannot be alienated; its essence is the general will, and will cannot be represented -- either it is the general will or it is something else; there is no intermediate possibility. Thus the people's deputies are not, and could not be, its representatives, they are merely its agents." Rousseau classified government by assembly as an elective aristocracy. The Social Contract, tr. Maurice Cranston (Baltimore, 1968), 141, 115.

36. Diary, I, 335; "Dialogue," M. XXVIII, 103.

37. Joseph Schumpeter, Capitalism, Socialism, and Democracy (third edition; New York, 1950), 250-283; "Additions, III," 37.

38. John Kenneth Galbraith, The Affluent Society (paperback edition, New York, 1958), 129-130.

39. "Hutchinson in America," 52; Burke, "Speech to Electors of Bristol" (1774), II, 96.

40. "Additions, III," 26.

41. Quincy, 236; Burke, "Thoughts on the Present State of the Nation" (1770), I, 271.

42. Burke, "Reflections" (1790), III, 560; H to Israel Williams, April 26, 1765, M. XXVI, 265; History, III, 125; Burke, "Thoughts on the Cause of the Present Discontents" (1770), I, 536. Richard Hofstadter's assessment of Burke's attitude toward parties, The Idea of a Party System (Berkeley, Los Angeles, and London, 1970), 29-35, does not consider that he only approved of a certain type of party; he would have abhorred the parties defended by Martin Van Buren.

43. History, III, 5, 232, 302, 6.

44. "Dialogue," M. XXVIII, 107-108.

45. Ibid., 103; Quincy, 307; Burke, "Reflections" (1790), III, 359.

46. Hutchinson's discussion of Indians is found in History, I, 388-400.

47. Bradford, 251 (see also 200).

VIII: CRITIQUE OF REVOLUTIONARY LANGUAGE AND LOGIC

Hutchinson believed that revolutionary theorizing presented a complete yet misleading view of the world. However, he also thought that it asked all the wrong questions, proceeded through contradictory reasoning, and had nothing to do with how the real world worked. Its principal fallacy, from which all others proceeded, involved erecting false, absolute standards to judge mutable reality. By seeking to discover the meaning of history, the fundamental nature of the English constitution, the correct form of government, and the rights of man, the American revolutionaries had embarked on a hopeless task. Hutchinson argued that every society had its own identity, which was flexible and yet consistent with its internal standards.

However, because revolutionary thought missed the mark by so wide a margin, Hutchinson could not accept his opponents' sincerity. He believed he had realized the contradictions of radical Whig thought and could not imagine that all sincere men would also do so. Hence, he did not attribute revolutionary ideas to mistaken good will but to conscious evil intentions. The instigators played havoc with the rules of language and logic -- the only means through which civilized man could communicate this tradition of morality and law -- as freely as they overturned political institutions. In their ambitious efforts to rule America, the Massachusetts incendiaries destroyed one world and created another.

Hutchinson recognized the power with which the revolutionaries' ideas appealed to the American people. He carefully analyzed the manner in which they manipulated words and sought to make outrageous behavior and "absurd principles of government" seem not only lawful but heroic. They ingeniously "adopted their arguments to the great purpose of obtaining the voice of the people." Hutchinson perceived that once they asserted a false principle such as natural rights a correct line of reasoning could follow and the argument would appear perfectly logical to the average man. He found in some manifestoes a "style [which] was correct" and "reasoning [that was] plausible." But "the facts" were "so represented and such a construction made of them, to give a favorable appearance to a system which was a mere figment."(1) For a democratic revolution to succeed, it had to alter meanings of words and modes of reasoning to break down obedience to traditional authority.

Hutchinson's treatment of the transformation of language in times of ideological politics still offers research possibilities for historians. He began by observing that "in political discussions, talents for compositions which would admit of a doubtful construction are exceedingly useful." For example, some writers had distorted the word subjection, which had never meant "any more than subject to the supreme legislative authority of Britain, in common with their fellow subjects in the island." But the radicals "improved" it and made it synonymous with oppression. A "Tory" had hitherto been someone who either favored restoration of the House of Stuart or believed in royal rather than parliamentary supremacy: "all on a sudden," everyone who opposed the revolutionary movement was branded with that name. The General Court distinguished between the "realm" and "kingdom" of England to show that the colonies belonged to the latter but not the former, and were therefore subject to the King but not to Parliament. Hutchinson dismissed this unprecedented idea as a "mere chimera," and instead argued at length that the King was both part of Parliament and subject to it himself.(2)

In another instance, the Massachusetts representatives "acknowledged their obligation to yield a <u>due</u> subordination to the legislative authority of Great Britain," and "considered a <u>constitutional subordination</u> to Parliament their great privilege and security." But since "no judgment could be formed to what acts of this authority subordination was <u>due</u>, or what degree of subordination was <u>constitutional</u>," these statements cloaked a denial of the sovereignty they pretended to assert. Hutchinson posed the question "who is to be the judge of" what extent the colonies were to obey Parliament. When the colonies claimed this power for themselves, they were thenceforth "submitting to just nothing."(3) The revolutionaries also inflated some words according to their purposes. They employed "big sounding words" without regard for their true meaning to captivate the populace:(4)

That which used to be called the "court house" or "town house" had acquired the name of the "state house"; -- "the House of Representatives of Massachusetts Bay" had assumed the name of "His Majesty's Commons"; -- the "debates of the assembly" are styled "parliamentary debates"; -- "acts of Parliament," "acts of the British Parliament"; -- "the province laws," "the laws of the land"; -- "the charter," a grant from royal grace or favor, is styled the "compact."

The thrust of the Massachusetts assembly's language was not that of a body defining traditional liberties, but that of a would-be sovereign body claiming "separate but equal" status with the mother country.

At the same time, words which described violence lost their impact. Hutchinson observed that terms such as "riots, routs, and unlawful assemblies" had ceased to excite "great horror in our minds" from frequent usage. He tried to convey their true importance to several of the juries he addressed as chief-justice: "if we were told that such a man's house was to be destroyed -- such a man to be killed -- it would fill us with great dread of the consequences."(5) Hutchinson realized that the counter-revolutionary must restore the correct use of language.

The American revolutionaries took their greatest liberties with the word "liberty" itself. Hutchinson considered it "very extraordinary to find the same persons contending for an unlimited freedom of thought and action which they would confine wholly to themselves." The loyalists could hardly "contradict what the other [side] advanced and [were] not permitted even to reason without being treated in the most abusive manner and vilified without bounds." "Every supposed advance" toward liberty "brought a restraint upon freedom of judgment in the power of attaining to it." The revolutionaries subordinated means to ends, and Hutchinson bitterly concluded that "nothing is more frequent than for men, in the height of their struggle for liberty for themselves, to deny it to others."(6) Hutchinson thought revolutionary "liberty" simply meant popular power, regardless of what the power was to be used for. He therefore confronted his opponents with another definition roughly synonymous with the modern notion of civil and personal liberty.

Hutchinson refused, however, to grant any moral validity to the revolutionaries' definition of "liberty." The contradiction between their theory and practice served as one of Hutchinson's "Strictures on the Declaration" of Independence. He wrote, "I wish to ask the delegates of Maryland, Virginia, and the Carolinas, how their constituents justify the depriving of more than an hundred thousand of their rights to liberty, the pursuit of happiness, and in some degree of their lives, if these rights are absolutely inalienable." Similarly, where was real freedom in the new state? Rather, as Hutchinson remarked sarcastically, "under the present free government, no man, by writing or speaking," could "contradict any part of this declaration without being deemed an enemy to his country and exposed to the rage of people." He thought the American Revolution fused two sorts of activity he abhorred: the morally corrupting effects of politics with the fanaticism hitherto reserved for religious movements.(7)

Hutchinson thus concluded that the revolutionaries either did not believe or could not understand any of their own principles since these were either internally contradictory or denied by their own activities. In the "Dialogue between an American and a European Englishman," Hutchinson demonstrated not only how the colonists' behavior negated their arguments, but he progressively exposed their fraudulent appeals to history, philosophy, and tradition. He thereby hoped to refute, in concentrated form, the major arguments which revolutionaries have always used to legitimate themselves.(8)

Hutchinson first showed how the shifting, escalating content of the revolutionaries' demands called their sincerity into question. To the "American's" insistence that the real grievance of parliamentary taxation lay at the heart of the quarrel, the "European" replied: "what guarantee have we that as soon as you are relieved from external taxes you will not alter your mind and not incline any longer to submit to regulations of your trade." The North Americans had always resisted the authority of the Navigation Acts, and showed no more disposition to obey trade regulations than to pay taxes. Referring to successful colonial requests for British assistance in the French and Indian War, the "European" summed up that "when you can make the authority of Parliament secure for your protection or benefit in any respect you have been ready to own and even to seek it," but "when any burden is to be laid upon you, however equitable, you shun and refuse to submit to it." Since the denial of parliamentary authority made no sense and revealed confused if not hypocritical reasoning, that principle could not be the Revolution's true cause. Rather, as the "European" noted, "we must move closer to the point."

Did the revolutionaries' appeals to ancient history, political philosophy, and the English constitution -- which they held up as precedents arguing that parliamentary taxation was unlawful, unprecedented, and a sign of impending slavery -- possess any more validity? Hutchinson thought not. When the "American" claimed that "the Greeks and Romans are worthy of the imitation of Englishmen" in their "love of liberty," Hutchinson denied that appeals to the remote past held any lessons for the present. The "American" argued that because Rome did not tax its colonies neither should Britain, but the "European" countered with an example from Livy showing that during the Punic Wars the Senate did in fact demand a payment from the colonies and severely punished those which refused. Hutchinson did not assert that his counter-precedent was correct, and therefore Britain should in fact tax the colonies. He merely introduced it to show the selective partiality of such historical citations. History taught men nothing apart from what they had already determined to wrench from context to support their own requirements. In fact, the "European" remarked that his opponent had assumed a greater knowledge of ancient history than the facts warranted: the modern world remained "much in the dark" about Roman history and did not even have an accurate idea of Rome's own tax structure, let alone that of its colonies. And granting everything that the "American" claimed for Roman colonial liberty, the "European" could not see "how it will conduce to your purpose." The situations were completely different. No uniform rules had been laid down at the beginning of time for governing dependencies. Every case had to be decided on the principles of a particular constitution. "The Roman colonies had their informal government," and "so have the English colonies." In this brief passage, Hutchinson summarily sought to destroy all revolutionary appeals to non-existent pasts which have been held up as models for impossible futures.

Hutchinson then attacked revolutionary natural

rights in the same manner. Locke's *Second Treatise of Government* contained far more ambiguities and more conservative thinking than the revolutionaries thought. It did not only speak of rights, but also of order, obligation, and majority rule. Hutchinson arranged to quote Locke against himself. When the "American" cited the *Treatise* to argue that "when property is taken away without the individual's consent" it "subverts the end of government," the "European" retorted that everyone living under a regime had "to submit to the determination of the majority and to be controlled by it, or else the original compact whereby he with others incorporated into one society would signify nothing." He concluded by stating "I reverence Mr. Locke as much as you." Hutchinson thus favored a majoritarian rather than a libertarian reading of Locke, as has Wilmoore Kendall. Kendall has pointed out that Locke believed the majority in any system of government would not wish to subvert the common good and could be counted upon to do justice. Otherwise the state would fall into chaos. As Parliament represented the majority, America had to submit. Only by defining itself as a separate society could the colonies get around Britain's opposite Lockean doctrine.

Nevertheless, while Britain threw America's reading of Locke back in its face, and Hutchinson found it useful to cite Locke against himself to show the anarchic consequences once individuals denied the majority's authority, he was no Lockean himself. He based his political theory on natural law and custom, not natural rights and compact. When the Massachusetts house of representatives began to introduce Lockean arguments into its debates, Hutchinson chided them that tossing around citations did not constitute rational argument, stressing in one instance that "the quotation from Mr. Locke, detached as it is from the rest of the treatise, cannot be applied to your case."(9) Hutchinson primarily used Locke to show the dubious interpretation Samuel Adams, James Otis and others had made of his works. Political philosophy, like history, did not dictate its application in any situation. The work of a great thinker could admit multiple interpretations which revealed more about the interpreters than the author.

Hutchinson found the revolutionaries' appeals to the British constitution equally ludicrous. When the "American" argued that certain fundamental documents such as Magna Carta constituted laws no subsequent Parliament could violate, the "European" slyly replied that were Magna Carta to be enforced, Americans would have to accept the bishopric they had so long opposed as a threat to their religious liberty, since the document expressly recognized the existence of bishops. The "European" posited instead that he could find "no principle in the English Constitution more fundamental . . . than that no act can be made or passed in any Parliament which it shall not be in the power of a subsequent Parliament to alter and repeal." There could be "no idea of any government being unalterable"; if a former Parliament could innovate, so could a contemporary one. In fact, "the rights of British subjects vary in every age and perhaps every session of Parliament." Like Roman history or philosophical tracts, British law could not be deduced for all time by wrenching a document out of its historical context and contending that it prescribed immutable standards. The selective quotation of authoritative texts, compounded with their misinterpretation, demonstrated the weakness and duplicity of revolutionary logic.

Hutchinson's theory of the mutability of government may seem at first glance to contradict his vehement assertion that the principles of a constitution had to be "fixed." But there need be no problem here. In fact, Hutchinson's very reverence for tradition implied social institutions and law did change to meet developing circumstances, but they altered in accordance with their own fundamental principles. British law had evolved through the interaction of parliamentary sovereignty, the common law courts, and the crown. Hutchinson's idea of traditional legitimacy did not imply stagnation. The balance between innovation and conservation had to be a function of prudence and flexibility, rather than rigid adherence to abstract standards. Deducing some or other rights from the tradition of English law and labelling them fundamentals conveyed nothing of its true nature.

Hutchinson's attitude that prudence and respect for the past, as embodied in living institutions, must govern but not inhibit change coincided with Edmund Burke's, for whom prudence was "the God of this lower world." Hutchinson similarly asked, "Is not prudence a part of morality," for rash alterations in government would produce unspeakable harm for which the innovator would be morally liable.(10)

Hutchinson's notion of prudence, however, operated in the limited sphere of permitting careful adjustments to circumstances within a traditional framework. It could never serve as an excuse to violate fundamental moral principles, but rather guided their institutionalization. Hutchinson could advise his friend Israel Williams to be "more of a willow and less of an oak" and gracefully sit with his political foes in the Hampshire Court of Sessions. But in the next breath, he assured Williams that "if it was a matter of religion or morality and there was room to exercise conscience, whatever the world thought of it, I would not urge you to give up your judgment."(11) Prudence functioned to determine how and when to articulate one's principles most effectively, or to permit flexibility on matters of lesser importance, not to dictate what moral or political principles ought to be. As in the case of impressment and the Stamp Act, Hutchinson refrained from pressing his arguments for colonial rights to the utmost because he feared that it would be counter-productive. But that did not mean he therefore readjusted his belief in them.

For Hutchinson, prudence differed vastly from pragmatism. Moral standards and social customs could not be altered for the sake of personal interest or even if someone thought that the common good depended on immoral behavior. Such people would find out, as did Governor Bernard when he flirted with the radicals early in his administration, "the truth of Sir Robert Walpole's saying that one expedient makes necessary a great many others." For his own part, Hutchinson confessed that he could have "kept upon terms with" the faction opposed to parliamentary supremacy by waiving his most cherished ideals, but he preferred "to bear the full weight of their resentment rather than to show them my countenance." Hutchinson's career and writings exemplified his own claim that "I have endeavored for thirty years past to maintain a steady uniform conduct in matters of government and to avoid all extremes."(12) He himself fully believed flexibility and moderation did not necessarily contradict a firm adherence to principle.

Within the limits of his principles, however, Hutchinson was extremely cautious. In practice as in his writings, he strove for balance, harmony, and reconciliation. These virtues required prudence, but their achievement would realize Hutchinson's principles. As early as 1751, he feared that his "prejudice in favor of myself and my friends carried me beyond the bounds of prudence," and fifteen years later remarked that "we are not always upon our guard, and resentment upon . . . injuries may lead me to dangerous expressions which I wish to avoid." He described his policy as follows: "I desire as long as I live to promote internal concord and harmony and to prevent unreasonable and intemperate zeal." Men were not themselves in the grip of passion, and "great zeal and warmth of temper . . . must subside before there can be any room to hope for an accommodation" of disputes.(13) But when the revolutionaries challenged the fundamentals of government and morality themselves, Hutchinson felt obliged to assume an isolated stance as a defender of virtue in a hopelessly corrupt world. He played this role during both the monetary crises of the 1740s and the Revolution.

Hutchinson's critique of natural rights, popular sovereignty, the politicization of government and society, and radical appeals to "history" and "philosophy" all tended toward the conclusion that revolution cannot be justified on principle. It had to be defended by such specious arguments that no man of good faith could propagate them. Hence the "Dialogue between an American and a European" concluded with an analysis of how men of neither wealth nor importance who wished to achieve prominence made the American Revolution. Déclassé individuals -- intellectuals -- who manipulated the political language and events of the age to take over the government destroyed one of the world's happiest societies. To topple a social order, they first had to annihilate its customary discourse.

If the population had understood their true principles, revolution would have been impossible. When he read the Declaration of Independence, Hutchinson wrote that "the reasons for their rebellion would appear to the last degree frivolous if the facts upon which they are founded were fully known."(14)

For a revolution to be just, like England's Glorious Revolution, it had to be limited to restoring law and morality in the face of wanton abuses of power. But Hutchinson saw revolutions occurring where they were least needed, in free governments:

A thirst for liberty seems to be the ruling passion not only of America but of the present

age. In governments under arbitrary rule
it may have a salutary effect but in
governments where as much freedom is enjoyed
as can consist with the ends of government
it must work anarchy and confusion.

Revolution contributed to another tragedy as well.
Observing the case of the Wilkes Riots in England,
Hutchinson remarked that "such licentiousness cannot
long continue without either carrying you into a state
of anarchy, or else, if suppressed, endangering your
just rights and liberties." Once revolutionary principles gained some measure of popular credence,
restoration of a government limited by law and custom
became a dim possibility. Tyranny could only succeed
anarchy.(15)

Hutchinson tried, in his own writings, to adhere
carefully to the rules of argument he criticized his
opponents of violating. He rarely used quotations from
classical, Biblical, constitutional, or philosophical
authority. Such citations, out of context, were
valueless. Their absence did not imply that Hutchinson
was ignorant of the political theory of others and had
none of his own, as has been argued.(16) His discussion
of Locke in the "Dialogue" and his use of Locke's
religious ideas in a letter and in the History
revealed that he understood not only the complexity but
also the inconsistencies of Lockean theory. Rather,
Hutchinson's refusal to substitute citation for
argument showed that, almost alone among his contemporaries, he had thought through the implications of the
use of undigested argument both for political theory
and its popular reception. He preferred to develop a
mode of thought which relied upon induction from the
observation of history and custom to supplant the
hodgepodge of arguments which he believed characterized his opponents' thought.

To be sure, Hutchinson occasionally did cite an
"authoritative" source, such as Livy, English statutes,
or the Bible. But he did so only to counter the
arbitrariness of his adversaries' usage, not to support
his own ideas. A rather amusing passage in the History
exemplifies his own manner of using quotations. The
Puritans based their opposition to long hair worn by
men upon the authority of a Biblical quotation.
Hutchinson countered with another: "ye shall not round
the corners of your heads." The moral, of course, was
not that long hair exhibited virtue, but rather that

"in every age indifferent things have been condemned as sinful, and placed among the greatest immoralities."(17) In Volume I of the History, Hutchinson occasionally cited classical authors in Latin to express moral platitudes, but he abandoned this practice as confidence in his own ability grew. He also cited a classical authority in his essay on the Stamp Act, but he wrote this piece to persuade a specific audience. Hutchinson probably used this sort of comparison because he thought it would carry weight with his readers, for he probably never used one again. The only sources Hutchinson cited regularly were historical documents or works by other historians, almost all of which pertained specifically to New England. Through his unusual mode of citation, far more typical of scholarly writing today than of eighteenth century practice, Hutchinson testified to his belief that ancient history and selections from political philosophy did less to illuminate contemporary circumstances than study of the specific institutions and customs of colonial America.

Hutchinson refused to adopt his adversaries' methods of argument in still another way. He would not discuss what he considered "points of mere speculation." He attacked the Declaration of Independence because it attempted to universalize and define the nature of government with a precision unattainable in practice: "I should therefore be impertinent, if I attempted to show in what case a whole people may be justified in rising up in opposition to the powers of government, altering or abolishing them, and substituting in whole or in part, new powers in their stead, or how far life, liberty and the pursuit of happiness may be said to be inalienable." Speculation on such matters proved not only fruitless but actually harmful. Rebellion occurred because "men in New England took sides upon mere speculative points in government, when there was nothing in practice which could give occasion for forming parties."

Popularly accepted metaphysical notions of politics only became common in America in the 1760s. Until then, the constitution of government had been "pretty well settled, and in a contented society, the people were "not apt to be disturbed by mere theoretical notions of government, or with the ideas of any particular degrees of natural liberty." But the combination of British legislation and the improvement made of it by ideologues altered this situation and New England found itself again in the same quandary as during the Antinomian controversy of 1636: "the town of [Boston] and country were distracted with these subtleties, and every man who had brains enough to form some imperfect conceptions of them, inferred and maintained some or other point." Hutchinson was exasperated by these disputes and found it useless to argue such issues as of "these rights of citizens" in general. These were "very uncertain seeing you will scarce find any two cities where they are just the same."(18)

Among the other "points of speculation" Hutchinson made it his business not to discuss were the nature of man and the pattern of history. Man had no fixed nature, and no one race or nation was peculiarly virtuous, God's country, or a "type" of the ancient Romans or Israelites. He considered his fellow Americans, "like all the rest of the human race," to be "of different spirits and dispositions, some more calm and moderate, others more violent and extravagant." Hutchinson was extremely "cautious . . . of condemning or even applauding" his fellow actors in what he termed the "grand comedy" of life. Men and nations could change so readily, or reveal different aspects of their characters to different audiences, that to categorize their actions marked a presumption equal to abstracting lessons from history or philosophy. It was a fallacy to "compare this world to a theater and to consider every man as a person." Not only was there no such thing as human nature, each individual did not even have a nature. Citing the two-faced behavior of Pompey and Cicero -- two of the mainstays of "republican virtue" whose devious private schemes contradicted their noble public utterances -- Hutchinson argued that when people confront "new connections" and "new scenes of life," elements of their "characters which always existed but did not come under observation before" appeared. Hutchinson therefore resolved to "suspend all determination upon the real state" of a man's personality until after "a long acquaintance." Even then he doubted whether he could "make a judgment of his real intention . . . with certainty enough to venture anything of moment from it." What held for man held for the state: hence, only after his "long acquaintance" with traditional Massachusetts did he deign to judge his native land and its major historical figures. Both men and societies were to a large extent creatures of circumstance, multiple role players lacking fixed identities.(19)

In what may well be Hutchinson's only other fragment of purely philosophical speculation, he again questioned the concept of personal identity. When he lost a tooth, he noted that "I now felt no more affection for [it], than if it had been the tooth of a stranger. I could easily imagine the case to be the same with a finger, or hand, and arm, and so on to every part of the body, even to the brain, my thinking part still existing, and perhaps assuming some other better form."(20) Hutchinson viewed the individual as the product of continuously operating societal processes and personal experiences, not as an autonomous being voluntarily entering into social and political arrangements of his own choosing. His notion of the self mirrored his idea of society as a flexible entity, although one with a basic "fundamental" core, continually molded by history. A state could not be identified with a few of its institutions or with some scheme abstracted from them and alleged to be its origins. Neither could "human nature" be reduced to some arbitrarily selected elements.

Hutchinson did, however, advance generalizations about the characters of individuals and societies he had studied in depth. He demonstrated the deleterious consequences of Indian society and revolutionary states for human morality, but he condemned with equal vehemence the tenets of the "hobb[es]ians and infidels" who identified human nature solely with its bestial elements.(21) A people governed by wise laws, such as pre-revolutionary Massachusetts, and those individuals such as Hutchinson himself who defended their convictions in the face of unpopularity, clearly rose above this level. Thus, while circumstances shaped man to a great extent, he could also, in some degree, choose those experiences and acquaintances which influenced him. Hutchinson's own desire to quit politics to avoid damnation and his condemnation of blasphemers and perjurers demonstrated than an individual who lived in a society where good institutions disseminated a knowledge of right and wrong was morally responsible for his actions, even if he usually followed social customs unthinkingly.

Hutchinson did not discover any moral progress or deterioration in history. When he cited the duplicity of Pompey and Cicero, he answered the question "is mankind really degenerated within a few years" with a definite "no." Elsewhere, he remarked that "what is very tolerable in one age is very ridiculous in another." Just as no form of government could be considered especially superior, neither could the customs of any particular age possess any claim to universal validity. Yet Hutchinson did find the morals of the revolutionary age looser than those of the period preceding it. They had to be, or the people could not have revolted. In 1765, he wrote "that a future writer will not be able to set the present age in so favorable a light as I have done the last." Such a decline appeared in England as well as America. When in 1779 a French fleet threatened the kingdom with invasion, Hutchinson was astonished by the "unconcern on this occasion" exhibited by "men of influence." He contrasted this with the situation in 1588, when leading men roused the countryside to prepare for the Spanish Armada. Hutchinson may have possessed an inkling that the world was on the threshold of great changes. In 1778, referring to the Revolution, he informed Lord Hardwicke that "a more strange and improbable turn in the affairs of any kingdom has not occurred since the creation of the world." Upon the destruction of his mansion in 1765, he observed the first instance of new ideological savagery: "some gentlemen of the army said they had seen towns sacked by an enemy, but never saw an instance of such hellish fury as was expressed here."(22) But because the contagion of revolution did not spread beyond America and, to a lesser extent, the British Isles, before Hutchinson died in 1780, he did not infer any world-historical trends from the case at hand.

To some extent, Hutchinson adopted a pessimistic philosophy of history at odds with either the progressive or cyclical theories favored by most thinkers in the "Age of Reason." Good societies, if they suffered moral decay, could experience revolutions which led to anarchy and then tyranny. But while such conclusions can be deduced from his thinking, Hutchinson did not stress them or search for institutional patterns which dictated when such a decline was likely. He attributed revolution primarily to circumstances created by specific individuals and events, and considered history far too complex for its greatest patterns to be discerned.

Hutchinson did admit occasional providential interventions into history, but he cautiously refrained from probing the divine mind. He <u>did</u> believe that the hand of God guided the settlement of America, arguing that just because the Puritans supposed an immediate interposition of providence in the great mortality among the Indians, was no reason for the modern age to "go into the contrary extreme" and deny the Almighty any role. Hutchinson could not explain "the Indians' universal extinction" -- even though the English sometimes "have made use of all means most likely to have prevented it" -- without postulating divine intervention.(23) Aside from this instance, however, I have been unable to find a case where Hutchinson linked God and history. And even here, he did not attribute any moral, millennial import to the founding of America. Although providential intervention could perhaps be inferred, its purpose was veiled.

Neither did Hutchinson believe that the past provided lessons which could guide the future apart from the ordinary teachings of moral law which were evident enough without historical reinforcement. For instance, after condemning Massachusetts' "transactions relative to agents" -- which consisted of expecting them to obtain impossible concessions from England and then vilifying them for their failure to do so -- Hutchinson concluded that "errors and failings, as well as laudable deeds, in past ages, may be rendered useful by exciting posterity to avoid the one and imitate the other."(24) But if his account in the History revealed anything, it was that Massachusetts in no way suffered whatsoever for this shameful behavior. The moral lessons were not inherent in the historical process; rather, certain actions were right or wrong regardless of the practical, mundane consequences for the actor. When Dr. William Robertson, a famous historian in his own right, decided not to write a history of the British colonies "on the grounds there was no knowing what would be the future condition of them," Hutchinson told him "be it what it may, it need make no odds on writing the history of what is past, and I thought a true state of them ought to be handed down to posterity." Hutchinson was perhaps the only major eighteenth century historian for whom history had value apart from its incorporation into a philosophy of history.(25)

In sum, Hutchinson condemned speculation as to the meaning of the history, the nature of man, the correct form of government, or natural rights. No one needed such knowledge to manage his affairs, which only required an understanding of the moral law and historical and institutional circumstances of one's own society. Metaphysical generalizations based on other criteria demonstrated the fallacy Hutchinson criticized in the Declaration of Independence, "of reasoning from the whole to the part." Edmund Burke shared Hutchinson's low opinion of a deductive political theory:(26)

> It seems to me a preposterous way of reasoning, and a perfect confusion of ideas, to take the theories which learned and speculative men have made from a [certain] government, and then suppose it made on those theories, which were made from it . . . to accuse the government as not corresponding with them.

Hutchinson too insisted that any valid political and ethical theory must be induced from the way in which institutions and customs of a particular state conformed to the immutable laws of justice and morality which mankind has historically, to greater or lesser degree, striven to approximate.

Apart from their firm belief in Christian morality and natural law, Burke and Hutchinson considered the world mysterious and confused. Knowledge depended on careful, detailed study of very particular circumstances. Even each man only revealed himself as the tip of an iceberg. The earth burst with diverse nations, races, religions, and customs, and men of every degree of moral and intellectual ability. Hutchinson and Burke found the Age of Reason presumptuous and dangerous. In the words of Carl Becker, it sought to build a "heavenly city" through discovering the correct principles by which states could govern themselves.(27) For Burke and Hutchinson reason itself, like freedom, only emerged from a morass of customs in rare circumstances. To be faithful to their origins, thought and liberty had to admit their fragility in a world which has generally respected neither.

FOOTNOTES

1. "Strictures," 42; History, III, 217, 273.

2. History, III, 108, 60, 74, "Additions, III," 52; Bradford, 373, 378. Hutchinson may have derived his discussion of the effect of social revolution on language from Thucydides' Peloponnesian War.

3. History, III, 121; "Dialogue," M. XXVIII, 106.

4. History, III, 108, 296.

5. Quincy, 261.

6. Ibid., 244; History, III, 179, 198.

7. "Strictures," 26, 42.

8. "Dialogue," M. XXVIII, 101-109, passim, is the basic source for all unattributed information in the next several pages.

9. Bradford, 250.

10. Burke, "Letter to the Sheriffs of Bristol" (1777), II, 226; H to ?, November 1771, M. XXVII, 440.

11. H to Israel Williams, August 5, 1759, Williams Papers.

12. H to Israel Mauduit, June 6, 1767, M. XXV, 164; see also H to John Pownall (early 1773), M. XXVII, 525 and H to ?, October 26, 1765, M. XXVI, 338; H to William Bollan, March 6, 1762, M. XXVI, 15.

13. H to Israel Williams, September 15, 1751, Williams Papers; H to ?, March 27, 1766, M. XXVI, 557; H to David Chesebrough, March 16, 1765, M. XXVI, 257; "Dialogue," M. XXVIII, 102.

14. "Strictures," 26.

15. H to John Hely Hutchinson, January 18, 1769, M. XXVI, 697; H to ?, September 16, 1763, M. XXVI, 135.

16. See Loewenberg, American History in American

Thought, 196; Bailyn, Hutchinson, 76.

17. History, I, 130.
18. "Additions, III," 73; "Strictures," 26; History, III, 74, 62; I, 151; "Dialogue," M. XXVIII, 107.
19. "Stamp Act Essay," 480. H to Richard Saltonstall, August 29, 1759, Saltonstall Papers, 429.
20. Diary, I, 346.
21. Hardwicke, November 6, 1779, 208.
22. H to Richard Saltonstall, August 27, 1759, Saltonstall Papers, 429; H to Robert Hale, December 22, 1755, Saltonstall Papers, 411; H to ?, October 26, 1765, M. XXVI, 341; Hardwicke Correspondence, August 23, 1779 and August 31, 1778, 150, 193; H to William Bollan [September 1765], M. XXVI, 307.
23. History, I, 32.
24. History, II, 99.
25. Diary, II, 194.
26. "Strictures," 42; Burke, "Reflections" (1790), quoted in J. G. A. Pocock, "Burke and the Ancient Constitution" in Politics, Languages and Time (New York, 1971), 228. Burke made many remarks against basing government on abstract principles. On the issue of "superiority in the presiding state and freedom in the subordinate," he agreed with Hutchinson that "those vexatious questions," which "in truth rather belong to metaphysics than politics . . . can never be moved without shaking the foundations of the best government." Speculation about "how far all mankind, in all forms of polity are entitled to an exercise of that right [taxation] by the charter of "Nature" was dismissed by Burke as a "deep question, where great names militate against each other, where reason is perplexed, and an appeal to authorities only thickens the confusion." Such points constituted "the great Serbonian bog . . . where armies have sunk." Burke, "Observations on a Late Publication on the

Present State of the Nation" (1769), I, 386; "Speech on Conciliation with America" (1775), II, 140.

27. Carl Becker, <u>The Heavenly City of the Eighteenth Century Philosophers</u> (New Haven, 1932).

IX. CONCLUSION

In his writings, Thomas Hutchinson expressed many principles which have characterized conservative or counter-revolutionary thought since the eighteenth century. Edmund Burke also advanced most of these ideas, and he is usually considered the first modern conservative theorist. Aside from the difficulty of locating the origin of any significant thought -- tradition, for example, was important to the seventeenth century common lawyers, if not to thinkers in antiquity such as Aristotle or Cicero -- Hutchinson anticipated many of Burke's arguments. He, too, represented a traditional elite fighting for its life against a democratic revolution. (If the mild violence of Boston in the 1760s and 1770s pales beside the seventeenth century religious wars or the French Revolution, it appalled Hutchinson, and the bloody internal war which accompanied the American Revolution exhibited a more typical fanaticism.) Hutchinson's most important ideas, which have been discussed in this volume, will remind readers of the characteristics described in Russell Kirk's The Conservative Mind and other books on conservative political theory:

1. The moral teachings of Christianity, and those which natural law makes known to all men, both intuitively and through social tradition, can never be justifiably violated.

2. Apart from this fixed starting point, political theory is an inductive discipline. The structure of existing states is the only legitimate field for gathering data to determine the nature of political institutions and the obedience due them.

3. Conversely, deductive political schemes based upon the nature of man, the "correct" form of state, or the original purposes of government, have no basis in fact and are invalid.

4. Therefore, variety is a necessary feature of both the world in general and any given society. Many forms of government are legitimate, as natural law is best maintained through traditional institutions. Each man has his own special nature. Disagreements and parties legitimately formed to promote the public good

which do not violate moral law are desirable.

5. If different political principles can be equally valid depending on the situation, men should tolerate other customs, religions, races, and points of view except insofar as they are criminal and threaten a society's conserving institutions. Hutchinson thus opposed a counter-revolutionary "particular" to the revolutionary "universal."

6. Sovereignty must be indivisible, but at the same time it should be restricted by the fundamental institutions, customs, and principles a society has developed, and by natural law.

7. History, the study of a given society's customs, is the test of its political theory.

8. History has no grand pattern and exhibits no steady progress. Particular trends, however, such as moral decline or revolution in a state, can be discerned.

9. Tradition and custom are the most important elements of a constitution, which ought to be altered only with reluctance and through the very means the constitution itself has provided.

10. Oppression does not cause all revolutions. They can be begun by unimportant individuals motivated by selfish ends; however, only when a population possesses real grievances against its rulers can the ever-present incendiary element become prominent.

11. Revolution is accomplished through the distortion of language and the destruction of moral standards.

12. The period which began in the late eighteenth century witnessed important changes. Ideas that governments are the creatures of their subjects, that they exist to actualize certain ideals or "natural rights," and that all other states are illegitimate, gained currency.

13. Among these false ideas is the doctrine that laws passed by the legitimate sovereign of a state may be judged by the individuals therein. (Individuals may, however, resist criminal behavior on the part of their rulers. The state is identified

with its laws and customs -- as opposed to the will of either the people or the governing officials. If the latter, under the cloak of authority, violate laws, they do not act in their formal capacity, but criminally.)

14. For a democratic revolution to succeed it must pervert religion into its service so people will suspend morality with respect to opponents of the rebellion. It must also politicize large numbers of people who then make politics a vital part of their lives.

15. Politics is an inherently immoral, corrupting activity. The less it has to do with the administration of government and society, the better.

16. Insofar as the principles described in 11, 12 and 13 are realized, government must either be perverted into an anarchic war of all against all, a tyranny ruling by force alone or -- what is most likely -- the successive existence of both.

17. The notion that one man can "represent" another through popular election is a figment.

18. Human knowledge -- of man's nature, the process of history, the correct form of government, the proper action to perform when the morality of the situation is not obvious -- is very limited. Therefore, prudence, moderation, and humility should characterize human behavior. Knowledge and liberty are best achieved through respecting tradition.

19. The proper cure for social disorder is the persuasion or punishment of individuals, not the sudden destruction or creation of institutions.

Similarities in the careers of Edmund Burke and Thomas Hutchinson are as striking as those in their thought. Both were practical politicians who never wrote a speculative treatise on politics but usually formulated their ideas in response to contingencies. Many counter-revolutionary theorists -- Joseph de Maistre, Prince Metternich, Juan Donoso-Cortes, and Konstantin Pobodoenostev come immediately to mind -- were statesmen before they set pen to paper in a serious way. As such, they based their ideas on knowledge of how traditional institutions and politics functioned in contrast to revolutionaries who usually viewed their operation from the outside.

In contrast to their counter-revolutionary successors, Burke and Hutchinson looked more favorably on popular freedom and hoped traditional European or American society could be preserved. By the end of the French Revolution, conservatives had to seek refuge in unqualified identification with the major European monarchies. As such, they were too apt to identify the "is" with the "ought" and postulate a nationalism above morality which to some extent resembled the very revolutionary principles they combatted. But Burke and Hutchinson, defenders of pre-revolutionary social orders which abhorred despotism as much as democracy, found monarchy which ignored custom and law as intolerable as revolution. For a brief period, then, in the latter half of the eighteenth century, conservative thinkers could balance liberty and authority, change and stability, tradition and sovereignty, particular customs and universal morality. The coexistence of these principles, precarious at best, would soon be transformed into irreconcilable conflict. Even conservatives are now divided between libertarians who stress popular freedom from a "leviathan" state and authoritarians for whom morality, law, and order are breaking down and the modern state must curb excessive liberty to survive radical challenges.

Today, scholars remember Edmund Burke as a theorist as well as a statesman whereas Thomas Hutchinson has only attained fame -- or rather infamy -- in the latter capacity. Several complete and abridged editions of Burke's works and correspondence have been published in addition to biographies and studies of his thought. But many of Hutchinson's writings are available only in manuscript, or -- with the exception of The History -- can be found only in scholarly journals or archaic editions.

Part of the blame must rest with Hutchinson himself, who did not write as extensively as Burke and lacked his flair for aphorism. In addition, he confined the theoretical elaboration of many principles implicit in his History to letters, unpublished pamphlets, and speeches. Burke's thoughts, too, appeared unsystematically in letters and speeches, but he published and circulated them more widely. But profundity and reticence are by no means incompatible. Hutchinson had thought through the major problems of political theory -- this is clear as early as volume I of the History -- but never felt the need to "systematize" his thoughts in the customary fashion. Indeed, given his belief in a diverse and unfathomable world, Hutchinson could not have propounded a "system." His emphasis on the uniqueness of each national tradition and denial of the usual categories of political theorists made systematic thought in the usual sense impossible.

Another reason for Hutchinson's neglect lies in the nature of American political culture. Until quite recently, Americans have suffered from amnesia with respect to the loyalists. Even those who have admired their integrity have been so convinced of the Revolution's legitimacy that the energy they have expended on the losers has been devoted to explaining why in fact loyalists existed, as though it were not an anomaly to be a revolutionary! Second, Americans -- especially conservatives -- have gloried in distinguishing their revolution as orderly and conservative from virtually all subsequent ones. The relative lack of violence and atrocity in the War for Independence has been overemphasized and attributed to the people's peculiar moral virtue and prudence. On the other hand, non-conservative Americans, including many historians, either praise the Revolution as radical and thus have no interest in the principles of the losers, or consider it conservative although unfortunately so. For liberals and radicals the loyalists are the pathological case of "counter-revolutionaries" such as Alexander Hamilton and Robert Morris. Finally, Hutchinson's thought was anomalous even among the loyalists. He held a complex theory of the Revolution's origins and refused to regard institutional reforms as a remedy, like most of his fellow exiles. He also rejected their belief in some form of natural rights and representative government. Hutchinson's true significance cannot be ascertained taking a few excerpts from his writings and incorporating them into a "loyalist mind."

Combining these elements, it can be understood why it has taken two centuries for serious studies of Hutchinson's career and thought by Malcolm Freiberg, Clifford Shipton, and Bernard Bailyn to appear. American conservatives have not deplored the Revolution as evil incarnate since 1783, whereas Burke and European counter-revolutionaries have had disciples aplenty. Hutchinson's critique of what have come to be recognized as American ideals may be uncongenial to patriotic citizens, yet in his defense of American liberty and loving articulation of New England institutions as he understood them Hutchinson took great pride in being an American. He had no illusions about British society and politics. In 1741, on the occasion of Hutchinson's first trip to England, Isaac Watts wrote to Benjamin Colman that the young agent "had found it very tiresome work to attend upon a British court." Thirty-odd years later, Hutchinson maintained that he "never met with anything which set the depravity of human nature in a more striking light, than the conduct of . . . heads of past administration" who had lost America. Another incident struck him as indicative of British moral depravity, when a carriage of ladies which ran over and killed a small child drove on without concern. Unlike his colleagues, former chief justice Peter Oliver and secretary Thomas Flucker, who ceased "to think of America," Hutchinson found "more of the old Athens" in himself, and "felt a fondness to lay my bones in my native soil." While in England, he endeavored "to live as much in the New England way" as possible. The last words he wrote from exile to his life-long friend Israel Williams spoke for themselves: "The cruel persecution I met with makes my absence from my country more tolerable than I thought it possibly could be, but still, of all parts of the globe, it is nearest to my heart."(1)

    Perhaps Hutchinson's cruelest punishment was to die before the United States established a workable and stable government. Many of his fellow exiles returned to their homeland. One who did not, Jonathan Boucher, dedicated his loyalist history of the Revolution to George Washington. As Hutchinson's analysis of the Puritan state indicates, he would have been the last man to judge the new nation by the principles which motivated its establishment in the first place. And while he may well have found much to condemn in the nation's history -- he had considerable reservations about how the Puritans treated Indians and dissidents -- it cannot be doubted that in general he would have compared the United States favorably with other modern nations. In fact, by recognizing that people best redressed legitimate grievances through legal channels, but in case of great abuses were justified in civil disobedience, Hutchinson's political theory would have provided a good framework for appreciating both the continuity of fundamental American institutions and the non-revolutionary protests through which minorities and oppressed groups have, albeit imperfectly, secured recognition of their claims to equality and justice.

* * * * * * * *

Until now, this work has sought to understand Hutchinson's thought without praise or blame. To be sure, the assumption that Hutchinson did have important and original things to say is an implicit form of praise, as is the assertion that he consistently guided his career by a devotion to tradition and morality. That he was a devious, self-serving politician who did not care if he advanced his career on the ruins of his country is belied by the fact that he behaved consistently throughout the 1760s and 70s and tried to persuade both America and Britain to look at the other side, even when it became obvious that such conduct only increased his unpopularity.

Recognition that Hutchinson provided valuable insights into his own times and the human condition does not require agreement with his principles. His history and political science are open to many of the criticisms that have been levelled against conservative thought. It would be most un-Hutchinsonian, therefore, not to mention legitimate objections to his ideas. By taking great pains to see every side of nearly every question, Hutchinson may have hoped to pre-empt all possible criticism. Still, several caveats may be raised.

First, while Hutchinson noticed that Massachusetts had real grievances such as imperial taxation or the Navigation Acts and that the lower classes benefited from paper money and suffered from impressment and war, he refused to recognize popular protest as a direct, genuine response to such burdens. It filtered itself through self-serving "demagogues" who perverted justifiable anger into immoral and potentially disastrous attempts to destroy society. Even granting that revolutionaries are not disinterested idealists and that natural rights theory is problematical, it need not follow that all movements for political change ought therefore be abhorred. It could rather be argued that Hutchinson misrepresented the case when he insisted Massachusetts enjoyed the world's happiest constitution. Such glosses must have rung hollow indeed to a province which had probably spent more money and lost more lives per capita than any European nation, even Frederick the Great's Prussia, in war from 1740 to 1763. British intransigence in the face of protests against impressment and the misuse of colonial armed forces, to say nothing of the mother country's blatant exploitation of India and Ireland, augured poorly for the future and convinced many Americans that even if, as Hutchinson contended, Britain responded positively to most colonial demands, it had only done so unwillingly and under duress.

Put another way, Hutchinson can be said to have created a tradition of Anglo-American reconciliation and limited conflict which was as much of an abstraction or fantasy as the wildest speculative flights of his opponents on the natural rights of man. If Britain and the colonies had actually compromised most issues, they only did so because neither possessed the resources to force total capitulation. Because no one in Massachusetts had previously looked at its history as such a balance, Hutchinson may have made a fortuitous outcome, not wished for by anyone, the measure of a tradition best defined by conflict.

Hutchinson may be criticized here on the same grounds as Burke or almost any conservative thinker. He viewed the past through rose-colored glasses, if not ignoring, at least de-emphasizing strife and the insensitivity of the upper orders to which he and most conservatives have either belonged or identified themselves. Readers of E. P. Thompson, George Rudé, and Dorothy George can discover an England they would never have suspected from reading Burke's paeans to a population protected unthinkingly under the shade of the British oak. No one could imagine from Burke, who wrote at the dawn of the Industrial Revolution, what violence to persons and customs the development of the factory system exacted.

Hutchinson, too, must have lived so long with the increasing poverty, rootlessness, and economic decline which began in eastern Massachusetts in the 1730s, if not earlier, that he accepted it as a fact of life which he preferred to overlook in his praises of America's general level of prosperity relative to the rest of the world. If Hutchinson's concept of Massachusetts' historical tradition may be criticized as much as his desperate efforts to create a family

heritage, then what becomes of his assertion that
liberty, prosperity, happiness, and morality reigned
in Massachusetts? Is it not then possible to argue
that what freedom and happiness the population did
enjoy came from its very combativeness, its "tradition"
of standing up for its rights -- no matter how
chimerical these might have been? By creating a false
counter-tradition based on consensus (even if it
admitted inconsequential strife) rather than conflict,
Hutchinson may be viewed, as his political opponents
regarded him, as an innovator who sought to institute
an unprecedented servility and compliance with
Britain. And if the colonies became less aggressive at
the very moment the mother country took the offensive,
all the "traditional" blessings would be lost. Thus,
Hutchinson is open to the general charge against
conservative thinkers that freedom and happiness do
not develop slowly in a traditional context, but are
achieved through protest and even violent reaction
against customary norms.

 Judgment of Hutchinson, as of the virtues and
defects of conservative political thought, depends on
one's own vision of history. With respect to
eighteenth century Massachusetts, evidence exists both
for against his interpretation. If war brought
suffering, much of the population joyfully joined in
the crusade; it can even be argued that military pay
and casualties alleviated poverty brought about through
natural increase. Most of the leading revolutionaries
suffered not at all. The ruling families to which
Hutchinson belonged can be viewed as either society's
traditional rulers who did a fine job of leading the
province through several catastrophic campaigns, or an
aloof, self-interested group that profited both
financially and career-wise from wars that hurt the
general population, and who took little interest in
alleviating the misery their policies had caused.

 In short, the principal criticism which can be
levelled at Hutchinson is not that he did not perceive
or was unconcerned with popular grievances, the
miseries of war, or attacks on American liberty. In
fact, had he been any more or differently sensitive he
would have been obliged to join the revolutionaries
wholeheartedly. He failed intellectually in not
carrying his love of reconciliation and balance one
step further and recognizing that the "fundamentals"
or tradition of a society can consist of both change
and adherence to tradition, and include unprecedented,

sudden changes which to some extent incorporate, to some extent supersede what had come before. Thomas Kuhn's <u>The Structure of Scientific Revolutions</u> provides an excellent example of the sort of reconciliation of authority and liberty Hutchinson could have achieved had he managed to work out his ideas to their fullest. Kuhn argues that revolutions in knowledge occur when the paradigms of an old order, valid and useful in their day, no longer explain reality. Then they are replaced by a new set of norms which proceed to define a new tradition. Similarly, Hutchinson could have shown that political revolution occurred when traditional "fundamentals" had outlived their usefulness, and that to survive a society had to regenerate itself untraditionally to meet unprecedented challenges. But had Hutchinson advanced this argument, he would not have been able to maintain the superiority of traditional Massachusetts to the new order. Even the harshest critic of Hutchinson, however, must grant that he scored some telling points against his adversaries. He repeatedly stressed the tremendous moral and physical costs which accompany revolutionary change. Innocent people will be killed or otherwise injured; good men whose only crime is defense of the only society they know will be defamed or destroyed. Regardless of how legitimate popular demands for change may be, a great deal of what Hutchinson called "anarchy and tyranny" must ensue. By pointing to the certainty that revolution must violate natural law, whereas its positive effects are at best uncertain, Hutchinson confronted his opponents -- and still confronts us -- with a reminder that good intentions (and he denied these to most revolution- aries) do not liberate men from moral responsibility for the consequences of their actions.

Further, once revolutionary principles of natural rights and popular sovereignty appeared in the world, it would be impossible to stop their spread. Hutchinson spoke far truer than he knew when on August 27, 1765, the day after he had narrowly escaped with his life from his ruined house, he warned his countrymen:(2)

> I hope the eyes of the people will be opened, that they will see how easy it is for some designing wicked men to spread false reports, raise suspicions and jealousies in the minds of the populace, and enrage them against the

innocent -- but if guilty this is not
the way to proceed -- the laws of our
country are open to punish those who
have offended. -- This destroying all
peace and order of the community --
all will feel its effects.

More than anything else, Hutchinson dreaded the penetration of politics into the general consciousness of society. A land excited by the chimerical ideals of equality and self-rule would only discover they could never be implemented, and that continued pursuit of natural rights would lead to an anarchy from which any tyranny would be a relief.

As a result, the past two centuries have produced nations existing in contradiction to the ideals which motivated their establishment. The situation introduced on a relatively mild scale in Hutchinson's Boston has repeated itself again and again with greater ferocity as regimes and leaders supposedly striving for human rights exercise despotic powers over the inhabitants of which the "Great Khan" himself would never have dreamed, forcing people to win their "freedom" through participation in revolutionary or nationalist crusades. Enemies to the regime become enemies to the ideals themselves, and hence to all that is good. Hutchinson spoke truer than he knew when he predicted that "all" will feel the effects of widespread politicization.

Having presented both as strong a critique and apology for Hutchinson as possible, I would be excessively timid to conclude that because both have merit we need not choose between tradition and revolution, liberty and authority, natural law and natural rights, conflict or consensus in history, economic well-being or principled idealism, or not think about how these concepts should be defined or whether these dichotomies can be reconciled. We are choosing daily by participating or refusing to join in the spectrum of possibilities for social change or preservation. If Hutchinson teaches us anything, it is that these choices are agonizing and fraught with unforeseeable consequences if diverse possibilities are considered with the seriousness they deserve. Hutchinson's vision of a tragic, complicated world where to act thinkingly man must somehow try to detach himself from extraneous influences and examine the situation from every possible angle reminds me, at any rate, of Max Weber's essays on "Science as a Vocation" and "Politics as a Vocation." For Weber, the scientist, or scholar, exists to call attention to the "inconvenient fact," the terrible consequence which political actors who fight uncritically for their principles rarely consider. But having raised all possible doubts, the scientist, like Weber and Hutchinson, can move on to politics. By doing so, and struggling for his own vision of the good society, he will then realize that he must accept full consequences for any harm wrought by his efforts before God (if a believer) or his conscience. In accepting that awesome responsibility, he can at least hope to approach disinterestedness and genuine good will even if he knows such an idea remains impossible.

If, in the last analysis Hutchinson's thought, like Weber's, can be interpreted as an elaborate rationalization for the political dominance of his own class or, on a psychological level, of rule by a peace-loving arbiter pretending to be purged of self-interest, it cannot only be interpreted that way without grave injustice. To show that Hutchinson tried to see the other side, except in cases where he could only see evil incarnate, has been one theme of this book. That he believed he lived in a society which had with some success synthesized the best of supposedly contradictory worlds and ideals is another. And that he tried to preserve this tradition of reconciliation in the face of those who would identify the good with a fraction of that heritage or even supplant it entirely with new ideals is a third. We can never know to what extent Hutchinson was sincere, but evidence of his willingness to examine and re-examine his ideas from different perspectives, even to the point (like Weber and James Otis) of risking madness rather than surrendering his intellectual struggle, must be a presumption in his favor.

Hutchinson's enemies were right: by their standards, his principles would indeed have enslaved Massachusetts. By accepting them, the province would have recognized his leadership and fulfilled his Caesarian ambitions as no one of importance held even remotely similar ideals. And he undoubtedly would not have hesitated, in such a case, to reward his handful of faithful relatives and friends. The revolutionaries had good reason to place Hutchinson among the four horsemen of the apocalypse and to compare him with the Anti-Christ: if their cause had merit he deserved such a fate as their most important opponent who not only denied the application of shared Lockean principles, but who rejected that entire world-view and substituted another. Hutchinson believed that he forced his adversaries to show their true cards: by his dogged persistence, he sought to maneuver them into situations where they either had to abandon their political ideals and accept his terms of reconciliation, or surrender their moral principles to destroy him. By compelling them to make such a choice, Hutchinson willingly sacrificed himself to their vengeance, confident that he had thereby revealed the diabolical motives of those who made natural rights theory the foundation of the state. We will never know, at least in human history, whether Hutchinson was right or wrong. But like the signers of the Declaration of Independence who pledged their "sacred honor" to testify to their sincerity, Hutchinson's own writings, and his enemies' warnings, revealed that he had also staked his soul that he had spoken and acted truthfully.

FOOTNOTES

1. Isaac Watts to Benjamin Colman, August 19, 1741, Proceedings of the Massachusetts Historical Society, XXIX (1894-1895), 386; Diary, I, 355, 477. H to Israel Williams, September 23, 1774, Williams Papers.

2. Quincy, 172.

INDEX

Acadians: H and, 90.
Acts of Trade and Navigation: see Navigation Acts.
Adams, James T.: on Puritans, 66.
Adams, John: 121-122; and impressment, 32-33; on H, 39, 52-53; and Boston Massacre, 38; as lawyer, 48-51; on Revolution, 125; on "canon and feudal law," 136; and "democratical despotism," 169, 172.
Adams, Samuel: 6, 122; and Knowles Riot, 26; and Revolution, 124-125, 143-144; on "Christian Sparta," 160; compared with H on rights of man, 180-181; on Locke, 202.
Admiralty Court: in Rex v. Corbet, 32, 33, 53, 141.
Admiralty, Lords of: and impressment, 30, 33.
"Age of Reason": 185, 210.
Alexander the Great: and H, 2, 39.
Allen, James: expelled from Massachusetts Assembly, 15.
American Revolution: see Revolution, American.
Anarchy and Revolution: 171-172.
Ancient history: 201.
Andros, Sir Edmund: 74-75.
Anglican Church: 91, 134.
Anglicization: 84.
Anti-Christ: H compared with, 39, 91.
Antinomians: 67-69, 99.
Antiquarians: 62, 97.
Apocalypse: 59; Four Horsemen, compared with H, 39.
Appeals: from colonies to Privy Council, H on, 51.
Aristotle: 212.
Army, Continental: character of, 131.
Asiatic government: 177, 182, 187.
Assembly (Massachusetts): see House of Representatives.
Augustine, St.: Confessions, 9; political theory, 168-169.

Bailyn, Bernard: on H, 16, 20, 221; on Massachusetts politics, 84; on origins of Revolution, 119, 124.
Baptists: toleration, 165.
Battis, Emery: on Antinomians, 69.
Beer, George L.: interpretation of Revolution, 120, 121.
Belcher, Jonathan: 2, 80.
Berkshires: land riots in, 171.

231

Bernard, Francis: 2, 13, 19, 40, 204; and
    impressment, 31-34, 38; and Revolution, 126-127,
    143-147.
Bible, The: H and, 206-207.
Blacks: see Slavery.
Blasphemy: and social control, 164-165.
Bolingbroke, Henry St. John, Viscount: on history, 61.
Bollan, William: and impressment, 27-30.
Boston: H on, 5; Caucus, 13; impressment in,
    22-27, 35, 84; soldiers in, 39; Town Meeting, 5;
    and Revolution, 126, 131, 145; Indian trade in,
    90; clergy, 165.
Boston Massacre: 4, 16, 18, 33, 128, 142;
    John Adams' case, 38, 39.
Boucher, Jonathan: history of Revolution, 134, 222.
Boundaries, intercolonial: 142.
Bowdoin, James and family: 126, 143.
Boyer, Paul: on witchcraft in Salem, 91.
Bridenbaugh, Carl: on Revolution, 119.
British Empire and imperial administration: see also
    Constitution -- British; 14, 18, 42, 87;
    and Puritans, 70-75; prosperity of, 72-73;
    H on, 92-95; Constitution of, and sovereignty,
    H on, 105-116; and Revolution, 128-129,
    144-147, 181; H's suggestions for reform, 137-147.
British Law: 41, 42, 46, 48, 54, 55.
Brown, Robert E.: on Massachusetts history, 84,
    119, 132.
Buren, Martin Van: on parties, 195.
Burke, Edmund: 17, 62, 134; compared with H on: --
    tradition, 42, 54-55; on Revolution, 144-147;
    and traditional liberty, 148; on British
    arrogance, 156; and natural law, 162-163;
    on religion and society, 168; on French and
    American Revolutions, 169-170; on popular
    power, 172-173; on traditional and natural
    rights, 177-178; on representation, 184;
    on parties, 185-186; on political obligation,
    187-188; on prudence, 203; general comparison,
    212-214.
Burnet, William: 80, 81.

Caesar, Julius: and H, 2, 187.
Calvinism: political theory, 159.
Canada: 73, 83; and Revolution, 121-122.
Carthage: 89.
Catholicism: H on toleration, 91, 166-167.
Chalmers, George: on Revolution, 135.
Charles I, King: H on, 10, 12.
Charles II, King: 73-74.

Charter, Massachusetts: 46, 71, 73-77, 112;
    and impressment, 28-31; suggestions for
    revision, 139-141.
Chief Justice: H as, 15, 18; see Superior Court.
Christianity: see also God, religion; 45, and history,
    59-61; and Massachusetts Indians, 89-90;
    toleration, 91; and political thought, 157, 158,
    160; and Revolution, 169-170.
Cicero: 208, 212.
Civil War (American): causes, 145.
Clarendon, Earl of: on history, 61.
Clark, John: 82.
Clark, Dora Mae: on impressment, 32.
Class: problem of in Massachusetts, 87, 123-127,
    130-132, 140, 171.
Clergy: 85; and Revolution, 133, 165, 169.
Coercive Acts: 4, 114, 127-128, 144-147.
Coinage, Massachusetts: 73.
Colman, Benjamin: on H, 222.
Commerce, Massachusetts: 71, 90, 92-95.
Committees of Correspondence: 15, 143-145.
Common Law: 41, 46, 54, 61, 115.
Commons, House of: 46.
Congregational Church: 133, 137, 169, 170. See also
    Puritans, clergy.
Connecticut: founding of, 66, 138, 164.
Conservatism: H and, 160-162; as political theory,
    217-219.
Constantinople: compared with Boston, 172.
Constitution (and law in general): 45, 61, 105-106.
Constitution (British): 28-29, 46, 54; of empire,
    105-116, 202-203.
Constitution (Massachusetts): H on, 43-48, 53-55, 75;
    and British, 105-116; suggestions for changes,
    139-141.
Constitution (United States): 46, 110, 171.
Cooke, Elisha, Jr. and Sr.: 2, 13-14, 82, 85, 86.
Corbet, Michael: impressment of, 22, 32-33, 50, 174.
Corruption: and politics, 61, 81, 219.
Council, Massachusetts: H on, 15, 46, 77; and
    impressment, 24; role in politics, 83-84, 87;
    in Revolution, 139-141.

Courts: role of in society, 43-46, 115, 165-169;
    see also Superior Court and Suffolk County
    Judiciary.
Critical Period: 207.
Crime: H on, 165-167.
Cromwell, Oliver: 73.
Crowd: see mob.

Crown, British: 45, 46; see prerogative.
Currency, Massachusetts: H and, 12, 14, 81-87.
Cushing, John: 49.
Cushing, Thomas: debates sovereignty with H, 112.
Custom (Massachusetts): 43-47, 176-180.
Customs House Officers: 49, 141.

Dartmouth, Earl of: 141-143.
Dawson, Christopher: on Revolution, 191.
Debt: law of, 47; province, 81.
Declaration of Independence: H's critique, 113-114, 177, 200, 212, 217, 229.
Declaratory Act: 105.
Declension: 75-76.
Deeds: as evidence, 6.
De Maistre, Joseph: 219.
Democracy: see popular government.
Demos, John: on witchcraft, 6.
Derby, Lieutenant: and Knowles Riot, 24.
Diggers: 161.
Donoso-Cortes, Juan: on sovereignty, 109-110, 117, 219.
Dudley, Joseph and family: 2, 13, 48, 80, 82, 84.
Dummer, William: 90.
Dutch: trade with, 94.

Edwards, Jonathan: 61.
Eighteenth Century: in Massachusetts, H on, 66-77, 218.
Endicott, John: 68.
England, English: 1, 7, 63; see Britain.
English Civil War: 100.
Entail, law of: 47, 48.
Erudites: see Antiquarians.
Erving, George: 126.
Evidence, rules of: 50.
Exchequer Courts: 50.

Family: importance to H, 1-17.
Fifth Monarchy Men: 161.
Fishery, Massachusetts: and impressment, 27-28.
Florentine political thought: 158-159.
Flucker, Thomas: 222.
Founding Fathers: political ideas, 162.
Fox's Martyrs: 10, 20.
France, French Revolution: 42, 63, 73, 83, 169-170, 179, 217, 220.
Franklin, Benjamin: <u>Autobiography</u>, 1; and French and Indian War, 29; and attitude toward Indians,

76; on trade, 93; on colonial growth, 122; on Revolution, 143.
Freedom: see liberty.
Freiberg, Malcolm: on H, 221.
French and Indian War: and impressment, 27-31; Massachusetts' effort in, 30; and Acadians, 90; and Revolution, 120-121, 200.
Fundamental Law: 43, 46, 54, 80.

Gage, Thomas: 128.
Galbraith, John Kenneth: 183.
Galloway, Joseph: 135, 147.
General Court (Massachusetts): 11, 46, 77, 79; and impressment, 27; disputes about powers, 46, 77, 79-88, 109-113; and Indians, 90; and Revolution, 127, 141-143.
General Search Warrants: 41, 50.
George III, King: on colonial taxation, 113; and Revolution, 136, 144-145, 148.
George, Dorothy: 224.
Gibbon, Edward: 61-63.
Gipson, Lawrence Henry: 119-122.
Glorious Revolution: 61, 74, 85, 148, 160, 205, 219-221, 224.
God: role in history, 59; and Puritans, 66, 76; and political obligation, 164-174; and history, 210-211.
Gookin, Daniel: 13, 83.
Gorton, Samuel: 70.
Göttingen, University of: historical writing at, 62.
Governor (Massachusetts): powers, 46, 77; political role, 80-83, 87, 140-141.
Grand Jury: see Superior Court, Suffolk County Judiciary.
Great Britain: see Britain.
Great Khan: 182, 187, 227.
Great War for Empire: 121-122; see French and Indian War.
Greece: 201.
Greene, Jack P.: on politics, 45, 99.
Greven, Philip: on colonial child-rearing, 6.
Gridley, Jeremiah: 41; and Writs of Assistance, 49.
Guicciardini: 158.

Hale, Sir Matthew: 49, 54.
Hale, Robert: 27.
Hamilton, Alexander: 221.
Hancock, John: 122, 125, 143-144.
Hancock, Thomas: 126.
Hansen, Chadwick: on witchcraft, 91.

Happiness: H on, and people of Massachusetts,
   111-113.
Hardwicke, Lord: 122.
Harvard College: 9, 171.
Hillsborough, Earl of: 136, 139-142.
History, Historians, Historiography: in civilization,
   59-62; H's general ideas on, 62-65; of colonial
   North America, 65-95; of American Revolution,
   119-137; and political theory, 157-162.
Hobbes, Thomas: 159.
Hofstadter, Richard: on parties, 195.
Hooker, Thomas: 64.
Hooper, Robert: 32.
House of Representatives (Massachusetts): see also
   General Court; 46, 77, 81-82, 87, 184, 199;
   quarrel with H, 109-112.
Hubbard, Peter: 69.
Hume, David: as historian, 60, 63.
Hutchinson, family: 1-17; Peter Orlando, 1;
   Foster (H's brother), 2; Eliakim (H's cousin), 2;
   Thomas, Sr. (H's father), 5-7, 13; H's children --
   Thomas, Sr., 6; Elisha, 6; William, 6; business
   ventures, 94, 103; Elisha (H's grandfather), 7,
   13; William and Eliakim, 13; Margaret (H's wife),
   5, 6; Margaret (Peggy -- H's daughter), 4, 6;
   Elisha (H's brother), 2, 50.
Hutchinson, Thomas: for comparisons with Edmund
   Burke, see Burke; and family, 1-17; and naval
   impressment, 22-37; as judge, 39-56; as
   historian (of colonial period), 59-95, (of
   Revolution), 119-137; on sovereignty, and
   relation of colonies to Britain, 105-116;
   remedies for imperial crisis, 137-150; political
   theory, 157-190; critique of revolutionary
   thought, 197-212; conservatism of, 217-229;
   critique of, 223-229; The History of the Colony
   and Province of Massachusetts Bay, 16-17, 20,
   25-26, 42, 59, 65-95, 119-137, 144, 164, 172,
   179, 186, 206, 207, 211, 219-221; "Hutchinson in
   America," 1, 7-8, 16, 76; "Dialogue Between an
   American and a European Englishman," 16, 47,
   134, 166, 182, 206; analyzed 200-203;
   "Strictures on the Declaration . . .," 79-80,
   212; political career, 2-5, 14-15, 40, 222;
   business activities, 6, 7, 20, 94, 103;
   childhood, 7-9; religion, 7, 8, 11, 76-77,
   164-174, 192; on crowds and violence, 27, 34,
   122-132; on loyalists, 10-11, 127-132;
   on Indians, 88-99, 88-189, 209-210; on blacks

and slavery, 90, 200; on toleration, 67-70,
74, 165, 178-179, 199-200; on political
parties, 185-186; on popular politics,
122-123, 181-184; contemporaries' opinions
of, 20, 39, 51-52; scholars' opinions of,
17, 23, 62-63, 97-99; on revolutionary
language, 197-200; on revolutionary logic,
200-206; method of citation, 206-207; and
metaphysical speculation, 207-208.

Imperial historians: 119, 120, 122.
Impressment: naval, 11, 18, 22-37.
Independent Advertiser: 2, 26.
Independent Reflector: 129.
Independents: see Presbyterians.
Indians: 69-70; H on, 88-90, 178, 188-189.
Industrial Revolution: 224.
Inns of Court: 41.
Instructions to legislators: 14.
Islam: 91.

Jackson, Richard: 139.
James II, King: 61, 64.
Jefferson, Thomas: 89.
Jenkins' Ear, War of: 27.
Joachim of Fiore: 159.
Johnson, Samuel: 161.
Jones, Thomas: on history, 135.
Jouvenel, Bertrand de: author of Sovereignty, 168.
Judiciary, Massachusetts: 42, 45-46, 141; see also
    Superior Court, Suffolk County Judiciary.

Kendall, Willmoore: on Locke, 202.
King George's War: 30, 83; impressment in, 22-27.
King Philip's War: 83, 88, 89.
Knowles, Commodore Charles and Riot: 24-28, 174.
Koebner, Richard: author of Empire, 122.
Koehler, Lyle: on Antinomians, 69.
Kuhn, Thomas: author of The Structure of
    Scientific Revolutions, 226.

Land Bank, Massachusetts: 83, 186; see currency.
Lasch, Christopher: author of Haven in a Heartless
    World, 5.
Law: see British, common, natural.
Le Bon, Gustav: author of The Crowd, 186.
Legal profession in Massachusetts: 40-41,
    51-52, 126-127, 135, 169.

Legislature: role of, 44, 46; see General Court.
Levellers: 160.
Lewis, C. S.: author of The Abolition of Man, 163.
Libels: 44, 53.
Liberty: 42; H on personal, 43, 44; and law, 50,
    77, 159, 169; in British history, 61; colonial,
    65, 68; and taxation, 120; colonial and British,
    105-106, 126-127, 129-130; and Indians, 188-189;
    revolutionary definition of, 199-200.
Liberties (Massachusetts): and impressment, 28-29;
    in colonial era, 71-75; Burke on American, 147-149.
Locke, John: Second Treatise of Government, 4, 162,
    177, 202, 206; on religious toleration, 166-167.
London, Great Fire of: 72.
Lords, House of: 46.
Louisbourg campaign: 28, 30.
Loudoun, Lord: 37.
Loyalists: residence of, 5; theory of law, 42, 44;
    judges, 53; historians, 134-136; and Revolution,
    127-132; interpretations of, 221.
Lukacs, John: on history, 62.

Mabillon: 62.
Machiavelli: 10, 39, 158-159.
Madison, James: 88.
Magna Carta: 61, 203.
Mary, Queen: 10.
Maryland: 132, 135.
Massachusetts: 17, 35, 71; see Boston; Charter;
    Council; Constitution; General Court; History;
    Hutchinson; Legal Profession; Liberties;
    Revolution; Stamp Act; Suffolk County
    Judiciary; Superior Court; Towns.
Mather, Cotton: 61.
Mather, Increase: 31.
Medieval: conception of history, 59; political
    theory, 157-158.
Meinecke, Friedrich: 60-62, 97.
Mercantilism: H on, 92-95.
Merchants: 47, 48, 66, 72; in Revolution, 126-127.
Metternich, Clemens von: on Revolution, 192.
Millennium: 59-60.
Miller, Perry: 62, 119.
Mobs: 15; H on, 24-27, 53, 95; in Revolution,
    125-132, 165, 168-171, 226.
Mongolia: 182.
Monroe Doctrine: 121.
Montesquieu: political ideas, 110.
Morgan, Edmund S.: 62.

Morison, Samuel E.: 62, 66, 98.
Morrall, John: on political theory, 157-158.
Morris, Robert: 221.
Murrin, John M.: on Massachusetts politics, 84.

Namier, Sir Lewis: on British politics, 88.
Nash, Gary B.: on Revolution, 119.
Nationalist Historians: on Revolution, 119-122.
Natural Law: H and, 159-190.
Natural Rights: 41; James Otis and, 48;
  H and, 159-190, esp. 178-182.
Nature, State of: H on, 188-189.
Navigation Acts: 71, 113; H on, 92-95, 167.
Nero: 74.
New Brick Church: H in, 76, 77.
New Hampshire: 71.
New Lights: H as, 77.
New Whigs: 61, 159-160.
New York: 138-142.
Newcastle, Duke of: 32.
Non-Importation: 53, 126-130.
North, Lord: 113, 147.
Nova Scotia: Acadians in, 90.
Noyes, Oliver: 82.

Obedience, obligation, political: H on, 173-176,
  179; Burke and H on, 187-188.
"Old Whigs": 61, 129, 159-160.
Oliver, Andrew, Sr. and Jr.: 2, 27.
Oliver, Peter: 2; on Superior Court, 49;
  on H, 51, 52; on Puritans, 68; on Cooke, 82;
  on Revolution, 119, 127, 135.
Oratory: H's, 14.
Ortega y Gasset, Jose: author of The Revolt of
  the Masses, 186.
Osborne, John: 27.
Otis, James, Jr.: and chief justice controversy,
  2, 21; impressment, 32; as lawyer, 41; Writs
  of Assistance, 49-50; political theory, 114-117;
  and Revolution, 122, 125-126; madness, 152.
Otis, James, Sr.: and chief justice controversy,
  2, 21, 39; and Revolution, 126, 129, 139.

Palmer, family: H's business associates, 103.
Parliament (British): on impressment, 22, 29-33;
  law and, 43, 61, 65, 73, 74; and trade, 92;
  sovereignty, 115-116; and Revolution, 124,
  128-129, 137, 140, 184, 199, 203.
Party politics: effects, 86; Burke and H on,
  185-186.

Pemberton, Ebenezer: H's minister, 77.
Pequot War: 69, 89.
Perjury: 165, 169.
Persia: 172.
Phips, Sir William: 2, 80, 82.
Physicians: and Revolution, 133.
Pilgrims: see Plymouth.
Pitt, William: 29, 130.
Pitts, James: 126.
Plato: 173.
Plumb, J. H.: on history, 62.
Plymouth (colony): 89, 135.
Pobodoenostev, Konstantin: 219.
Pocock, J. G. A.: on history and politics, 54, 55.
Political theory: see Burke, Hutchinson.
Pollard, Benjamin: 24.
Popular government: 77, 84; H on, 172-173, 181-184.
Pownall, Thomas: 13, 31, 38, 80, 82.
Pratt, Caleb and William: 23.
Prejudice: H and overcoming, 64-65, 173, 205.
Prerogative, royal: 45, 184.
Presbyterians: 134-136.
Press, Freedom of: 44.
Privy Council: appeals to, 51.
Professionals: in Revolution, 133, 169.
Progressive historians: 119, 126.
Proud, Robert: on history, 134-135.
Puritans: H on, 10-12; 67-77, 94; society, 67-70, 75-76; religion, 70-74; declension, 75-76; and Indians, 88-89; and witchcraft, 91-92; and Revolution, 134, 166.

Quakers: 67-70.
Queen Anne's War: 27.
Quincy, Josiah: 15, 33, 40, 49, 51.
Quo warranto: against Massachusetts charter, 43.

Reformation: historical views of, 59; political theory, 158-159.
Religion: H's, 7, 8, 11, 76-77; and Revolution, 133-134, 137; and government, 164-174; toleration, 165, 178-179; established churches, 166.
Renaissance: historical views of, 59; political theory, 158-159.
Resistance to authority: H on legitimacy of, 174-175.

Revolution (American, Massachusetts): 44;
    H on, 54, 63, 105-116; H's interpretation,
    119-137; remedies, 137-150; loyalists and,
    134-136; modern historians and, 119-122;
    contemporaneous historians and, 134-137;
    and imperial policy, 122-126; legitimacy of,
    171-175.
Revolutions of 1848: 109.
Rhode Island: 69.
Rights: see liberty; natural rights; tradition.
Riots: see mobs; Stamp Act.
Robertson, William: historian, 123; 211.
Rockingham Whigs: 148.
Rogers, Nathaniel: 4.
Rome: 63, 89, 201.
Roosevelt, Theodore: 128.
Royal Commission of 1664: 73-74.
Rudé, George: 224.
Russell, Charles: 27.

Salem: 15, 141; witchcraft, 91-92.
Saltonstall, Nathaniel: 12.
Savage, Samuel P.: 26.
Schlesinger, Arthur M., Sr.: on Revolution, 126.
Schumpeter, Joseph: author of Capitalism,
    Socialism and Democracy, 182.
Scott, James: and impressment, 23-24.
Sennett, Richard: author of Families Against
    the City, 6.
Shaffer, William: author of The Politics of
    History, 136.
Shays' Rebellion: 171.
Shelburne, Earl of: and Revolution, 129.
Sheriff of Suffolk County: 49.
Shipton, Clifford K.: 221.
Shirley, William: 13; and impressment, 23-26,
    36-37; and Writs of Assistance, 50;
    administration, 80-85.
Shute, Samuel: 80.
Slavery (African): H on, 90, 200.
Smith, Adam: author of The Wealth of Nations;
    on commerce and defense, 92-93.
Smith, William R.: author of History as Argument,
    136.
Smuggling: 94, 165.
Social compact: and Revolution, 125-128.
Soldiers: British, in Boston: 124, 128, 130,
    137-140, 142, 174.
Sons of Liberty: 34, 91.

Sovereignty: 53, 54, 146; H on, 105-116,
    177-178, 226.
Spain: colonies, 111.
Spanish Armada: 210.
Stamp Act: 13, 53, 113; riots, 10, 16, 18, 45,
    85, 226; H on, 28-29; and Revolution, 120,
    123, 129, 135, 148, 167.
Starkey, Marion: on witchcraft, 91.
State of nature: H on, 188-189.
Statute Law: 42-44.
Stoughton, William: 13, 84.
Strauss, Leo: on law and tradition, 55, 191.
Stuart, House of: 55, 65, 74.
Sugar Act: 106.
Suffolk County Judiciary: 41, 42, 49, 53.
Superior Court (Massachusetts): 2, 127, 167;
    H's speeches before, 10, 11, 42-54, 111;
    and Writs of Assistance, 50; on Appeals, 51.
Swain, Philip, Jr.: on Bostonian soldiers, 131.
Swift, Jonathan: 161.
Swift, Samuel: 167.

Tao: and C. S. Lewis, 163.
Taxation, colonial: see Stamp, Sugar, and Tea Acts;
    71, 105-107, 112-113, 123, 164.
Tea Act and Party: 18, 131, 142, 151, 167.
Temple, the Earl: 126.
<u>Tenth Federalist</u>, The: 88.
Thacher, Oxenbridge: 41.
Thompson, E. P.: 224.
Thucydides: author of <u>The Peloponnesian War</u>, 213.
Toleration: see religion, Hutchinson, parties;
    H on, 64, 90-91; religious, 166-167; racial,
    178; political, 184-185.
Tories: see loyalists.
Towns (in Massachusetts): 77, 81; and Revolution,
    132-133, 182, 184.
Trade: see commerce, impressment.
Tradition: see Burke; H on, 18, 42, 54-55.
Triangle Trade: 72.
Truman, Nathaniel: on H, 39.
Tryon, William: 130.
Turkey: 122.
Typology: and Puritan thought, 60.
Tyranny: 45; in British history, 61, 108-111;
    in revolutions, 172.

United States: see Constitution; early historians
   of, 136, 221-222.
Utopian political thought: 159.
Utrecht, Peace of: 22.

Vane, Sir Harry: 70.
Vaughan, Alden T.: on Indians, 88.
Vice-Admiralty Courts in Massachusetts: 141.
Virginia: 121, 138.
Voegelin, Eric: political theory, 191.
Voltaire: on history, 60, 63.

Walpole, Sir Horace: 204.
Warren, Joseph: 124.
Warren, Mercy Otis: on H, 51.
Washington, George: 222.
Watts, Isaac: 222.
Weber, Max: on scholarship and politics, 228.
Wentworth, John: and impressment, 34.
West Indies: British, 72; trade of, 92-93, 121.
Whigs: see New and Old Whigs; historical writing, 17;
   political thought, 44, 61-62, 74, 79, 129,
   159-160.
White, William: and impressment, 24.
Whitefield, George: and Revolution, 134.
Widows: law pertaining to, 49.
Wilkes, John: 50, 129, 148-150; riots, 206.
Willard, Josiah: and impressment, 37.
Williams, Israel: 3, 53, 84, 127, 173, 204, 222.
Winthrop, John: 42, 69, 71.
Witan: 61.
Witchcraft: H on, 91-92.
Writs of Assistance: 40-41, 49-50, 53, 126.

Young, Thomas: 125, 130.

Zemsky, Michael: on Massachusetts politics, 84.
Ziff, Larzer: on Puritans, 66.
Zuckerman, Michael: on Massachusetts, 84;
   on Revolution, 119, 132.